Shaping an Urban World
Planning in the Twentieth Century

Shaping an Urban World

edited by

GORDON E. CHERRY

ST. MARTIN'S PRESS, New York

© Mansell Publishing 1980

All rights reserved. For information, write:
St. Martin's Press., Inc., 175 Fifth Avenue, New York, NY 10010
Printed in Great Britain
First published in the United States of America in 1980

ISBN 0-312-71618-4

Library of Congress Cataloging in Publication Data

International Conference on the History of Urban and Regional Planning,
1st, London, 1977.
    Shaping an urban world.

    Includes bibliographical references.
    1. City planning—History—20th century—Congresses.
2. Regional planning—History—20th century—Congresses.
I. Cherry, Gordon Emanuel. II. Title.
HT166.I6113   1977a   307.7′6   80–17276
ISBN 0-312-7168-4

Foreword

While today there is considerable questioning about the future directions of planning, there is a parallel and growing interest in the origins and history of the planning process and its effects on our environment. In this series, *Studies in History, Planning and the Environment,* we intend to provide in-depth studies of some of the many aspects of that history, to reflect the increasing international interest, and to stimulate ideas for areas of further research.

We shall focus on developments during the last one hundred to one hundred and fifty years and attempt to examine some of the questions relating to the forces which have shaped and guided our contemporary environment—urban, rural and metropolitan—and which demand answers not just for critical analysis in the advance of scholarship, but also for the insights they can provide for the future. Planning policy is constructed from knowledge of the *origins* of problems, as well as the *consequences* of decisions. Planning history therefore looks at processes over time; how and why our contemporary environment is shaped as it is. The broad outlines may be known; exercising an interpretative judgement on the details provides a fascinating field of study in which there are not a few surprises and many lessons for academics and practitioners alike.

In shedding light on the recent past we hope to understand the present; in fusing insights from different subject fields we hope to strengthen the synoptic traditions of both history and planning; in being avowedly inter-national we will reflect the different cultural attitudes to planning and the environment over time.

It is right that the first three volumes, which make up the trilogy *Planning and the Environment in the Modern World,* should derive from the papers presented at the first International Conference of the Planning History Group, held in London in September, 1977. Other conferences and meetings of the Group can be expected to provide material for the series, while individual initiatives will release the fruits of personal labour.

Gordon E. Cherry
Anthony Sutcliffe
July 1980

Contents

The Contributors

GERD ALBERS studied architecture and town planning at Hannover and Chicago, taking a doctorate in town planning at Aachen. From 1952 to 1962 he was a town planner in various capacities in the municipal service of three cities. Since 1961 he has been Professor of Urban and Regional Planning at Technische Universitat, Munich. He is a member of several German professional and scholarly societies, Honorary Corresponding Member of the Royal Town Planning Institute, and Past President of the International Society of City and Regional Planners. In addition to teaching, he works as a planning consultant and in research, especially in the field of urban structure and planning procedure, as well as in history of modern town planning.

BLAINE A. BROWNELL is Associate Professor of History and Urban Studies at the University of Alabama in Birmingham, and Associate Dean and Co-Director of the Graduate School. He received a Ph.D. from the University of North Carolina at Chapel Hill and served as Visiting Fulbright-Hays Professor in Hiroshima University, Japan, 1977–78. He is Editor of the *Journal of Urban History* and of numerous publications, including: *Urban America: From Downtown to No Town* (1979); *The City in Southern History: The Growth of Urban Civilization in the South* (1977); and *The Urban Ethos in the South, 1920–1930* (1975). He is now working as co-author of a revised edition of George E. Mowry's *The Urban Nation, 1920–1960*.

GORDON E. CHERRY read geography at the University of London and subsequently took professional qualifications in town planning and surveying. Between 1956 and 1968 he worked in a number of local planning authorities in England, latterly as Research Officer in the City Planning Department, Newcastle upon Tyne. He moved to the University of Birmingham as Deputy Director of the Centre for Urban and Regional Studies. In 1976 he was elected to a Chair in Urban and Regional Planning. He has served on the Council of the Royal Town Planning Institute for many years, and was President 1978–79. His many publications include *Town Planning in its Social Context* (1970), *Urban Change and Planning* (1972), *The Evolution of British*

Town Planning (1974) and *Environmental History Vol. 2. National Parks and Recreation in the Countryside* (1975). He is currently Chairman of the Planning History Group.

JOHN COLLINS read architecture at Cambridge and from 1965 to 1968 was an architect on the staff of Lusaka City Council, Zambia. From there he went to New York where he took a Master's degree in urban planning at Columbia University. He then lectured for two years at the Project Planning Centre for Developing Countries at the University of Bradford. In 1972 he became an Associate Research Fellow at the Development Planning Unit of University College London, from which he returned to Lusaka in 1973–74 as leader of a research team studying planned urban growth on a project financed by the Ministry of Overseas Development. He now works in local government in London.

SUSAN M. CUNNINGHAM read geography at the University of London and after a year's teaching read for a Masters degree in 1974 when she examined some aspects of Brazilian industrial geography. Subsequent doctoral research at Birkbeck College, London, was concerned with the planning, policy and spatial aspects of industrial development in Brazil since 1960. During 1979 the author gained a scholarship to Brazil based at the Federal University of Rio de Janeiro for a post-doctoral project on Brazilian private industrial enterprise. In October 1979, she took up a post as Research Officer at St. Antony's College, Oxford, on an SSRC-funded project researching into the financing of urban development in Buenos Aires, Argentina from 1870–1910.

ROBERT FISHMAN has a Ph.D. from Harvard (1974) and is now Associate Professor of History at Rutgers/The State University of New Jersey. He is the author of *Urban Utopias in the Twentieth Century: Ebenezer Howard, Frank Lloyd Wright and Le Corbusier* (1977) and is now working on a History of Suburbia, 1780–1980.

W. HOUGHTON–EVANS is an architect and town planner. He was first employed in local government in London and Coventry, where his work gained two Civic Trust awards. He has taught at Schools of Planning in Birmingham and Leeds. He is now Senior Lecturer and Head of the Architectural Engineering Group in the Department of Civil Engineering at the University of Leeds. His research is mainly into historical, quantitative and technical aspects of town planning. His publications include *Planning Cities: Legacy and Portent* (1975) and *Architecture and Urban Design* (1978).

ANTHONY KING, sociologist and historian, teaches at Brunel University, London. Previous research and teaching posts have been held at the Universities of Leicester, London, Washington, South Carolina and, between 1965–70, at the Indian Institute of Technology, Delhi. He is author of *Colonial Urban Development* (1976), *The Bungalow. A Cultural History and Sociology* (1980); he has edited *Buildings and Society: Essays on the Social Development of the Built Environment* (1979). He is interested in comparative studies of urban development and the social and cultural production of built form.

PETER MARCUSE is Professor of Urban Planning at Columbia University in New York. A lawyer and former President of the Los Angeles Planning Commission and now a member of a Community Board in New York, he has written extensively on issues of housing policy and city planning. His most recent article is entitled *The Myth of the Benevolent State*. His study, *Rental Housing in the City of New York,* was released by the Division of Rent Control of that City in February, 1979. He is currently working on a comparative historical analysis of the determinants of housing policy in the United States and Western Europe.

DIETER REBENTISCH is Assistant Professor of History at the University of Frankfurt, specializing in urban history and the history of administration. He is a member of the advisory council of the Institute of Comparative Urban Studies in Münster and member of the historical study group of the Akademie für Raumforschung und Landesplanung. His writings include a biography of Ludwig Landmann who was chief executive official of Frankfurt during the Weimar Republic. He is now engaged on a study of Nazi party's influence on the central government of the Third Reich.

SHUN-ICHI J. WATANABE is Head of the Building Economy Division of the Building Research Institute, Ministry of Construction, Japan. He graduated in architecture (Tokyo, 1961), took a Masters in city planning (Harvard, 1964) and a Ph.D. in urban planning (Tokyo, 1973). A book, based upon his dissertation on American urban planning and the 'community ideal', won the annual award of the City Planning Institute of Japan in 1978. He worked for the Government of Puerto Rico (1963–64), was a research fellow at the University of Tokyo (1965–78), a visiting lecturer at the University of Sheffield (1973–74), and a visiting scholar at the University of California, Berkeley (1974). He is now working on comparative studies of urban planning from American, British and Japanese perspectives. He is presently interested in Japanese planning history and is conducting a group called Planning History Group in Japan. He is also an active member of the Academic Committee of the City Planning Institute of Japan.

Acknowledgments

The studies in this volume were first presented at the First International Conference on the History of Urban and Regional Planning, which was organized by the Planning History Group at Bedford College, University of London, 14th–18th September, 1977. The Group wishes to extend its gratitude to the bodies whose generous grants allowed the conference to take place: the Anglo–German Foundation for the Study of Industrial Society, the British Academy, the Nuffield Foundation, the Rockefeller Foundation, and the Social Science Research Council.

A record of the discussions at the conference was made by Martin Gaskell, James Read, Stephen Ward, and Madge Dresser for the Planning History Group. This record has proved most valuable in setting the context for the papers collected in this volume, and grateful acknowledgment is made for their hard work at that time. I should also like to express my thanks to the contributors for their careful re-editing of their papers for publication.

Finally acknowledgment is given for permission to reproduce a number of illustrations in the paper by W. Houghton-Evans: figure 5.2, Oxford University Press; figure 5.8, Longmans Green; figure 5.11, Edward Arnold; figure 5.13, Thames and Hudson; figures 5.14, 5.21 and 5.27, the Controller of Her Majesty's Stationery Office; figure 5.15, *Architectural Review;* figure 5.17, Alcan Industries Ltd.; figure 5.18, Buckinghamshire County Council; figure 5.19, Runcorn Development Corporation; figure 5.20, Barrie and Rockcliffe; figure 5.22, Redditch Development Corporation; figures 5.24 and 5.25, Washington Development Corporation; figure 5.26, Milton Keynes Development Corporation; figure 5.29, Sheffield Corporation; figures 5.30 and 5.31, Athlone Press.

Gordon E. Cherry

1

Introduction: aspects of twentieth-century planning

GORDON E. CHERRY

Anthony Sutcliffe has explained the background to the publication of the trilogy *Planning and Environment in the Modern World* in his Introduction to the first volume, *The Rise of Modern Urban Planning, 1800–1914*. As it was impossible to reproduce all the papers given at the First International Conference on the History of Urban and Regional Planning, held in London in 1977, it was decided instead to select essays which were representative of the ground that was covered. This second volume, *Shaping an Urban World*, brings together eleven papers which highlighted the debates surrounding twentieth-century developments in planning. The papers have been revised where necessary in the light of comments offered at the Conference and also to accord with editorial suggestions, but basically they still reflect the freshness with which they were first delivered and the liveliness of the discussions which surrounded them.

The overall message of the first volume is one of continuity, in that elements of planning can be detected throughout the nineteenth century. There is debate as to how significant the years of 'progress' around 1900 really were, but the contributors agreed that planning was in no way firmly established in urban affairs by 1914. This second volume is a logical successor because it deals with some of the ways in which, and to what extent, the twentieth century has in fact been shaped by planning thought and activity.

An immense field is covered, and almost every topic which is the subject of the eleven papers could itself be extended to book length. But the essays are not superficial, they are studies in depth of particular aspects and have been selected to illustrate a certain theme in planning this century. To give

coherence and structure to the volume, the papers are grouped in five
sections, as follows:
  (a) recurrent themes (papers 2 and 3)
  (b) planning method (papers 4 to 6)
  (c) establishing the planning tradition (papers 7 to 9)
  (d) international transfers (papers 10 and 11)
  (e) assessment (paper 12).
  This introduction provides background reflections and a commentary on
the content of the papers included in these five sections.

RECURRENT THEMES

Despite the continuities from previous decades, many of the origins of
contemporary urban planning can be traced to a twenty-year period round
the turn of the twentieth century. The critical years were 1890–1910, though
for some particular aspects 1885–1905 may be more significant. Each
country in the Western world has its own story to tell, though national or
local determinants were so affected by the diffusion of ideas and experiences
from country to country that many common themes may be detected.
Nonetheless, there were quite distinct centres for particular formative aspects
of planning. For example, American planning was strongly shaped by the
City Beautiful movement, the landscape tradition and the influence of the
Chicago Exposition. German planning owed much to an engineering
tradition and municipal action in city extension plans. British planning was
heavily influenced by the problems posed by working-class housing and the
context of vigorous social reform movements. Elsewhere, across Europe and
North America new approaches to civic design and the planned regulation of
city growth, sometimes in highly imaginative ways as on the outskirts of
Madrid (Soria y Mata's *cuidad lineal),* illustrated the ferment of ideas and
innovation.
  From the very start then, there were a number of different foci in the
emergence of the planning movement and these released many themes
throughout the industrialized urban world. As the twentieth century unfolded
these themes continued to be explored and became recurrent in various
guises, affording both a continuity and an internationalism to planning. The
remarkable consequence was that the forest fires of curiosity, speculation,
reforming drive, zeal and inventiveness took hold; what could have been an
ineffective spluttering of disconnected fashions and fads turned out quite
differently. It could have been another instance of a haphazard upsurge
articulated by intense idealists, like one of the rash of nineteenth-century
utopian communities recently described by Hardy[1], but events conspired
differently. This remarkably innovative period produced a set of ideas which

took root in government and they subsequently flourished in the twentieth-century explosion of State involvement in community affairs. To this extent town planning has been one of the major forces to shape our modern environment.

As we have hinted, one of the reasons for this success was that in the origins of town planning issues were seized upon which, while common to a world of growing cities, were not just of transitory importance but proved to be of long-standing significance. In short the themes were recurrent over time and throughout many countries. The first, and probably most important was that represented by the housing question in the late-Victorian city, almost irrespective of which country we select. As a theme its significance was that it expressed most of the other issues which had also bubbled to the political surface of the time.

They were all interrelated. First there was the need for health and amenity improvement, a logical continuation to sanitary reform, which linked new standards in community health to the eradication of ugliness and squalor. Then there was the search to give order to a chaotic, disordered city: the aim to separate out unneighbourly land use, and on the one hand reduce high residential densities and to limit overcrowding, while on the other to search positively for the decongestion of city populations through redistribution and dispersal. Additionally there were conscious efforts at environmental improvement through civic design projects, ranging from statuary work and ornamentation to new developments in architecture and planned layouts for whole districts of cities. All these factors came together in a concern for land and its proper and effective use, and this remains a characteristic of planning today, enshrined in a focus on environment and its quality, the 'right use of land', and a spatial perspective to a rational ordering of urban complexity.

The motives behind this broad canvas were largely social and cultural and stemmed directly from the social, economic, political and technological conditions of the late-Victorian city in the West. They were powerfully underlain by reform movements, the ideology of which came through to colour town planning itself; and they were concerned with the perceived links between environment (and particularly housing conditions) and individual morality and behaviour. The Victorians were not so much concerned with the causes of poor housing but the consequences, and problems were tackled from that direction. It was therefore necessary to improve housing conditions, particularly for the impoverished third of the population, in order to protect their moral position; it was not as imperative to restructure the capitalist basis of a society which redistributed its rewards in a grossly inequitable manner, to cushion people from grinding poverty and to move towards a more egalitarian society. We might be guilty of oversimplification and of omitting another important factor, namely the political expedience of maintaining social stability and order for a reasonably contented workforce through improved housing, but the point is still a fair one and it indicates the

importance of housing as one of the key recurrent themes in the origins of
modern town planning.

Marcuse brings out this question in paper 2. As in Britain and the new
industrial cities of Europe, housing problems in America at the turn of the
century were critical; the accounts of housing poverty there were as graphic
and as moving as elsewhere. In every country the housing question has been
intimately tied to developments in urban planning, but Marcuse finds that in
the United States developments in planning failed to contribute much to
solutions to the housing problem, indeed rather they exacerbated it. He
argues that events in the professionalization of American planning served to
deflect some of the reformist zeal; that zoning proved inimical to the solution
of the worst housing situations; and that regional planning (as typified in the
Regional Plan for New York and its Environs, 1931), with its prescription
for deconcentration, again failed to address the hard core of the problem. The
separation of housing reform from planning and the resultant failure to deal
adequately with the problems of the ill-housed may be a partial explanation,
but Marcuse takes us further. He argues that fears about public health, of
social unrest and of the need to Americanize the large numbers of
immigrants, had all begun to recede by the first decade of the twentieth
century; and the rationale for a city planning movement to be concerned so
intensely with housing questions had perhaps begun to lose its force.
Moreover both the subordination of the problems of the ill-housed to real
estate values, and the political failure to resolve conflicts over the appropriate
uses of land at a metropolitan scale contributed to a lack of fit between
planning strategy and the housing problems with which the strategy was in
part concerned.

Marcuse admits differences with Europe. Within Europe there were also
differences between States. This comparative element is the very stuff of
international planning history. In Britain, for example, housing and planning
have been relatively close. The first two Planning Acts (1909, 1919) were
composite pieces of legislation in which housing figured first in the title. Not
till 1925 was there a Town Planning Act in its own right, and that was only a
consolidating measure. Subsequent legislation has largely been titled 'Town
and Country Planning' (for example, 1932, 1947, 1968).

The closeness of housing and planning in Britain was particularly well
defined in the years of origin, and indeed helps to explain a subsequent focus
on land, land management and the rational ordering of space[2]. By the
1890s the British urban crisis centred on the problem of working-class
housing: the provision of healthy, adequate housing and at rents that could
be afforded. The high cost of land had all but brought house building by
private developers in the centre of cities to a standstill; politically it was not
yet possible to provide significant numbers of dwellings through local
councils; philanthropy and experimentation in 'model' dwellings or estates
could not contribute more than they had done. Meanwhile the problem of an

ageing, unfit housing stock, inhabited by the least able of the population, remained. The solution that emerged was the promise of cheaper housing on the periphery of cities, and this led in Britain at least, to a style of suburban land-use planning in which, through town planning schemes, land was allocated for low-density housing. After World War I the full logic of this came to fruition with legislation in 1919 which obliged local authorities to begin a council housing programme, and for a while a town planning scheme and a housing scheme were almost synonymous. This was typical of the early part of the interwar period, but later in the century the two threads were again very close. The new towns programme dating from the Act of 1946 was a specific element in the planning strategy for Greater London, following Abercrombie's Greater London Plan, 1944, as was the town development programme (the Act of 1952, and 1957 for Scotland) in the more flexible arrangements for dispersal from conurbations. Later, too, programmes in respect of housing improvement have been keyed in with urban renewal programmes from a city planning point of view.

In paper 3 we turn to two further recurrent themes: the professional organization of the planner, and planning's capacity and, indeed, obligation to react to changing circumstances. Brownell neatly brings these two points together. His thesis is that American planning drifted away from the goals of broad reform and towards more 'practical' activities. It became committed to special and focused skills on the path of securing a professional identity, and in this process the impact of the motor car was crucial; it helped to shape an emergent profession of planning almost as much as planners have helped to shape the form of American cities.

His paper tells us much about the way planners organize their corporate life and structure. It also illustrates how the field of activity which we have come to know as town planning has taken on accretions of knowledge and skills, much wider than its original remit. As our urban world has been shaped this century, so both points have become important. Planning is strong in countries where the ideology of planning is well grounded and where planners themselves are in positions of some power through good organization; also planning, in as much that it deals with the rational ordering of land, now deals inescapably with traffic, transport and transportation, which is such a vital element in the determination of land use.

Once again the American experience is not necessarily that of Britain and in the international perspective which this volume embraces it is important to identify differences. An examination of why differences exist helps us to understand developments unique to one country. Brownell remarks that American planners soon became 'restrained professional consultants' rather than 'worldly philosophers or eager reformers'; part of the explanation was that the car and the urban transportation crisis helped to determine the evolving role of planners in that they provided a convenient body of knowledge and range of activity to which it could lay partial claim.

The American City Planning Institute was founded in 1917. In Britain the Town Planning Institute appeared in 1914[3]. The early days must have been very similar: a small number of devotees from other professions fired by enthusiasm but with no singular professional role. But the two bodies went different ways, largely due to divergent political and social circumstances in the two countries. In Britain the TPI grew in the British mould as a qualifying association, and membership was soon accorded by virtue of success in a qualifying examination and a qualifying period of experience. It was also shaped by close association with local government and the particular British characteristics of 'statutory town planning' whereby local authorities discharged mandatory or permissive planning powers over the use of land and related environmental matters. In due time it shed the constraining links exercised by other professional bodies, notably the architects, engineers and surveyors, encouraged the growth of educational curricula, regulated the conduct of its own members, gained its Charter (1959) and Royal status (1970) and has come to occupy a position of considerable influence in both local and central government.

This sense of professional recognition and status is typically British; other countries which do not have it may regret the loss of influence which is entailed. In Europe planning is for the most part in the hands of other professions, notably architecture, engineering and the law, and a number of national organizations proclaim their subject field. In Eastern Europe planning is largely the preserve of the architects organized as in the USSR or Romania, for example, as the Union of Architects. In Poland a separate organization exists, the Society of Polish Town Planners, which is recognized by the State and given certain functions. In the British Commonwealth and former Empire States the British professional idea is strongly entrenched and varieties of Town Planning Institutes exist on the British model.

The extraordinary automobile developments in United States from even before 1920 was not reflected in Western Europe to nearly the same extent. Urban development in Europe after World War I was conditioned rather by other factors, notably economic and political, and it took some time before urban transport was anything like a major question, at least outside London, Paris, Berlin and other large cities. Certainly there was the problem of arterial roads for London even before World War I and in the 1920s and 1930s a British roads programme encompassed modest road improvements, although not accepting the need for major new roads to match the German autobahns. But government legislated rather for speed limits, road accidents, enforcement of penalties and the relationship of these to motorists' behaviour, as Plowden has shown[4].

Likewise British planning adopted no great stance towards the car or the wider question of transportation until the mid-1940s. Once again the British characteristic of planning in a local-authority mould affords part of the answer. The chief technical officer of a city was the city engineer first and the planning officer second (or even third or fourth, if he was also architect, surveyor and water engineer); and as city engineer he adopted the approach of a professionally trained municipal engineer. Roads and road traffic were his concern; the planner applied the cosmetic of widened roads, geometric layouts and grand manner vistas to his city plans. Strangely enough the first conceptual breakthrough came not from the planner but from a police commissioner, Alker Tripp, with his influential publications, *Road Traffic and Its Control,* 1938, and *Town Planning and Road Traffic,* 1942. During wartime Britain the question of road layout assumed a new significance with the rebuilding of towns and cities, and the planner came more into his own. However, it was not really until the generation of land-use transportation plans from the mid-1950s and the work of Buchanan in the 1960s (*Traffic in Towns,* 1963), seeing the motor car in an environmental setting, that the planner had a specifically original and separate contribution to make. But all that is another story; Brownell keeps us to the early twentieth century.

PLANNING METHOD

We have already suggested that inherent in the idea of planning is the rational ordering of space—the search for order out of complexity. This imparts to planning both its spatial perspective as a key note and its concern for land management at both macro and microscales. The ways in which spatial ordering has been undertaken may be considered the methods whereby the objectives of planning have been achieved.

Three papers in this section consider certain examples of planning method adopted in the shaping of our urban world. Rebentisch looks at land planning at the regional scale with a German example; Houghton Evans reviews architectural concepts in city form with particular reference to British new towns, though his review is relevant to other countries in Western Europe too; and Watanabe shows how Japan borrowed the Western garden city as a term, but imperfectly as a concept, in a Tokyo suburb. All are examples of how an approach to land planning developed in three different countries— with particular constraints and particular results.

Rebentisch in paper 4 shows how regional planning developed in practice in the Rhein–Main area of Germany in three very different political periods: the Kaisserreich, the Weimar Republic and under the Nazis. The area has an economic unity but is fragmented by several administrative boundaries; forms of regional planning were therefore slow to become effective, illustrating how inconsistencies and imperfections in forms of local, provincial and State government can seriously constrain the rationale of regional planning.

This German example is a vivid reminder that planning, if it is to have any claims to effectiveness at regional scale, must have an unambiguous role in decision-making processes of government and in the network of political

interaction that shapes both policy formulation and subsequent implementation. Non-federal countries which have developed forms of local
government over many years, with a resultant complex mixture of central and
local powers, and with variations including *ad hoc* authorities in between, find
it very difficult, if not frankly impossible to develop a regional arm of government. Attempts at regional planning are consequently rarely successful.

But in all countries marked by complex, overlapping, interpenetrative
governmental systems, coordination at regional scale is acutely difficult.
For example, Rondinelli[5] has described abortive attempts in north-east
Pennsylvania during the 1960s when development planning agencies created
with the assistance of the Economic Development Administration, the
Appalachian Regional Commission, the Office of Economic Opportunity,
Model Cities, and other federal initiatives all had to find a place within
existing organizational structures. The organizationally-complex environment, reflected in fragmentation, decentralization and pluralism, meant that
control over resources and decision-making was dispersed. Similarly in a
study of the planned expansion of Droitwich, England, in a subregional and
indeed regional context, Friend *et al.*[6] have powerfully reminded us that the
making of strategic decisions is not just a corporate, but an inter-
organizational process. To this extent regional planning ideally consists of a
whole range of actions by local authorities, national and other agencies of
government and public bodies generally, in a thoroughly interactive process.
Regional planning is really regional management and relations between
institutions of government is crucial; when the key note of these relations is
independence rather than interdependence, effective regional planning is
impossible.

So far, regional planning has been long on prescription and short on
attainment. The history of planning this century is marked by the publication
of plans of seminal importance: New York 1929–31, Greater London
1929–33 and again in 1944, Moscow 1935, to name but three cities.
Implementation of these and other plans has been imperfect often because of
an inappropriate machinery of government, and unfavourable political and
institutional settings. Rebentisch, with his study of the Rhein–Main area,
neatly reminds us of these reasons for failure in regional planning.

Houghton Evans deals with another way in which planning has attempted
to influence land use, in the search to impose order on the course of development. His illustration is that of the architect and his influence on urban form.
From earliest antiquity town planning has existed in the sense that there have
been conscious attempts in urban civilizations to create ideal cities in visual
aesthetic terms as well as from the point of view of purpose, structure and
achievement as a community. City building is the earliest of the major arts of
civilization, as Hiorns[7] asserted; and he is just one example of many
synoptic reviewers of town development through the ages. One can see
throughout the world countless examples of man's creation of an

environment that is a projection of his abstract ideas; geometrical forms such as the square and circle are particularly repetitive. In this sense cities are a form of landscape art and the civilizations of Ancient India, China, Japan, Pre-Columbian America, Egypt, Greece, Rome, Islam and the West all produce impressive examples.

The twentieth-century world has been shaped in art form, too. Our contemporary planning movement is full of examples of influences of new design approaches. Sometimes it is at macroscale and expressed in general terms such as the clarion call for low-density suburbs; sometimes it is at microscale, as with the general prescription for residential architecture in the English cottage vernacular tradition as offered by Unwin, or compact living in city blocks of the machine age as advocated by Le Corbusier. Alternatively the influences have come more directly in particular schemes, and no richer tradition has been offered than the New Towns movement. Houghton Evans selects the British postwar new towns for his examples, and certainly they are noteworthy for creativity of a high order. The Mark I new towns of the late 1940s and early 1950s produced residential environments of considerable quality, within the context of an English tradition but counteracting the openness and untidiness of the previous interwar decades. Subsequent standards may have fallen somewhat, but innovative solutions have continued in a fruitful link between ideology and design. Our architect-planners today are doing no more than their predecessors over three millenia, imposing order on environment.

What is of interest to the historian is the ideas of those designers, how they took root and in what political, economic, social, moral and cultural climate. This is what makes twentieth-century planning so rich a vein of scholarship because we have had such astonishing variety of prescription over less than a century. (No better comparison is there than that offered by Fishman[8] of Ebenezer Howard, Frank Lloyd Wright and Le Corbusier in their plans for three very different types of cities.) From architecture's traditional concern with geometry we have interestingly come to pay more regard to use zones and spaces, which has given rise to the development of the neighbourhood or the urban cell in city structure. Additionally we have come to focus on route-lines and urban traffic. The British new towns offer almost an ideal case study to reflect all these trends.

The chapters by Rebentisch and Houghton Evans can be mirrored in the experiences of many other countries. Keeping our perspective to North West Europe, France, for example, has developed a New Towns programme in an on-going experiment of planned population distribution. As Merlin[9] has described, the beginning was the publication of the outline scheme for the comprehensive development of the Paris region in 1965; five years later an Act of July 1970 laid down the procedure governing the creation and development of new urban areas. Nine new towns were due to receive aid: five were in the Paris region (Evry, Cergy-Pontoise, Trappes, Vallée de la

Marne, Melun-Sénart) and four were provincial (Lille-Est, L'Isle d'Abeau near Lyon, Le Vaudreuil near Rouen, L'Etang de Berre near Marseilles). A decade later we can detect the weaknesses in the institutional structures of decision-making and implementation on a regional scale which have resulted in imperfections in attaining the plan in terms of coordinated investment. Furthermore, while there is still hope and promise, there is also disillusionment in architectural achievements, with reliance on design concepts transmitted from other experiments in other countries.

New towns have come to occupy a unique and perhaps over exaggerated place in international planning circles. The opportunity to build new cities has rightly captured the imagination of the architect-planner. Walter Burley Griffin's Canberra, and Le Corbusier's Chandigarh, are grandiose, alien creations. Other new towns are almost anonymous, simply part of a vast programme of population resettlement, as for example the Soviet expansion in Siberia. In Britain by comparison the postwar new towns represented a conscious step in the construction of a new social order after the war, and as such were accorded great significance. They were new communities of great purpose. They represented in large part a determined strategy of population redistribution from over-congested, high density conurbations, London, the West Midlands, Merseyside/Lancashire, Tyneside/Wearside, Clydeside and Edinburgh. In other words they were seen as answers to megalopolis and played a role in creating a dispersed regional city; they were a conscious design element in channelling growth, expansion and change; as social laboratories they were to be examples of what could be achieved as 'balanced communities'; and as new settings for urban living they were to provide for a quality of life in an environment of high technology.

The results for British new towns are ambivalent. One and a half million people live in new towns, double the population living in the towns when they were first designated, an achievement surely much less than the 1946 Act envisaged. Balanced communities have only partially been created (the definition is so obscure) and self-containment has been sacrificed at the altar of expediency as far as commuting is concerned. Satisfaction in living conditions is high, but not necessarily any higher than in most attractive, middle-class suburban areas. The lesson is that this particular planning method is only as good as the institutional arrangements through which the developments are channelled, only as attractive in design terms as the creativity of the designers and the times in which they work, and only as acceptable to the consumer as a widening range of consumer choice dictates. Decision-making processes of New Town programmes can go awry, as Levin[10] has chronicled in his study of the Central Lancashire New Town. Germany's experiments in regional planning, and Britain's in New Town programmes, emphasize the complex relationship between administrative systems (which enable or constrain) and the economic or social purpose behind public policy.

Watanabe's paper completes this section. He records the founding and early years of Den-en Chofu, a Tokyo garden city, built under the inspiration of Eiichi Shibusawa in emulation of British and other experiments internationally. The purity of Howard's idea and the achievement of Unwin and Parker at Letchworth were misunderstood, perhaps intentionally so, by suburban speculators, and it was the words 'garden city' that were transmitted rather than the concept. The Tokyo results certainly are not as at Letchworth or Welwyn, but rather more like Hampstead and Forest Hills, embedded in the urban fabric of London and New York respectively. Nonetheless, the Den-en Toshi Company represents at micro scale an example of how a particular district of a Japanese city came to take on a distinctive character.

The seminal importance of Howard's *Tomorrow: a Peaceful Path to Real Reform* (1899) reprinted under the better known title *Garden Cities of Tomorrow* (1902), together with the founding of the Garden City Association (1899) is a striking feature of the events surrounding the origins of the town planning movement. British town planning may have taken its early characteristic not from garden cities but from statutory arrangements and planning legislation in which the preparation of schemes was all important, but planning and the Garden City Association shared many common objectives. In other countries, however, replicas of the Garden City Association flourished to the point of very often being the chief stimulus in planning developments. In 1913 an International Garden Cities and Town Planning Association was formed, and no less than eighteen countries were represented, even at that early date.

A different concept was 'garden suburb', of which in Britain Hampstead is a masterpiece. In other countries garden cities and garden suburbs were terms and concepts that became confused, as Tokyo's example illustrates. Some of Howard's principles were lost: communal ownership and separateness from a parent city by agricultural land in particular. Those retained were adherence to small size and conscious planning to provide community facilities and a high standard of residential environment, often at low density. The purity of the goal of dispersal may have been unattainable, given the scale of the problem, but the achievements in garden suburbs are not to be dismissed lightly; enlightened estate development is worthwhile in itself, and Den-en Chofu is an interesting example of it.

ESTABLISHING THE PLANNING TRADITION

This section brings together three papers in which we consider some of the factors involved in establishing a planning tradition in a particular country. Albers reviews the main landmarks in German town planning since the middle of the last century; they appear remarkably similar to those in other Western countries and it may be suggested that the international trends exhibited in the industrially advanced countries of Western Europe have been sufficiently strong to override other local factors. Indeed, Albers concludes that a turbulent political history in Germany has not resulted in any loss of continuity of planning ideas and practice from one political phase to another, and that when there are breaks they are paralleled by similar breaks in other countries.

Nonetheless, there is no automatic, inevitable course for the planning tradition to follow, even in the Western democracies, united as they are by many common links, customs and opportunities for cultural interpenetration. The macro pattern might bear close resemblances across countries, but the detail and departures from a common theme will depend on the particular influences of key actors in the national story. I offer the example of Neville Chamberlain who contributed greatly to the evolving path of British town planning for over twenty years, cementing a link with statutory processes in local government, and reflecting an ideology about housing conditions and slum environments which kept alive a radical stance in planning about city form and structure.

Cunningham presents a case study of Brazil; this shows how different things can be. A strong urban tradition was established by the Portuguese, but town planning in the Western European and, indeed, North American sense was slow to take root in the twentieth century. Her chapter is therefore a counterpoint to the previous two, and it obliges us to consider the reasons for failure to establish an effective planning system, even when faced with severe urban problems. Urban growth in the last quarter of a century has outstripped the capacity of the country's planning structures to deal with the problems with which that growth is associated. Cunningham considers this with reference to four particular cities: two old, Rio de Janeiro and Sao Paulo; and two new, Belo Horizonte and Brasilia.

Albers' broad sweep of German town planning covers its goals and tools, its principles and its results. From the early days of police regulation of development in the mid-nineteenth century to the emergence of local authority administration at the end, to postwar redevelopment and the conscious control over urban spatial systems, the story is a familiar one to West Europeans. The objectives of land management, housing improvement, regulation of city form and visual enhancement of the environment, all strike common chords. The methods of planning also show common features: zoning, the city plan and the regional strategy, all implemented through integrated forms of public administration. The underlying ideology of planning, made explicit in the value stances towards both the city (a source of evil or of hope for the future) and its social problems is also mirrored in other Western countries. The results of planning are likewise common to many; it is an important influence on environmental change, but at most a useful complement to other forces, social, economic and technological, more formidable and enduring. And all this similarity has been followed, almost irrespective of political changes in a nation more turbulent than others in Western Europe.

This suggests that countries at a similar stage of industrial development, with ready facility for intercharge of ideas and experiences, and with a broadly similar pattern of social and political democracy, whereby community and environmental problems are the responsibility of a broadly-based, accountable government, may develop common approaches to planning. A similar path for planning might also evolve from a set of common origins and underlying objectives, with common traditions of social welfare and with a governmental system responsive to community needs. Given these strengths political turbulence seems not to have a major influence.

Certainly there are many points of convergence with Britain, as just one example[11]. A period of Victorian environmental management saw governmental initiatives to safeguard public health (the Acts of 1848 and 1875), to deal with poor housing (Acts of 1868, 1875, and 1890), and to provide public utilities. This was followed by a period at the turn of the century marked by a particular reaction to the urban crisis, when the first efforts at planning in a modern sense mobilized disquiet at environmental and social problems into a coherent movement. As the twentieth century unfolded, the next stage, first between the wars and then after 1945, witnessed a strengthening of interventionist policies with regard to housing and related city problems, and increasingly a broadening of their wider application; it reached its high-water mark in the late 1940s with the strategic thinking behind postwar reconstruction. A final period is our contemporary one in which the centralist approach has been eroded as the consensus that formerly surrounded the objectives of planning has weakened. Recognition of the various preferences that exist in a pluralist society has broken down single-minded approaches to planning solutions; the community with its varying needs now forms a stronger element in the planning system. Planning has become adaptive, flexible, pragmatic and reactive, instead of normative and prescriptive. As in Britain, so in Germany and in other Western democracies.

But history does not follow immutable lines; history is made by individuals who occasionally are of outstanding significance in their contribution to a particular course of events. The case study of Neville Chamberlain is an illustration. As Chairman of Birmingham's Town Planning Committee before the First World War he was responsible for his city's use of planning powers in the 1909 Act; Birmingham proceeded to use that Act more than any other local authority, and its preparation of town planning schemes was an important spur to progress nationally. He contributed to a wider planning philosophy, having an important view about the need for the eradication of bad housing and the decentralization of overcrowded populations. As a reforming Minister of Health he gave new strength and purpose to local government and gave planning an important place within it. He successfully nurtured a tender, growing field of activity and professional concern.

More attention devoted to the biographies of key figures in British planning will reveal the very great importance of a number of them[12]. Amongst the professionals we should certainly mention Thomas Adams, first President of the Town Planning Institute and subsequently a contributor to both Canadian and American planning; also George Pepler, a quietly persuasive civil servant from the days of the Local Government Board to the Ministry of Town and Country Planning; and Patrick Geddes, an intellectual impossible to label and categorize but a stimulant to so many aspects of planning. Also F. J. Osborn, life-long propagandist for garden cities; Raymond Unwin who left his imprint on forms of low-density residential architecture, a radical break from the past; and Patrick Abercrombie, strategist extraordinary for the dispersed city. Likewise Thomas Sharp, passionate devotee of the romantic urban tradition set apart from a preserved countryside; William Holford, civic designer and international entrepreneur; and Colin Buchanan, protector and manager of the environment against the motor car.

But politicians have also made their mark. J. S. Nettlefold, a Birmingham councillor before his cousin Chamberlain, urged the idea of the 'town planning scheme' in emulation of German town expansion plans, a method taken up by John Burns, President of the Local Government Board and architect of the first Town Planning Act. Herbert Morrison, Leader of the London County Council in the 1930s invigorated planning and local government in London, while E. D. Simon brought a planning perspective to Manchester's problems. In the early 1940s Lord Reith blazed a radical trail for reconstruction and later in the same decade Lewis Silkin was a pivotal politician for new towns, national parks and the new development plan system. Since then Duncan Sandys' contribution to civic amenities, that of George Brown to regional economic planning and of Peter Shore to inner city initiatives, have all been significant. Neville Chamberlain takes his place in this sort of roll of honour, all of whom have made inputs to British planning in ways which have shaped the course of events.

However, while there may be a common canvas, with threads of personal significance in the planning history of certain countries, there are many examples where a planning structure fails to get established in any effective sense. Cunningham reminds us of this in her case study of Brazil. Portuguese influence in the colonial period certainly imparted an urban tradition with a rudimentary system of town management. But the evolution of planning in the administrative structures of government, local or central, failed to materialize; the German or British path was not followed. The consequence has been that when urban and economic growth 'took off', accompanied by dramatic increases in population, the Brazilian planning system failed to cope with the problems. The planning solutions which have been adopted have often proved insensitive to the basic needs of the urban population, particularly in terms of housing and public amenities. Instead, emphases, often dramatic and spectacular, have been rather on urban projects like new highway developments or grandiose new towns, with welfare planning for low-income groups of rather less priority.

The reasons for this state of affairs explain how a satisfactory planning system can develop in one country but not in another. Gilbert[13], in his study of Latin American development, suggests a number of factors which might have a bearing on the situation. First there is the heritage of centuries of subordination to Portugal, when the colonial period may have given an economic and social foundation, as well as an elite psychology, that fulfilled the needs of the home country rather than the colony. After political independence, there was still economic dependence on the industrialized West. Then there is the distinctive political system throughout Latin America, the typical features of which are military intervention, limited political participation, and centralism in the administrative system. Few people participate in the political process, and the democratic tradition, beloved of the West, is limited. There is authoritarianism in both Church and State; local government is weak. Thirdly there is the legacy of the population structure. Nearly every Latin American country has a predominantly European ruling class and an Indian or Negro lower class. Race, poverty and class are highly correlated.

Given also the population explosion, the rural drift to the towns and (until quite recently) the poor industrial growth rate, we can begin to understand how housing poverty remains a problem while spectacular highway projects and new capital cities are favoured by autocratic regimes. It is not surprising that concepts of land and social planning, as developed in the West, have failed to take root in Brazil. Furthermore, the political system could not nourish the planning structures that would feed on those concepts.

INTERNATIONAL TRANSFERS

The shaping of our twentieth-century urban world has been considerably influenced by the international transfer of ideas. We have already seen that within Western Europe at the turn of the century there was a considerable borrowing from others' experience. In the first decade Britain had a close interest in Germany for example, and throughout Europe there was a creative exchange of ideas regarding design and technology. Furthermore Western Europe itself exported planning and planning concepts to other parts of the world; the garden city is probably the best example.

The two papers in this section consider this international transfer from the particular point of view of the export of planning to colonial countries. Britain is the home country selected but the general points raised refer broadly to the Westernization of the environments of other cultures and societies. King offers a wide-ranging review of the factors concerned with the establishment of British planning in its colonies. Collins deals with the particular case study of Lusaka, showing how the imported values of planning helped to shape a city's physical form.

King suggests that the 'history of export planning' can be divided into three phases: a period up to the early twentieth century when settlements were laid out according to military-political traditions; a period in the first half of the century in which British planning ideology, legislation and professional practice were prominent in the network of colonial relationships; and a post-colonial period when the export of planning values, though with wider political and economic contexts, has continued. In this useful historical frame we can place the work of the planning entrepreneurs (Lutyens at Delhi or Le Corbusier at Chandigarh, for example); the use made in British colonies of British planning legislation, particularly the Town and Country Planning Act, 1932; and the different styles of planning according to the traditions of the exporting country (Britain in Africa or India; Russia in Inner Asia).

King goes on to offer theoretical considerations for the nature of exported planning. The political and economic framework is clearly important, with 'dependent capitalism' accounting for certain forms of spatial development. Then there is the cultural, social and ideological context, in which ideas about such matters as health and social organization are superimposed by one culture on another. The social dimension itself is important, particularly aspects of segregation, by race, colour or creed, in the community structure. Next there is the question of the interaction of environment and behaviour through which we see the influence of imported legislation with implications for life styles. Last, there are the mechanisms of exporting planning: professionals, propagandist societies, government (the Colonial Office, for example), universities, and the United Nations organizations.

This overview with its emphasis on political and cultural interchange between countries at different stages of economic development should encourage empirical case studies of particular cities. One might envisage a whole generation of student theses with this approach! The example offered by Collins is of Lusaka, 1931–64, and he illustrates how imported values of the colonial power (Britain) were translated into the physical form of the city. Lusaka became the new capital of Northern Rhodesia (now Zambia) and the first Plan was prepared by the British planner, Adshead. As a disciple of the Garden City tradition, he strove to avoid the rectilinear layout of Salisbury and Bulawayo. Subsequently the growth of the town was greatly affected by 'circulatory labour migration' which established the practice of towns for whites and the rural areas for blacks, but the Urban African Housing Ordinance of 1948 changed that situation. More consultants were appointed and a statutory development plan prepared.

These two papers confirm the view that planning in the twentieth century has been international in scope. This has been because the world's urban population has expanded greatly, and the growth of major cities has been accompanied by intractable urban problems of social, economic and political significance. The Western World, itself having gone through an acutely painful phase of industrialization and urbanization, had, by the end of the nineteenth century, begun to tackle successfully the worst problems of health, sanitation, housing and public-utility provision through systematic forms of urban management. In the twentieth century the West was in a position to export its ideas and skills. If this seems too altruistic, it is necessary to say that at that time the West economically and politically dominated the non-industrialized, non-urbanized, underdeveloped territories in a colonial relationship. In the export of good government to the dependent nations, the values, ideology, methods and skills of planning were transmitted. The transplant was often alien to a culture and to a set of economic and social conditions quite different from the advanced West, though this is not to say that many of the results were not beneficial. Planning history is not called upon to make that judgement (although it may), rather it has to painstakingly unravel, through empirical work, the ways in which the export of planning was actually conducted and with what consequences for the shaping of particular cities. This will lead to theoretical re-assessments in due time as scholarship advances.

The post- or neo-colonial phase of international history continues and opportunities for this kind of study are well nigh limitless. Urban problems in the Third World are acute and all countries are faced with the need to set up administrative programmes and planning structures, within the constraints of their political systems and financial and technical resources. There is now an international network of agencies and consultants giving advice, exchanging ideas, and communicating skills in forms of city, regional and economic developments. The urban world is still being shaped, and the planning historian's prospectus is almost unbounded.

Urban populations in the developing countries are now growing twice as fast as those in industrialized countries. Moreover the rates of growth of 'spontaneous' settlements (squatter areas) in many countries are accelerating in relation to urban growth rates as a whole. We saw in Cunningham's chapter how Brazilian cities are faced with the enormous problems of the ill-housed; perhaps it is this feature above all which will call for a quickening of interest in forms of comprehensive city planning. When adopted, the story will provide an even richer field for research.

But what forms of city planning? If we are critical of the insensitive application of styles of Western planning in the past, should we not be equally critical of contemporary attempts? Dwyer, whose experience of Third World situations is considerable, summarizes thus:

... master plans for Third World cities are often excessively rigid and antiseptic in concept. Most fail to give due weight to the growing significance of spontaneous settlement within the urban form or, where they do, tend to look forward to a millenium where all squatter huts will be eliminated and replaced by regularly laid out housing in the image of the Western city, without specifying the immediate rungs on this particular ladder to urban heaven.[14]

The Westernization (as well as Americanization and Sovietization) of other people's environments continues.

ASSESSMENT

It is too early to evaluate twentieth-century planning, but a number of critical perspectives may be legitimately offered. Fishman's paper has this objective. His starting point is to acknowledge a number of unspoken orthodoxies about planning: broadly speaking, these would be the view that planning can attempt a rationality over the complexities of environment and economic and social life; that it can attain social welfare objectives; and that from its consequences it can be termed 'progressive'. Fishman challenges these assumptions, pointing to a failure to fulfil expectations, querying the social benefits derived and preferring diversity to regulated order. A mistrust of experts and bureaucracies would lead him to be sceptical about government, the wisdom it mistakenly assumes and the power it increasingly wields. At the heart of the matter is the conflict between collective action and individual initiative; planning perhaps has claimed the benefits of the former too readily.

Fishman is an American academic observer, and other people will have different viewpoints; it is not easy to stand aloof from the influences and constraints of one's own ideological persuasion about planning, one's professional stance, or one's place in a cultural or political system. A British professional, keen to be loyal to and represent his own Planning Institute, or equally keen to align himself with the values of the government office or private firm in which he works, will answer one way; a detached academic observer will answer another. A planner in the USSR or a Socialist Eastern bloc country will be committed to centralism, State intervention and a high level of integration; it will not be easy for him to acknowledge the pluralism of contemporary society as observed in the West, and lean towards planning systems which take into account the need to be responsive to private preferences. The planner in Australia, South Africa or Latin America will have different value judgements and will have to work in different socio-economic and political systems.

However, there are some general objective points to be made, directly to Fishman's observations. In the first place we may readily concede that in the twentieth century there have been important political changes which have provided a crucial context within which town planning itself has developed. These vary from country to country but the example of Britain may be taken as an illustration. Apart from the 'municipal socialism' of cities in the later years of the nineteenth century, when public utilities were municipalized and there were other forms of municipal action for community welfare, the role of the public sector in crucial aspects of planning, notably land management and housing, was very slow to develop. There was political resistance to the view that this was in any way an appropriate area for government or local councils. World War I was a stimulus to a developing public sector role in housing and social welfare, and the Depression years a further encouragement, particularly in economic affairs. World War II was another powerful influence in extending the role of the State, so much so that Britain's postwar reconstruction years represented a high-water mark in approaches to housing and land planning. Since then there have been twists and turns, with developments in related aspects of planning (notably transportation, economic affairs and recreation), but environmental management has tended increasingly to lack sharpness and precision of objectives as the interests of separate community groups have assumed greater importance than a national consensus. All this very neatly reflects the fundamental conflict that Fishman notes, between the tradition of collective action and that of individual initiative. In countries and political systems where the former is strong, styles of urban planning will be different from those where it is weak. The distinction between the United States on the one hand and the socialist countries of USSR and the Eastern bloc is pronounced from this point of view. Britain stands with the benefits and weaknesses of both, and moreover it changes its stance over time.

A quarter of a century ago a British socialist, Crosland, could point out that it was no longer believed that a free price-mechanism led in practice to a maximization of economic welfare[15]. On the other hand he could recognize that excessive growth of bureaucracy could be economically inefficient. Extreme positions were not then adopted, and while differences of emphasis remained, generally the issue was not whether, but how much and for what purpose, to plan. That was the measure of progress made over the previous twenty-five years; it was a far cry from the different political positions adopted at the beginning of the 1930s. Twenty-five years after Crosland we find that the political ground has shifted again, as the frontiers of government intervention are rolled back. The public sector is distrusted on the grounds of alleged waste and inefficiency and there is a preparedness to have greater reliance in collective results of private actions. Over this fifty-year period, 1930–80, the vicissitudes of political change have provided the backcloth against which town planning itself has functioned, the powers which have been given to it, and the expectations which have been ascribed.

Quite apart from this political context (and there will be different ones in other countries of the world) the activity of town planning has to be conducted in a setting subject to popular approval. The changing value judgements of society are brought to bear critically on the planners' achievements. I have written elsewhere[16] that there is currently an awareness of the importance of the qualitative aspects of life rather than quantitative gains. This has led to some unpredictable reactions to planning achievements, recorded through public opinion. A major highway project may represent technological progress one decade, an environmental nuisance the next; a housing design can first be hailed as innovative, and later as a sociological disaster; a fast breeder nuclear reactor may be seen initially as a major scientific contribution to the energy crisis, but subsequently as an ecological hazard.

Public preferences in an affluent age can be fickle. The planner can be urged to provide for choice and opportunity; once provided, he is then charged with the consequences. Mass car ownership, unrestrained car usage, choice in housing location, freedom in recreation and tourism, all come to represent flash points in clashes of social values which then become the planning problems of a new generation.

I went on to remark that

the social climate of planning has changed over time, and we must expect this instability to continue... On the one hand there is a widespread view that planned change no longer represents an improvement: what is new is not necessarily better than the old. This discontent with the results of our environmental achievements has fostered both a spirit of conservation and scepticism against the claims of change.

These remarks were directed by a planner, a committed professional to his professional Institute. They accord with Fishman's critical observations, written to a different audience for a different purpose. There is a common ground of preparedness to challenge inherited assumptions, to question the social and economic benefit of plannned action, to acknowledge the failure to achieve high expectations, to recognize that excessive zeal for planned order can be counter-productive and to have a healthy distrust of technical objectivity.

The critical observations do not lead to a demolition of the achievements of planning. Planners need to be modest, for their inherited ideology has given a misplaced sense of unrealistic utopianism. They may be considered as experts, but they are best regarded as expert advisers to politicians in a delicate balance of power, influence and responsibility. While they must not claim too much of themselves, they should not claim too little for what can be, and indeed has been, achieved. The long-standing sense of common concern for environment and the setting it provides for individual life chances and community satisfactions makes planning one of the significant movements in the shaping of the twentieth century.

NOTES

1. Hardy, Dennis (1979) *Alternative Communities in Nineteenth Century England.* London: Longman.

2. Cherry, Gordon E. (1979) The town planning movement and the late Victorian city. *Transactions,* Institute of British Geographers, **4** (2), pp. 306–19.
3. Cherry, Gordon E. (1974) *The Evolution of British Town Planning.* Heath and Reach: Leonard Hill.
4. Plowden, William (1973) *The Motor Car and Politics in Britain.* Harmondsworth: Pelican.
5. Rondinelli, Dennis A. (1970) *Urban and Regional Development Planning.* Ithaca: Cornell University Press.
6. Friend, J. K., Power, J. M. and Yewlett, C. J. L. (1974) *Public Planning: The Intercorporate Dimension.* London: Tavistock.
7. Hiorns, Frederick R. *Town Building in History.* London: Harrap.
8. Fishman, Robert (1977) *Urban Utopias in the Twentieth Century.* New York: Basic Books.
9. Merlin, Pierre (1971) *New Towns.* London: Methuen.
10. Levin, P. H. (1976) *Government and the Planning Process.* London: Allen and Unwin.
11. Cherry, Gordon E. (1974) The Development of Planning Thought in M. J. Bruton (ed.), *The Spirit and Purpose of Planning.* London: Hutchinson.
12. Cherry, Gordon E. (ed.) (forthcoming) *Pioneers in British Planning.* London: Architectural Press.
13. Gilbert, Alan (1974) *Latin American Development. A Geographical Perspective.* Harmondsworth: Penguin.
14. Dwyer, D. J. (1975) *People and Housing in Third World Cities.* London: Longman.
15. Crosland, C. A. R. (1956) *The Future of Socialism.* London: Jonathan Cape.
16. Cherry, Gordon E. (1978) Prospects for the profession. *The Planner,* **64** (6), pp. 178–82.

2

Housing policy and city planning: the puzzling split in the United States, 1893–1931[1]

PETER MARCUSE

THE PUZZLE: WHERE IS HOUSING IN U.S. CITY PLANNING?

The relation of housing to the early stages of city planning in the United States presents a puzzle. The problems of housing in the late nineteenth century in the major cities were critical. One has only to read contemporary accounts:

> The Tenement House Committee of 1894 disclosed that the population of Manhattan Island—143.2 persons per acre—exceeded that of the most crowded cities of France, Germany, and England. The residential tenth ward, with a density of 626 per acre, was 30 per cent more congested than a similar section of Prague, generally considered the worst in Europe. One section of the eleventh ward had a density of 986.4 per acre and was even more crowded than the Koombarwara district of Bombay, which in 1881 had a density of 759.66 persons per acre and was one of the most overpopulated spots on earth.[2]

The housing built to these densities was shoddy indeed, as a report in the *New York Tribune* in 1884 shows:

> The walls are thin and made of inferior brick, the mortar is mere sand, the plastering flakes off, the woodwork warps, the panels of the doors show streaks of light in them, and the window casings let in cold drafts of air. As for the plumbing, it is indescribably bad ... Traps evaporate or siphon out, and tenants will often put a cloth held down by a brick over the sink openings to keep out the stench.[3]

23

The consequences were inevitable: a social worker described them in 1891:

> Scene after scene is the same. Rags, dirt, filth, wretchedness, the same figures, the same faces, the same old story of one room unfit for habitation yet inhabited by a dozen people, the same complaint of a ruinous rent exacted by the merciless landlord, the same shameful neglect of all sanitary precautions, rotten floors, oozing walls, vermin everywhere, broken windows, crazy staircases—this is the picture of the homes of hundreds of people in the tenement districts of New York ... An extreme case? If it only were—but these are tenements built within a comparatively recent period, and thus nominally more comfortable than older dwellings.[4]

The picture, indeed, is familiar to any student of urban life in England or in any other industrial country in Europe at the turn of the century.

One would thus expect, at least viewed with hindsight, that housing would be a primary concern of a city planning profession beginning to emerge at the very time that these desperate problems were being forcefully brought to wide public attention by crusaders and publicists such as Jacob Riis, Lawrence Veiller, Robert deForest, and others. One would expect that zoning, perhaps the first and still most important contribution of the city planning profession to the governance of the American city, would be designed and used to the fullest extent possible to improve the conditions of housing. And one would further expect that regional planning, as exemplified by such classic documents as the Regional Plan of New York and Its Environs published in 1931, would place housing high among its list of priorities, would attempt to put the housing problem in its regional context, and suggest means by which the full resources of the region might be brought to its solution.

Politically, throughout this period municipal reform movements often saw housing as a key issue calling for redress. The passage of increasingly restrictive and sophisticated regulatory measures controlling both tenement-house construction and occupancy was evidence of the political support available for governmental action dealing with housing problems. The stage seemed ripe for active contributions by planners, struggling in any event to carve out a role for themselves in the evolving urban scene and to achieve recognition and status for their profession.

Yet, contrary to all expectations, neither the city planning movement as it moved from intellectual crusade to practical influence, nor zoning, nor the Regional Plan of New York, contributed much to the solution of the housing problems of the ill-housed, and arguably each actually worsened it. Edith Elmer Wood, one of the earliest, most consistent, and most astute of the housing reformers, noted in 1931 that 'it is regrettable from every point of view that housing and city planning should be divorced to the extent that they have always been in the United States'[5]. It was not until the aftermath of the Great Depression that public policy in the United States dealt explicitly with the general problem of providing housing, and even then for reasons having more to do with employment than with housing. Not until the late 1940s did planners begin to deal with housing as a matter of national policy, and not until the late 1960s did planning for housing become a recognized and legitimate part of city planning at the local level.

This then is the puzzle to which the paper is addressed: why did city planning in the United States, confronted in its early days with critical problems of housing in virtually every place it worked, and displaying in its spoken and written words a vital concern with these problems and desire to contribute to their alleviation, in fact drop its concern with housing in each of the three cases examined here, and even contribute to its exacerbation, ultimately needing the turmoil of the 1960s to bring it back to those concerns to which it had paid such eloquent tribute at its inception?

That the puzzle is real, and not just the product of hindsight, may be seen by putting it in comparative perspective. Housing and city planning have been linked since the earliest days of modern planning in Europe. One can go back to the writings and schemes of Fourier and Owen to see the central place of housing; the very name of the Housing, Town Planning, etc. Act of 1909 in Britain, which gave city planning its formal charter in that country, shows the connection. The sequence of aims set forth in debates on the Act is significant; it is intended to promote 'the home healthy, the house beautiful, the town pleasant, the city dignified and the suburb salubrious'[6].

Ashworth summarizes the British evolution this way:

> Housing reform had gradually been conceived in terms of larger and larger units. Torrens' Act (Artizans and Labourers Dwelling Act, 1868) had made a beginning with individual houses; Cross's Act (Artizans and Labourers Dwellings Improvement Act, 1875) had introduced an element of town planning by concerning itself with the reconstruction of insanitary areas; the framing of bye-laws in accordance with the Public Health Act of 1875 had accustomed local authorities to the imposition of at least a minimum of regulation on new building, and such a measure as the London Building Act of 1894 brought into the scope of public control the formation and widening of streets, the lines of buildings frontage, the extent of open space around buildings, and the height of buildings. Town planning was therefore not altogether a leap in the dark, but could be represented as a logical extension, in accordance with changing aims and conditions, of earlier legislation concerned with housing and public health.[7]

City planning practice in Germany, as well as in other countries, was also far ahead of U.S. efforts in dealing with housing issues in the first decade of the twentieth century. While the integration of housing and city planning no doubt still leaves much to be desired in any given European country also, the difference between, say, England or Germany and the United States is nevertheless a striking one.

The fact that leaders of both the housing reform and the city planning movements in the United States were aware of these quite different European developments does nothing to make the puzzle easier. In a paper entitled 'Is Government Aid Necessary in Housing Finance?', Edith Elmer Wood told the National Housing Association in 1929 that the United States is

> at the point where Great Britain was 78 years ago, where Belgium and Germany were 40 years ago, France 35 years ago, and Holland 28 years ago, debating whether or not nation, state and city should provide housing credits, on an at-cost basis, to cut down the price of wholesome housing to be within the reach of lower-income groups that cannot otherwise attain it.[8]

Benjamin Marsh, a major figure in early housing reform efforts and secretary of the influential Committee on Congestion of Population in New York, went on a study tour of Europe as early as 1902, and Frederick Howe reported enthusiastically on German planning and housing programmes to the third national conference on city planning in 1911[9]. 'The Germans . . . have built the most wonderful cities in modern times', he said[10]. Others were equally impressed, and discussions of European practices were common in U.S. planning circles between 1909 and the First World War. Yet the linkage between housing and planning found in Europe was not applied in the United States. Why?

The puzzle is reflected in policy and practice as well as in planning. In every industrialized nation of Western Europe, government entered the housing field either before or during the First World War, and has remained in it, with retreats in the level but not the nature of involvement, ever since. In the United States, government at best put one toe in the housing field in the First World War, and withdrew it with unseemly haste as soon as the war was over. The difference in the impact of that war hardly explains the subsequent difference in policy. Policies during the prosperity of the 1920s, the Depression of the 1930s, the wartime and postwar recovery in the 1940s and 1950s, and long-term policies in the whole post-World War II period, show the same contrast in approach. As recently as 1973, the percentage of new housing construction subsidized directly by government stood at less than 1 per cent in the United States[11], while in West Germany the corresponding figure was 16.7 per cent and in the United Kingdom, 37.5 per cent[12].

How are these differences to be explained?

THE MILESTONES EXAMINED

Three milestones in the evolution of planning in the United States may give some clues to the answer. The first is the birth of the modern city planning profession in the movement starting with the Columbian Exposition in Chicago in 1893 and ending with the formation of what was to become the American Institute of Planners in 1917. The second is the development of zoning, from its first discussions within the city planning movement to the adoption of New York City's pioneering zoning ordinance in 1916. The third is the publication of the Regional Plan for New York and Its Environs in 1931, with antecedents going back to discussions of decongestion and deconcentration in housing and planning circles in the early 1900s. In each case, similar patterns appear, suggesting similar factors at work. In the third section of this paper we will then attempt to look at those operative factors in perspective, and see what solution to the puzzle they suggest.

THE EARLY CITY PLANNING MOVEMENT

Three intellectual concerns contributed to the initial shaping of the city planning movement in the United States: one aesthetic or architectural, one concerned with housing, and one promoting civic reform and scientific management, what William Alonso has called technocratic planning[13].

The aesthetic is the easiest to trace. The World's Columbian Exposition, held at Chicago in 1893, brought millions to the 'White City' to admire an 'enchanting spectacle', a 'thrilling revelation of the power of architects, landscape architects, sculptors and painters to evoke rapture and delight'[14] in a city hitherto known for its slaughterhouses and grain shipping facilities. Its elaborate civic centres, treelined boulevards, waterfront plazas and parks, and overall design of balance and beauty showed in the words of a contemporary observer 'what an ideal city might be'[15].

But the City Beautiful concept, which grew out of the Columbian Exposition[16] and dominated city planning in the United States for the next fifteen years, had scant attention to pay to housing.

Housing was indeed included among the list of concerns of the City Beautiful movement. When Charles Mulford Robinson, a leading apostle of city planning and municipal improvements, spoke of the requirements of good cities, he spoke of 'those that had to do with circulation, those that have to do with hygiene, and those that have to do distinctly with beauty ...' Hygiene, in this context, was intended to include 'sanitary' housing. But when it came to discussing the city plan that Robinson foresaw as combining these requirements into a 'single scheme comprehensive and harmonious', there were only two key elements suggested: 'circulation and community buildings'[17]. As Benjamin Marsh pointed out in 1908:

> The grouping of public buildings, and the installation of speedways, parks and drives, which affect only moderately the daily lives of the city's toilers, are important but vastly more so is the securing of decent home conditions for the countless thousands who otherwise can but occasionally escape from their squalid, confining surroundings to view the architectural perfection and to experience the aesthetic delights of the remote improvements.[18]

The plans that came out of the City Beautiful movement, like its rhetoric, contained occasional mention of housing[19], but few were shaped by

housing policy. Even defenders of the City Beautiful movement's contribution concede that it 'did little with housing'[20]. The best-known city plan
it produced illustrates the point.

Daniel Burnham's plan for Chicago, completed in 1909, a pioneering effort
in the history of U.S. planning, contained only one concrete suggestion
dealing with housing: that space be set aside for future residences. As Mel
Scott, in the history of city planning officially commissioned by the American
Institute of Planners to commemorate its fiftieth anniversary, said of the
Chicago Plan:

> It is [a plan for] an essentially aristocratic city, pleasing to the merchant
> princes who participated in its conception but not meeting some of the basic
> economic and human needs. In this metropolis for businessmen there are . . .
> no model tenements for workers, much less model neighborhoods. Not that
> Burnham, Bennett, and Moore were oblivious to the housing problem. Slums
> are mentioned, but only in one paragraph suggesting that 'It is no attack on
> private property to argue that society has the inherent right to protect itself
> [against] gross evils and known perils' by imposing restrictions on over-
> crowding, enforcing sanitary regulations, and limiting lot coverage. There is
> even an assertion that if private enterprise cannot rehouse persons forced out
> of congested quarters, the city itself may have to do so, 'in common justice to
> men and women so degraded by long life in the slums that they have lost all
> power of caring for themselves'. But this daring idea is tucked into the report
> almost surreptitiously, as if it were an irrelevancy to be overlooked in the
> contemplation of magnificent boulevards, imposing public structures, and
> splendid parks.[21]

The City Beautiful movement, then, and the essentially aesthetic,
architecturally-oriented view of planning which it represented, had little
direct impact on housing problems. Its rhetoric, where it included housing,
was not carried into reality; in most cases even rhetoric about housing was
absent. What impact there was in the event was probably unintentional: it
diverted attention from problems of the ill-housed to other problems
affecting other groups. Sometimes the problems of the ill-housed were even
aggravated in the service of those other groups. When Daniel Burnham
transferred the Columbian Exposition type of civic centre design to
Cleveland, slums had to be cleared to make way for the new public buildings.
There is no record of what happened to the occupants of those slums. And
when $5 million was appropriated in New York City to buy up unfit
tenements, parks were put in their place. Urban renewal has a long lineage
indeed!

Not that the proposals of the housing reformers, the second of the three
major influences on the early planning profession, were so radical. In fact, the
most general formulation of their major proposal, decongestion or deconcentration, was one that met with virtually unanimous approval within planning

circles. We shall see later on, in the discussion of the Regional Plan for New York, that deconcentration may in fact mean many different things to different people, and agreement on the concept may cover wide disagreement on its meaning. The housers' concern with decongestion, however, had two major thrusts: the improvement of conditions in the slums, and the provision of alternative housing for slum dwellers in the outer parts of the city. The former concern seemed to be being met, at least at the very beginning of the century, by restrictive regulation. As to the provision of alternative housing, however, only a small handful of reformers were willing even to entertain the notion that public efforts should be appropriately involved. At most, they saw philanthropy as playing that role; at the conservative end, as with Veiller, they felt negative regulation to be quite adequate.

The most specific programme for providing improved housing outside the slums that the housing reformers urged was based on the English industrial villages and garden cities. But the United States was not England. The Garden City idea was nowhere seriously adopted, and even proposals modelled on such well-accepted patterns as Port Sunlight and Bournville met with no great success. Gary, Indiana, built by the U.S. Steel Corporation on former marshlands and dunes, with homes developed by private speculators and no concern for planning or social consequences shown anywhere along the line, was much more typical of what happened in the United States in those instances where employers became involved with housing to secure for themselves an adequate labour force. Forest Hills Gardens, in New York, designed by Frederick Law Olmsted, one of the key figures in early U.S. city planning history, was the foremost accomplishment along Garden City lines; and it simply demonstrated, in Roy Lubove's dry words, 'the obvious—that attractive suburban communities could be created for those able to afford them'[22].

The third influence on the early evolution of the city planning movement, coming later than the aesthetic and the housing but of equal importance, was the managerial, or technocratic. It was concerned with the City Practical, rather than the City Beautiful, and it harmonized easily with the political currents of municipal government reform that were the hallmarks of urban politics during the Progressive Era. Planning was a technical process, going objectively from factual analysis of problem to inevitable and scientific solution.

The relation of these three threads: aesthetic, housing, and technocratic, is exemplified in the career of George B. Ford, one of the leading early planners and a brother of James Ford, who taught housing at Harvard[23]. An architect, George studied at the Ecole des Beaux Arts in Paris, but took as his thesis problem 'A Tenement in a Large City'. He spoke on housing and residential layouts at the first national conference on city planning, organized by Benjamin Marsh in 1909. He spoke passionately about the problems of housing: The City Beautiful was desirable, indeed, but can we with equanimity stand by and help the city spend its money on . . . frills and furbelows when only a step away the hideous slum, reeking with filth and disease, rotten with crime, is sapping the very life-blood of the city[24]?

But Ford also earned a degree in mechanical engineering from the Massachusetts Institute of Technology, and his belief in science began to indicate to him the path city planning should travel. Specific facts had to be collected (the twelve main headings were susceptible of objective definition); methods of analysing that data formed the subject matter of particular sub-categories of scientific city planning, or could be supplied by related disciplines, e.g. highway engineering; and such analysis would lead, in his classic phrase, to the 'one, and only one, logical and convincing solution of the problems involved'[25].

The underlying realization was that the businessman, who had to pay the bills, had to be impressed by the competence with which the activity of city planning was conducted.' The definition of competence in the business community was at that time heavily under the influence of Frederick Winslow Taylor and his *Principles of Scientific Management.* Ford presented the possibility of 'Taylorizing' municipal administration much as business-men were trying to 'Taylorize' manufacturing.

In the process, the concern for improving housing conditions dropped by the wayside. City planning became, in Mel Scott's words, 'a matter of altering spatial relationships to achieve the practical ends of efficiency and convenience'[26]—but efficiency and convenience primarily for the business community. The approach to planning for housing indeed sounded efficient and business-like. Surveys would show which existing housing was 'below minimum standards', and thus needed removal. As to new housing, other surveys would show the incomes and places of employment of residents of an area. By mapping land costs and employment locations together, one could determine the location of particular types of new housing[27]. On to the next category of surveys required. The hideous slum, as to whose consequences Ford had expressed his concern so vividly just four years earlier, could thus conceivably be removed. Concern for what happened to the slum-dweller, however, whose income would not even then[28] support new construction to contemporary minimum standards, is not as apparent.

Scientific, or technocratic, planning was more suited to developing efficient infrastructure to meet the needs of the private market (to making improvements in urban sanitation, for instance) than it was to interfering with that market and its results in the housing field. Like the City Beautiful before it, the City Practical seemed not to have, in the end, much to contri-bute to the improvement of the housing conditions of the worst housed.

The organizational history of this early period of the planning movement may be taken as symbolic of the substantive developments we have traced. It was concern with housing that first promoted the formation of the Commit-tee on Congestion of Population in New York in 1907. The Committee on

Congestion, in turn, convened the first National Conference on City Planning in Washington, D.C., in 1909. Successive annual conferences were held until, in 1917, it was decided at the ninth conference to form the American City Planning Institute (later the American Institute of Planners, itself a significant change of title suggesting the growing professionalization of the field)[29].

Simultaneously, the housing movement was beginning to take separate organizational shape. In 1907 Veiller had already suggested to the Russell Sage Foundation the desirability of forming a national organization to spread the word on housing reform. In 1909 the Foundation agreed to underwrite it, and the National Housing Association was formed. It was at the beginning largely a one-man operation, with Veiller speaking for it, editing its paper, convening its meetings, and drafting legislation on its behalf[30].

At first, the National Conferences on City Planning and the National Housing Association had a very heavy overlap of membership and shared very similar concerns. The same individuals read papers at each other's meetings, and they pressed for similar types of public action. But the separation of the paths of housing reform and city planning can be traced back to the conference sessions and organizational activities of 1909-11. The 1909 National Conference on City Planning focused on social problems, housing being prime among them. Social surveys, on the order of Charles Booth's *Life and Labour of the People of London*, were much in the air. Benjamin Marsh told the conference that planners should

> make a survey, if we may adopt this term, [certainly a more hesitant approach than Ford's!] of the economic and industrial conditions in the city, and pre-eminently of housing conditions and the ownership and control of land, since the land question is fundamental to a proper solution of the housing question.[31]

In 1910 John Nolen, one of the key figures in the history of city planning in the United States, was saying in his Plan for Madison, Wisconsin:

> The most important features of city planning are not the public buildings, not the railroad approaches, not even the parks and playgrounds. They are the location of streets, the establishment of block lines, the subdivision of property into lots, the regulations of buildings, and the housing of the people.[32]

But what Nolan had in mind was planning for new middle-class residential areas, rather than dealing with the problems of slums. The emphasis at national conferences was also moving in this direction, and the sessions after 1910 were, according to James G. Coke 'dominated by architects and landscape architects'. Coke continues:

> The New York Committee (on Congestion) independently organized the National Housing Association, which, beginning in 1911, held its own conferences. The two groups diverged, not to find common interest again until the 1930s.[33]

The account is slightly oversimplified, but substantially accurate.

In 1917, when the American City Planning Institute was officially founded, only two of its fifty-two charter members were such as to be called 'housers' in Mel Scott's summary[34]. Not till well after the Second World War, and then only under the pressure of Federal legislation and funding regulations, did 'housing elements' begin again to be seen as an important and standard component of a city plan. Whether even today housing has the prominence in most actual city plans that Benjamin Marsh would have assigned it is a debatable question.

THE BEGINNINGS OF ZONING

Zoning is the next major milestone in the history of modern city planning in the United States. It was the most immediate and effective fruit of the organized efforts of the early planning conferences and the organization of planners. It was, in a sense, that product of planning that had the most real impact on housing in the early years.

The history of New York City zoning illustrates the more general evolution. The pattern repeats that of the early city planning movement itself. An initially voiced concern with the condition of the ill-housed is conjoined with other concerns germane to city planning. The new professionals take up the challenge, make studies, and produce recommendations. The recommendations are subject to the influences of practicality, and are debated and modified after their issuance. In the end, the initial concerns with housing have disappeared, and the contribution planning has made has been to the solution of other problems.

Benjamin Marsh, concerned in New York in 1909 with slum conditions and the improvement of the condition of the ill-housed, saw congestion as a major cause of the problem, and agitated successfully for the appointment of a Commission on Congestion of Population. It produced a set of urgent recommendations to reduce congestion; zoning and the preparation of a comprehensive city plan were prominent among them.

Zoning appeared to be a planning device that would solve both problems of housing and other problems then plaguing New York. The other problems were readily visible. Fifth Avenue merchants were disturbed at the encroachment of garment manufacturers above 23rd Street, congesting the street with lower-class and immigrant workers, making their prime commercial locations less attractive and less accessible. The garment factories and their lofts

> are crowded with their hundreds and thousands of garment workers who swarm down upon the avenue for the lunch hour . . . They stand upon or move slowly along the sidewalks and choke them up . . . and as work ends at the close of the day, thousands of these operators pour out upon the sidewalks within a short space of time, and congest the side streets with a steady stream of humanity that moves its way to the West Side . . . Shopkeepers complain bitterly of financial loss [because many] women shoppers tend to avoid the section.[35]

Downtown property owners were simultaneously concerned at the pro-liferating skyscrapers; being able to build high on one's own property was fine, but a skyscraper next door blotted out light and air. The large insurance companies, the title and trust companies, the Bowery Savings Bank and other banks complained in a petition that haphazard development had already impaired the 'capital values of large areas', thus 'affecting the market value of real estate for investment'[36].

The combination of housing and other interests made zoning seem appealing indeed. George McAneny was reform borough president of Manhattan from 1910 to 1913 and one of the most influential supporters of housing reform and planning in New York City. He was, in his own words, 'bent on reducing the volume of misery or dependency in the city through the correction, so far as possible, of the conditions that breed misery'. McAneny saw zoning as a way of providing 'benefit to the tenement population as well as Fifth Avenue merchants'[37]. He lent it active support.

After extensive debate, a zoning resolution was adopted by the City, in 1916. Its focus was on the regulation of the height of skyscrapers and the exclusion of manufacturing uses from higher quality commercial areas. The improvement of slum housing was not a part of the resolution. The Advisory Commission which drafted the resolution 'stressed the fact that zoning was designed to promote business interests, not injure them for the benefit of the working class poor'[38]. Scott summarized the atmosphere in which the final regulations were drafted as 'dominated by the financial and commercial interests of the city'[39]. The final product was so ineffective in dealing with slum housing conditions that even Lawrence Veiller, the most conservative of housing reformers and life-time opponent of public housing, refused to sign the Advisory Commission's report, although he was a member of it[40].

Zoning was not only not helpful to the ill-housed, it had negative conse-quences for them. For one thing, like the earlier Tenement House Act regulations, it increased the costs of housing. Felix Adler had warned, thirty-five years earlier, that more restrictive plumbing requirements for new construction would 'legislate the poor out of the better houses'[41]. Similarly, in 1916, the adoption of zoning restricted the locations available for cheaper housing and imposed building requirements that were not tailored to specific sites or specific needs[42].

In addition (and of increasing importance as time went on), zoning excluded the poor entirely from most new residential areas. Originally pressures for residential zoning came from middle-class homeowners concerned to keep conflicting industrial or commercial uses out of residential areas. Los Angeles in 1909 passed an ordinance keeping brickyards out of residential areas, and applied it successfully to existing as well as future operations[43]. The Civic League of St. Louis, the state legislatures of Wisconsin, Minnesota, and Illinois, and numerous speakers at National Conferences on City Planning were all concerned even before New York enacted its zoning resolution 'to protect single family residential areas from invasion by factories, stores, and apartment houses'[44].

But zoning more explicitly to exclude certain types of residents from desirable residential areas has a history at least as old as zoning aimed at excluding types of uses. As early as the 1880s, the City of Modesto, California, passed an ordinance which provided:

> It shall be unlawful for any person to establish, maintain, or carry on the business of a public laundry or washhouse where articles are washed or. cleansed for hire, within the City of Modesto, except within that part of the city which lies west of the railroad tracks and south of G Street.[45]

There was no doubt at whom the ordinance was aimed: the Chinese immigrants, imported into California to build the railroads and work in the mines, for whom laundries served not only as one of the early business enterprises in which they could engage, but also as social centres and gathering places[46]. Since then, the use of zoning to discriminate against minority group members and poorer households has become a national scandal in the United States. The extensive political, judicial, and legislative controversies on the issue have almost pre-empted discussion of land-use controls in suburban areas for the last decade[47]. The net effect in increasing the segregation, congestion, and costs of housing in the ghettos and slums of the inner cities, and accelerating their physical deterioration, has been incalculable.

Zoning, despite the early support it received from housing reformers, and the concerns sometimes voiced by planners espousing it for the conditions of the ill-housed, in the end did more to worsen those conditions than to improve them.

THE FIRST REGIONAL PLAN FOR NEW YORK

If positive concern with the problems of the ill-housed dropped out of view, after promising beginnings in the formative years of the planning movement in the United States, and if planning's first and most used tool, zoning, similarly ended up hardly contributing to the improvement of those conditions in the slums to which some hoped at first it would be addressed, what can be said of the impact of regional planning on housing in the early years of the twentieth century? In particular, how did the Regional Plan for New York, published in 1931, and the third milestone in the history of planning examined here, relate to housing?

In the early days of housing reform in the United States the simple numerical concentration of population in the slums was seen as a major cause of substandard housing. 'Decongestion' became an early slogan of the reformers, and when Benjamin Marsh became secretary of the New York Committee on Decongestion of the Population, decongestion became the focal point of many housing-reform efforts. The Committee had been formed in 1907 by a group of social workers and their allies. One of their first acts had been the organization of an exhibition that demonstrated graphically the consequences of congestion in the slums of New York. That exhibition had been supported by the Tenement House Department, the Charity Organization Society, the Association for Improving the Condition of the Poor, the City and Suburban Homes Company—in short, virtually every major force in the housing reform movement.

The exhibition generated enough political support to get the appointment of a formal Commission on Decongestion of the Population by the Mayor in 1910. The report of that commission in 1911 was a major step forward in the effort to find regional approaches to the problems of central cities, and particularly to the housing problems of their poor. It recommended restrictions on the lot coverage of tenements, changes in the property tax to remove incentives to over-building, extension of the rapid transit system to encourage suburban migration, and the municipal acquisition of land prior to development to preserve for public benefit the fruits of public infrastructure investment. Most emphasized, however, were two other recommendations: the preparation of a city plan, and the adoption of zoning controls over the height and density of new buildings, the latter being so urgent that it should even precede the completion of a general plan for the city[48].

The evolution of concern for regional decongestion thus began to follow the same pattern with which we have already become familiar: an initial concern for housing, the conjunction with other concerns, the relegation of housing to the background and final action to meet only such other concerns. The housers in this case were slow to see the evolution, but see it they did. At first, Benjamin Marsh was enthusiastic, for instance, about the Metropolitan Improvement Commission of Boston. That commission had been set up by the Massachusetts legislature to

> investigate and report as to the advisability of any public needs ... which in its opinion will tend to the convenience of the people, the development of local business, the beautifying of the district, or the improvement of the same as a place of residence.[49]

But when the Metropolitan Commission reported, its recommendations dealt with harbour development, terminal problems, belt lines, dock systems, and passenger terminals[50]. Just as with New York City, the initial suggestion that regional approaches be used to help solve housing problems was not reflected in the outcome.

Not only was there disappointment with the practical results of the effort to use regional approaches to solve slum-housing problems; the theoretical underpinning of the effort was also questionable. 'Decongestion' suggested that density itself was a cause of bad housing. But when, at the Second National Conference on City Planning in 1910, the secretary of the Massachusetts Civic League took city planners to task for failing to deal with the problem of congestion of population, Veiller was forced to answer that he could not tell how to define undue concentration of population: 'Frankly', he told the conference, 'I do not know. I doubt if anyone knows'. He went on to suggest that, with sound planning, he saw no reason why families could not be housed at 1500 to the acre[51]. Yet the Tenement House Committee of 1894 had considered one area in the Lower East Side of New York, with a density of 986 persons per acre, to be one of the most crowded spots on earth; the highest density in Manhattan in 1910 was about 1300 per acre, and the average density was only 166.1[52]. Decongestion, in the sense simply of reducing gross density, did not logically seem the best, or even a necessary part of, a solution to the problems of bad housing—even had that been the prime concern of the proponents of regionalism.

   The publication of the Regional Plan of New York and Its Environs by the Committee on the Regional Plan of New York—later the Regional Plan Association—was a major milestone in the history of regional planning in the United States. It picked up where the Committee on Congestion had intellectually left off. It marks what Robert Fitch has called 'the most ambitious planning effort ever carried out under private auspices'[53], at least in the area of city or regional development. Relying heavily upon social science research, it was sponsored by the very apex of the business and financial pyramid in New York; more than half its members represented institutions like J. P. Morgan & Co., the Rockefeller Institute, and the First National Bank of New York. Into its work were woven the contributions of almost all of the earlier developments we have traced in this paper: Charles Norton, the key instigator of the Plan, had been president of the Chicago Commercial Club, which had financed Daniel Burnham's Plan for Chicago of 1909, the flower of the City Beautiful movement. Frederick Delano, Franklin Delano Roosevelt's uncle, had also been involved in the Chicago Plan; he was on the Regional Plan Association's ten-man board (RPA—the organization that undertook the publicizing and effectuating of the plan's recommendations). Edward Bassett, the conservative lawyer who had largely written New York City's zoning resolution of 1916, was a major figure on the staff of the Regional Plan Association. George McAneny, the municipal reform borough president of Manhattan who had supported zoning as a way of dealing with housing problems, was also on the board. Thomas Adams, originally from Britain and then Canada, was one of the most prominent and nationally respected professionals in city planning, and a regular speaker at the National Conferences on City Planning from their inception. He wrote the *Monographs on Building and on Housing Conditions* that comprised part of the RPA's multi-volume *Regional Survey,* a planning document described by Harvey Perloff as being almost twenty years ahead of its time[54].

   The Regional Plan Association was clear, at least in its general statements, as to the importance of housing, and its view of the intimate relationship between city planning and housing. Its language gives the flavour of its views:

Bad housing in the main is haphazard city building, and its cure lies in more city planning with the right social objectives. No financial consideration should stand in the way of a city in providing the basic conditions necessary to make home life healthful for the family.

Macaulay once said that the Huns and Vandals that would destroy the Christian states of Europe were being bred not in the wilds of Asia, but in the slums of great cities. It may be that the worst menace to civilization is not the ignorance and savagery of uncivilized countries, but the depressing housing conditions of the big cities in civilized countries.

Bad housing conditions lead to extensive sickness, social restlessness and crime. They cannot be considered to be necessary from a financial point of view because the cost of avoidable sickness and crime is probably greater than the cost of ameliorating the physical conditions that lead to them.[55]

But the details show a narrower focus:

The primary need in connection with housing is adequate open space about buildings for light, air and recreation . . .[56]

The chief problem is that of providing satisfactory houses for the large proportion of the population *that can afford to pay an economic rent.* (emphasis added)[57]

The specific recommendations that follow show the narrowness: enforce restrictive legislation, demolish unfit buildings, acquire open space in the slums, and encourage planning for

rehousing the *moderate income groups* that must remain in the center in healthful dwellings, and . . . creating at the same time new housing developments in open areas *for the same groups.* (emphasis added)[58]

Such proposals, contended the Association, would do more 'to solve the housing problem than . . . public building, tax exemption, or subsidy'. Unless they are adopted,

there seems to be no escape from the uneconomic methods which other countries have had to adopt to solve the evils of haphazard housing developments.[59]

A far cry indeed from the days in which Frederick Howe was lauding the German and English approaches of his day.

What concrete recommendations to deal with the housing problems of those not able to afford adequate housing did the Regional Plan Association in the end put forward? They are striking:

To the extent that better housing accommodation for those who suffer from poverty needs to be provided by public aid it should be regarded as a charity, for the same reasons that giving food or clothing is a charity. One of the great mistakes in the past has been in regarding this charitable work in housing as distinct from other forms of charity.[60]

This then is the end product of the RPA's view of what regional planning can do for the worst housed. It seems hardly necessary to quote its corollary recommendation:

> When it is necessary to grant public aid, it should be given as a last resource after other means of supplying accommodations have failed, and it should be given in a form that will assist rather than impede private operations in house buildings.[61]

The actual results of the Regional Plan Association's work probably contributed to aggravating the low-income problem more than to relieving it. Housing had never really been a high priority for the RPA in its overall work. Edith Elmer Wood had commented as early as 1931 that, in its ten-volume *Report and Survey*, 'housing is practically omitted from the picture'[62]. The specific recommendations that did refer to housing were only partly implemented, and where they were, they added to its costs, and limited its locations, as did zoning.

The highway programme was the chief and proudest achievement of the Association[63]. It included provision for 630 miles of circumferential routes, as well as major radial and cross-town segments. It included the proposal for the Cross Bronx Expressway, resulting in major residential relocation when Robert Moses imposed it on an unwilling community after World War II[64]. If RPA's housing proposals, partly executed, failed to alleviate the problems of the ill-housed, its highway proposals and their execution clearly served to aggravate them. Again, in the end, the recommendations and results of planning diverge from the interests of improving housing.

THE HISTORICAL DETERMINANTS OF HOUSING POLICY

This then is the shape of the puzzle. Housing, proclaimed as a major concern at the beginning of each of three milestones in the evolution of planning in the United States, in each case becomes joined with other issues; in each case solutions ultimately emerge either unrelated to housing or in fact aggravating those very housing conditions that had seemed to beget the effort. The pattern is reflected in the origins of the city planning movement and the birth of the professional organization of planners: the original focus on the problems of the slums gives way to the aesthetic and technocratic concerns of the City Beautiful and the City Practical. The pattern is reflected in the evolution of zoning: the attempt to improve housing conditions through comprehensive land-use planning becomes a device to protect land values in commercial and higher-income residential areas. And the pattern is reflected in the transformation of regional planning: it moves from its early concept of attacking slums by attacking slum density to recommendations that result in the demolition of existing cheaper housing, both directly and through highway construction, with no provision made for its former residents.

In all three cases, the aspirations of city planning to ameliorate the condition of the ill-housed seem, after a noble start, to have gone badly astray. How is this pattern to be explained? Why has not housing been as integral a part of city planning, and of government policy, in the United States as it seems to have been in Europe?

Certainly these developments do not seem consistent with any simple view of city planning and the search for ever increasing knowledge and sophistication about how cities function and for better and better tools to improve the conditions of life in them. In none of the three milestone cases examined was the changing attitude of planning theory and activity towards problems of housing the result of any intellectual development, any enriching of understanding or new perception. If anything, the failure to deal with the problems of the ill-housed was a recurring one; the lessons of prior failures do not seem to have led to subsequent improvements; deviations from a central focus do not seem to have been progressively corrected. The facts recounted do not make sense if seen solely in terms of the history of the city planning movement or the thinking of professional planners.

Neither do the developments traced here seem consistent with the view of history that I have elsewhere called the Myth of the Benevolent State[65]. According to that view, government is ultimately concerned with the improvement of the conditions of life of all of its citizens. City planning and social policy are specifically concerned with the alleviation of conditions which cause hardship to significant segments of society. In housing, thus, the benevolent state theory would expect government to be concerned about the problems of housing faced by those in physically, socially, or economically inadequate housing, and unable or unlikely to improve their conditions through their own means. Governmental policies would then be expected to tackle these problems, contending with conflicting pressures, lack of data, inadequate theory, and changing circumstances as it proceeded, but moving in the long run towards optimizing their contribution to improving conditions for the ill-housed. United States housing policy generally seems quite inconsistent with any such view[66]. Certainly the developments traced here are in flat contradiction to it: government policy, as reflected in public actions responding to planning initiatives, seems more to back away from efforts at improving housing than to head towards them.

The best approach to an explanation lies in an analysis of the concerns that historically produced the results we have witnessed. Three subheadings provide a convenient and not entirely arbitrary way to classify these concerns. The first includes concern with the physical externalities of bad housing. The second is the political concern to avoid unrest and assimilate the immigrant and the potential discontent into the mainstream of society. The third includes concern to provide for arrangements of land use that would enhance real estate values and accommodate the changing demands of business enterprises in the city[67].

PHYSICAL EXTERNALITIES

The physical externalities of slums first brought about governmental involvement in regulating housing. Fire and health hazards were major fears. They account for the earliest building controls, which in New York involved the fire-resistant nature of the roofs of houses built in New York as early as 1766. The cholera epidemics of the early nineteenth century, and particular incidents such as the panic that was evoked by the discovery of cholera among German immigrants on board the steamship *Atalanta* in New York harbour in 1865[68], account for the main drive for tenement-house reform and building regulation through the last decade of the century. The history is very much in parallel with that in the industrial countries of Europe, and also parallels developments there in public health and municipal sanitary engineering, in Britain and Germany in particular, very closely. It is a history that has been extensively and ably documented in the United States[69].

There is significant evidence that these concerns abated very sharply in the last decade of the nineteenth century. In the first place, both conditions of health and protection against fire seem to have improved sharply by this time, despite the rapid and continuing growth of cities and concentration of housing within them. Good figures are hard to come by, but public health statistics show a lessening infant mortality and improving life expectancy rate, and by 1900 the death rate had been brought below its lowest nineteenth-century level[70]. In Massachusetts, the infant mortality rate peaked in 1870-75, remained at a high plateau to about 1895, and then began a steady and continuous decline[71].

These developments are reflected in the housing reform movement. The tide of concern over problems of health and fire led to the first Tenement House Act of 1867 and the second major advance of 1901. But by that time it had already crested; its momentum carried through to the implementation of health and safety standards in cities throughout the country in the period from 1900 to 1910, but by the end of that time it was no longer a matter of public controversy. Technicians could be entrusted with the job: Veiller's effectiveness was precisely because he combined competence as a technician with conservatism of approach to the problem of housing.

Informed opinion of the day believed that housing standards had achieved a level obviating the health hazards earlier feared from tenement housing. A Massachusetts Institute of Technology civil engineering professor spoke of the

> constant advance in tenement-house designs, induced by a steady raising of the standard of requirements on the part of the Board of Health, until there has come to be about as much contrast between the best recent designs and the designs common ten or fifteen years ago, as there is between light and darkness.[72]

A magazine suggested that statistics showed the death rate to be less in 'the large modern tenement ... than in portions of the city devoted to private residences'[73]. A Board of Health report in New York in 1890 already concluded that everything was under control, and a U.S. Department of Labor survey published in 1895 concluded that New York City's progress in tenement design was 'wonderful'[74].

Housing improvement beyond tenement-house regulation had to await concerns other than those for the community's physical health. This was the situation confronting us at the beginning of the period here covered. Jacob Riis[75] symbolized the change. Warner points out, in the 1890s:

> The working-class and middle-class voters lost their fright and with it their enthusiasm for aggressive public-health measures. Housing reformers were forced to fall back more and more on appeals for public support on the grounds that overcrowding led to drink, crime, and prostitution, rather than urging a community of interest in safety from disease.[76]

POLITICAL IMPACTS

Political concerns about social order and domestic tranquillity are the second concern that shaped housing and planning policy in the United States in the period under discussion. 'Drink, crime, and prostitution' are the micro-formulations of that concern. Civil unrest, riot, and revolution are the macro-formulation. Immigrants, during the period reviewed in this paper, were a common focal point both of micro and macro concerns, just as blacks and Spanish-speaking persons are today.

The political implications of planning at first were expressed in rather rarified terms. Charles Mulford Robinson, the architect who was for many years a major propagandist for the City Beautiful movement, expressed them thus:

> The moral and spiritual standards of the people will be advanced by this art, and their political ideals will rise with a civic pride and a community spirit born of the appreciation that they are citizens of 'no mean city' ...[77]

Slum dwellers in particular would be affected:

> ... to make the homes not only livable but attractive, to awaken ambition, to encourage the life of the beautiful—would not this, this glorious aggregate, be the first task that civic art would undertake?[78]

The early city planning movement regularly linked 'civic orderliness and beauty' together, in the words of the plan for St. Louis in 1907[79]. The concept of order is similar to that intended in the more current phrase, 'law and order'. It has explicit reference to bringing the slums and their residents into a constructive, predictable, and safe relationship with the rest of society, ordering the teeming tenements from which unrest could otherwise be feared. The Draft Riots of 1863 had a direct relationship to the adoption of the first

Tenement House Act of 1867. A contemporary eyewitness account is so vivid and so classic as to be worth quoting in full:

> The high brick blocks and closely packed houses where the mobs originated, seemed to be literally hives of sickness and vice. It was wonderful to see, and difficult to believe, that so much misery, disease and wretchedness can be huddled together and hidden by high walls, unvisited and unthought of, so near our own abodes ... To walk the streets as we walked them, in those hours of conflagration and riot, was like witnessing the day of judgment, with every wicked thing revealed, every sin and sorrow blazingly glared upon, every hidden abomination laid bare before hell's expectant fire. The elements of popular discord are gathered in these wretchedly constructed tenement houses where poverty, disease and crime find an abode.[80]

'Popular discord', and the fear, if not the actuality, of 'conflagration and riot', following the economic dislocations of the late 1890s, had a similar effect in producing support for the young city planning movement and the talk of housing reform.

Jacob Riis, harking back thirty years later to the Draft Riots, warned that 'the sea of a mighty population, held in galling fetters, heaves uneasily in the tenements', and Roy Lubove writes that, in the view of the housing reformers,

> the tenement slum was a potential volcano, its inhabitants the willing recruits of the demagogue and revolutionist ... the unenlightened foreigner, a potential anarchist or criminal, was more likely to become a respectable middle-class American citizen if housed decently.[81]

Dispersal of the concentration of potential hostility and unrest through a policy of decongestion and deconcentration become a logical policy. The early espousal by planners of the Garden City idea, the desire to deflect immigrants from the large cities and settle them in rural areas, with appropriate agricultural training to help them settle down as independent small farmers, shows clearly the linking of planning recommendations to concerns for political unrest.

Immigrants were a particular focus of these concerns about political unrest, and suggest a major reason for the difference between developments in the United States and the industrial countries of Europe. The assimilation of immigrants into 'American' society is a consistent theme in the background of all three of our milestone cases. The attractions of the City Beautiful were to provide inspiration to the immigrant, and help show the possibilities open to those joining in to work within the system. Christine Boyer speaks of planners' equation of 'city-making' and 'citizen-making' and describes the ways in which they hoped to use environmental determinants to support a programme of 'Anglo-conformity'[82]. Zoning, restricting densities, was likewise appropriate to prevent dangerous concentrations of potential malcontents; excluding such malcontents (identified by race or national origin or income) from the better residential areas would provide an added margin of safety. Regional planning gave a broader context and rationale for these same policies.

But the immigrant problem was a temporary one, and was soluble through other means also. One was simply restrictive legislation: the scope of immigration, rising in a secular trend from the first settlement in the United States by Europeans to hit its peak in the decade between 1900 and 1910, declined steadily thereafter until the advent of fascism in Europe in the 1930s[83]. Significantly, the current of immigration ran to the agricultural areas and the new territories of the mid- and far-West, and to smaller towns, until the 1880s; it then shifted to the older cities, and Warner comments that

> during the years after 1890, a feeling was prevalent that a man's chances to get ahead had dwindled with the coming of the giant metropolis and the factory. For the first time, the waves of European immigrants appeared as a threat: perhaps to the workers of the time, certainly to their children.[84]

But starting some time after the Panic of 1907, and certainly by the time of the First World War, that threat had receded remarkably, or at least the measures that were needed to bring it under control seemed apparent. They did not include housing reform[85].

Just as the fears about public health that had produced the tenement-house reforms began receding by the 1890s, the fears of social unrest and the need to Americanize the immigrants into the large cities that had helped provide a rationale for the city planning movement seems to have begun receding in the 1910s. The possibility of going further in attacking the problems of slum housing generated by these pressures thus also receded in the same periods.

REAL ESTATE VALUES

The third concern underlying housing and planning policy involves real estate values and the uses of land. It has two aspects: one dealing with the preservation and enhancement of real estate values for the benefit of property owners, speculators and developers, and the other dealing with the arrangement of the uses of land—and, more important, its rearrangement—to meet the evolving needs of the business community.

Real estate interests have always been one of the dominant influences on municipal policies in the United States. The City Beautiful movement was early supported by property owners because they saw it as giving a significant boost to property values, both generally and specially. City plans were seen as a form of local boosterism, aiding business and increasing property values throughout a city generally. This was the type of appeal that made George B. Dealey, general manager of the *Dallas News*, such a successful promoter of a comprehensive plan for Dallas[86], and was repeated in St.

Louis, Minneapolis, and cities throughout the country. More specially, at a neighbourhood level, Fitch speaks bluntly of

> the Burnham technique of using parks and highways to transform the class character of neighborhoods in the interest of real estate values.[87]

Even John Nolen, most respected of the early leaders of the planning movement in the United States, noted in 1919 with some unease that 'to purchase large public parks and to develop civic centers adds to the value of the privately owned land and buildings in the city'[88]. No wonder businessmen and real property owners contributed over $200,000 to the preparation and publicizing of Burnham's Plan for Chicago[89].

Zoning is the aspect of planning that is the pre-eminent servant of real estate in the U.S. planning story. In New York, a formal petition by the largest real estate investors in the city spoke of haphazard development impairing the capital values of large areas, thus affecting 'the market value of real estate for investment purposes'[90], and requiring zoning as a cure. The details of the extensive behind-the-scenes involvement of real estate interests, as well as the public efforts of groups like the Fifth Avenue Association, in obtaining passage of the New York resolution, are described in fascinating detail in Makielski's study[91]. There is no doubt that the owners of real estate property were well aware of their vital interest in zoning.

The importance of real estate concerns in the Regional Plan Association's work is portrayed in detail in Robert Fitch's study of the origins of the Regional Plan for New York. He speaks of the 'renting, constructing and financing of office space'[92] as New York's main industry—a striking if overstated formulation of the importance of downtown real estate ownership and investment in the city's economic life. The City Rentable, he suggests, supplanted the City Beautiful as the goal of planners. The composition of the Board of the Regional Plan Association, described earlier, reflected that analysis, and clearly influenced its results.

It is not surprising, in view of these influences on the early planning movement, on zoning, and on regional planning, that in each case attention to the problems of the ill-housed was subordinated to proposals that would enhance real estate values. That the alliance of real estate interests with middle-income home-owning voters was easily made only guaranteed its ultimate success. As two of the leading students of the history of planning in the United States have recently said, the promoters of zoning wanted to 'give legal sanction to the status quo'[93], 'not to disturb existing conditions but [to] project current trends into the future and perpetuate them'[94].

CHANGING LAND USES

Property owners, speculators and developers are of course not the only parties interested in real estate: so are the ultimate users of land. In a perfect market, all demands for the use of land would be reflected in its price. Thus, selling land freely for its best price would guarantee that each separate parcel is also devoted to its highest (most profitable) use. But the market in land is notoriously not free. Externalities, ignorance, monopoly, government intervention, the exploitation of public goods, are all permanent parts of the scene. If land is to be devoted to its most profitable use, then something other than the free market must be relied on. This is particularly true when the issue involves changing from one land use to another, and when sunk infrastructure costs retard conversion—or, perhaps more serious, when less profitable uses such as housing, with little economic but much political clout, stand in the way. It is against this background that the concerns with land use must be seen, as they influenced the evolution of planning, zoning, and regionalism.

Housing is a key part of the story, but as passive object, or unwelcome constraint, rather than as a central concern. Land occupied by tenements is needed for commercial use: it can be let at a higher rent to businesses than to households, once the households are removed. Not only do the particular parcels of land have to be cleared; residential uses, particularly lower-class ones, have to be eliminated from the surrounding area. As early as 1917, a consultant to the City of Berkeley on its zoning ordinance reported to the Ninth National Conference on City Planning:

> Some manufacturers said to us, 'Why, if the city keeps factories out of residence districts, should not residences be kept out of factory districts? We find in most cities the most abject poverty and the worst tenements and bad housing conditions in the factory neighborhoods. When we want heavy traffic pavement for heavy hauling with spur tracks in the sidewalk areas, these ... home owners appear before the City Council and holler so loud that the improvements are held up. So we have dejected housing and hampered industry'.[95]

The New York Committee on the Regional Plan, more than a decade after the first zoning ordinance was adopted, was also concerned about conflicting and changing uses. In some cases, the desire was to replace old tenement house uses with modern houses, including 'high class residences' on the Lower East Side because of its ready access to the business areas of Manhattan[96]. In other cases, the conflict was between commercial and industrial uses. Robert Fitch quotes a revealing and unusually personal observation in the Economic Section of the Regional Plan's ten volumes:

> Some of the poorest people live in conveniently located slums on high priced land. On patrician Fifth Avenue, Tiffany and Woolworth, cheek by jowl, offer jewels and jimcracks from substantially identical sites. Child's Restaurants thrive where Delmonico's withered and died. A stone's throw from the stock exchange the air is filled with the aroma of roasting coffee; a few hundred feet from Times Square, with the stench of slaughter-houses. In the very heart of this 'commercial' city on Manhattan Island south of 59th Street, the inspectors

in 1922 found nearly 420,000 workers employed in factories. Such a situation outrages one's sense of order. Everything seems misplaced. One yearns to re-arrange the hodgepodge and to put things where they belong[97].

Fitch, in fact, recounts the history of the Regional Plan Association's activities as very much a campaign against manufacturing interests in the city. The Plan, in his view, was largely conceived as an effort to protect commercial (as well as real estate) interests against manufacturing encroachment. He calls it 'an economic plan hostile to manufacturing'[98], and speaks of the New Yorker's desire to 'expel heavy industry from the city'[99]. The story is, however, more complex, and requires greater clarity about the concept of decentralization if the evolution is to be properly understood.

'Decentralization' is a common word in city planning. Similar words range from 'decongestion', as used by the New York Committee on Congestion of Population in 1907, to 'deconcentration', used in the Housing Act of 1974 as a euphemism for promoting integrated housing in the suburbs. 'Regionalism' is often linked to the concept. The Garden City movement, the effort to develop a national urban policy influencing the extent of growth of cities, density controls, regional planning efforts, all use similar concepts, if not identical terms. More recent efforts to deal with the urban fiscal crisis, or plans of somewhat older vintage to 'revitalize the central city', have sometimes been called policies of 'recentralization', and reflect a trend apparently in the opposite direction.

Yet the word 'decentralization' involves an element of ideological obscurantism. 'Decentralization' as a general goal of policy exists only in the minds of planners, publicists, and some politicians. In practice, decentralization is a term that covers a number of quite different policies and approaches, espoused by quite different interests, having quite different consequences, and in most cases being quite unrelated to each other. They include:

1. *Efforts to relieve downtown traffic congestion.* The issue here is not to reduce the level of activity downtown. Quite to the contrary, it is to reduce certain activities so that other activities can better flourish there. Thus, Fifth Avenue merchants wanted the garment industry 'decentralized' not so as to reduce traffic on Fifth Avenue, but to remove garment workers so shoppers might take their place. Only specific users are the targets for such decentralization; for other uses, improved access through improved transportation is the chosen solution to the problem of congestion. There may occasionally be errors in judgment as to the choice of transportation modes, for instance automobile versus mass transit, or West Side versus East Side subway lines, but the general principle is clear: decentralize some uses so other uses can better operate centrally.

2. *Slum clearance, in areas with locational advantages for other uses.* Parts of the Lower East Side in New York are examples. So are the areas immediately

adjacent to many central business districts. The concern here is not with improving housing for slum residents, or reducing the residential density of the living quarters of the poor; it is with clearing them out, so others can live or work there—at the same or higher densities, most of the time. Thus Stuyvesant Town in New York placed more middle-income families per acre in an area than had been the average before, an area previously condemned as overcrowded; but they were different families. Urban renewal, in this sense, is decentralization of poor people's housing: decentralization away from a particular desirable location, not decentralization because of the quality of the new opportunities thus opened for those being decentralized.

3. *Suburbanization of housing.* Both the housing construction industry and its major ancillary consumer and supplier interests heavily stimulated the actual decentralization of housing from central city areas to suburbs. These interests were not in the least bit concerned with the problems of the central cities. They wanted to maximize the number of houses they could sell, and the appliances and cars and gadgets; in doing so, they wanted to pay the least tribute to property owners demanding high land prices. The outskirts of the cities were the logical answer. Pressures from these interests had nothing to do with city planning principles, and were continuous, whatever the ebb and flow of central city fortunes or fashions in regional planning.

4. *Control over the location of employment.* This is, from the viewpoint of city planning, the most sensible meaning of decentralization. It could have real impact and be the subject of real disputes over policy. But it is not an area relevant to the United States, although in cities like London or Paris it is a major issue.

5. *Slum clearance arising out of concern for the living conditions of slum dwellers.* This final possible meaning of decentralization or regionalism was one of the idealistic components of the Garden City movement. Planned and balanced communities, combining city and country, improving health, providing more open space, letting mothers (sic!) see their children at play, all are often seen as components of, or reasons for, a policy of decentralization. In practice, the results have been disappointing. The New York experience with garden cities, i.e. Forest Hills Gardens which was as far as the city went in that direction, showed the approach, without substantial governmental aid, usable only for more prosperous families. And the requisite governmental aid was never forthcoming; indeed, it was rarely requested, and certainly not by the Regional Plan Association.

These then are the possible issues involved with deconcentration and regional planning. The search for a logical link to housing policy is fated to fail, despite the prominence given to housing in the early statements of the Committee on Congestion, the comprehensive planners, the zoners, and the regional planners, because the most important issues are not concerned with improved housing. Housing is only a pawn in conflicts over the appropriate uses of land.

DIFFERENCES OF THE PUZZLE IN EUROPE

The comparative aspects of our puzzle have only been occasionally alluded to thus far. It might now be reformulated in terms of two quotations, each from respected and business-wise participants in the planning movement in the United States.

> Germany has decided that the housing question is too important a problem to be left to the free play of capitalistic exploitation.[100]

> New York City . . . is too big a city, the social and economic interests involved are too great, to permit the continuance of the laissez faire methods of earlier days.[101]

The first quote is from Frederick C. Howe, a member of the Cleveland City Council and the Ohio State Senate, speaking before the Third National Conference on City Planning in Philadelphia in 1911. The second is from Robert H. Whitten, Secretary of the New York City Commission on Building Districts and Restrictions, writing in its final report in 1916. Both statements are true. Yet the evolution of housing policies in the United States and Europe have been remarkably different. Why?

At first, the puzzle seemed to be why more was not done to deal with the problems of the ill-housed in the United States through the vehicle of city planning. A number of factors have been adduced that seem to explain adequately why housing was not in fact more centrally addressed. But now too much has been explained, in terms of the comparative aspect of the puzzle: for why were not the factors that limited U.S. housing policies at play with equal force in Europe[102]? Neither time nor knowledge permit full-scale discussion of the question. Only a few possibilities will be briefly listed here, more as an agenda for future discussion and research than as any definitive outline of an answer.

Most importance would probably have to be placed on the differences in political development. In most European countries, going back as far as the emergence of a bourgeois class out of the feudal system, class consciousness had been a feature of political history. Housing policy everywhere shows the impact of directly political conflicts, conflicts heavily ideological and class-oriented. The early Labour Party in England, for instance, differed sharply from the Liberals as well as the Conservatives in its housing proposals (if not always in its housing policies when in power). The events of Glasgow during the First World War, which played such a large role in shaping subsequent national legislation, linked housing to other working-class political demands.

No such events have taken place in the United States. Pressures from the ill-housed themselves have never constituted a major force in U.S. housing policy. With the exception of rent controls[103], specific housing pro-grammes have never formed a substantial basis for organized political activity. Housing planks periodically appear in the platforms of the political parties, and certainly major political battles are fought over housing issues[104]; but housing is not central to any significant set of political demands. In none of the three situations discussed in this paper has the voice of the ill-housed been a major factor; indeed, the absence of that voice is undoubtedly a significant contributing factor in explaining the puzzle of housing default with which we are concerned. In Europe, the effectiveness of the reaction of those most directly affected has been different.

This evolution is of course part of a much larger picture, not just confined to housing; as Richard Hofstadter notes, it was not until 1937 that American reform movements acquired even a 'social democratic tinge'[105]. This is hardly the place to explain this critical but much broader phenomenon; as it affects housing and city planning, however, the ability to separate off immigrants (and subsequently blacks and Spanish-speaking persons) from the bulk of the working class and the poor in the cities made the housing problem convertible into an immigrant or a black problem, and know-nothing ethnic prejudices and racism then helped overwhelm efforts to deal with it on a more general basis.

The role of the land question is also quite different in the European experience compared with the American. Private control of land is much more enshrined in the Pantheon of civic virtues in the United States than in Europe. The delicacy of the suggestion for tampering with 'the land question' in the United States is summarized in a little story: When Robert deForest, the lawyer for banks, railroads, and insurance companies, whose philanthropic interests carried him to the chairmanship of the Charity Organization Society and then to be New York City's first Tenement House Department head, first met Benjamin C. Marsh, just come from Philadelphia to New York to head the Committee on Congestion of Population, Marsh was introduced to deForest as someone particularly interested in 'the land question'. Marsh recalled later,

> Mr. deForest looked at me with the maddening tolerance of a wise old man for a well-intentioned young fool and said, 'If you touch the land problem in New York, you probably won't last two here two years'.[106]

In Europe, on the other hand, the right to impose controls on the use of land, or to acquire it for any public purpose, is taken for granted. The difference may lie in several sources: a different legal history, going back to the feudal era, of land ownership in Europe; differences in constitutional and judicial processes; and different patterns of land holding, with the European being more concentrated, and probably more directly identified with commercial and manufacturing uses, than in the United States.

Pure land speculation, and the rise of a development industry with no direct interests in the ultimate uses finally occupying the land and buildings developed, does not seem to have been as strong in Europe—at least not in Germany—as in the United States. The greater role of national government at the outset in the development of cities, not only in public/private terms but also in central/local terms, undoubtedly played a role. In the United States local government is unusually susceptible to real estate and developmental pressures, while manufacturing and finance tend to operate on a national political level. The very decentralization of governmental powers thus tends to give prominence to real estate interests.

Employers' role in the supply of housing has been sharply different in Europe. As both Britain and Germany industrialized, they faced the problem of attracting workers to the new industrial locations. The need for housing for such workers brought many employers heavily into the housing business, from Robert Owen to the coal and steel firms of the Ruhr. Similar developments took place in the United States, but on a very much smaller scale. Company towns in the United States were relatively few, and have always stood in poor repute; Gary and Lowell have been much more typical than Pullman or Hershey[107]. Employers indeed recognized some impact of housing conditions on work performance; the Regional Plan of New York summarizes in 1931 by saying:

> The worst effect of bad housing in a city is the demoralization and consequent lowering in productive power of a great proportion of the inhabitants.[108]

But the needs of employment seem never to have influenced housing policy in the United States nearly as directly as they did in Western Europe.

Landlords as an interest group seem much more influential politically in the United States than in some of Europe. Most of the housing built for the migrants to U.S. cities—who came by themselves, and in numbers immeasurably swelled by the national inmigration—was built by real estate speculators, whose interests were single-mindedly in profit maximization. These tenement house owners, 'slumlords'—a phrase which conjures up only large-scale operators, while some of the actual owners of the worst tenement housing in New York and other cities were in fact themselves poor individuals struggling in one of the few ways open to them to improve their fortunes—thus became a significant independent force on the local housing and planning scene. While a similar development to some extent took place in Europe, its scale seems significantly different, and its effects remarkably different, from that in the United States.

A final difference between the United States and Europe relevant to housing policies is in the level of prosperity. For a variety of reasons, including the absence of restrictive feudal legacies to the availability of an entire naturally rich continent for virtually unchallenged exploitation, the increasingly strong international position of the U.S. economy, and the handling of immigrant and black and Spanish-speaking workers referred to earlier, prosperity in the United States has enabled everyone to receive some share of a quite large pie. Even if the relative slice received by most of the poor did not grow, its absolute size did. Economic developments in Europe did not always have the same result, and expectation levels in any event were traditionally quite different. The American ideal of a single-family house on an individual lot, owned by the household that occupied it—an ideal, incidentally, assiduously cultivated by all of the institutions of the society in the United States[109]—was held out as a real possibility for absolutely everyone, sooner or later. In Europe, a little more realism seems to have been in the air for a much longer period.

None of the differences suggested above is entirely clear-cut, and adequate documentation is certainly not available on any. Further comparative study, which would attempt not only to establish and provide an order of magnitude to these differences, but also offer evidence as to the impact of each on housing policies, is very much needed.

Summary

In the light of the factors we have just traced, the puzzle suggested at the outset of this paper hardly seems a puzzle at all: why the early city planning movement, zoning, and regionalism all began with commitments to improved housing and ended with policies tending in quite the opposite direction— more generally, why city planning, in a situation in which housing conditions cried out for remedial action, has paid so little effective concern for them in the United States.

The explanation suggested here has been that the expectation that planning would respond to housing needs rests either on an implicit theory of planning's autonomy, that planning's evolution would be determined by its own concerns and its own intellectual progress; or the expectation rests on an implicit theory of a benevolent state, holding that government in the long run will act to alleviate the most pressing problems of its citizenry. Neither of these theories meshes with the history here recounted. The concerns that in fact dictated the evolution of housing and planning policy in the United States revolved more about the avoidance of gross dangers to public health and safety, the avoidance of political unrest, and the enhancement of real estate values and the arrangement of land uses for the maximization of profit, than they do around any concern for the conditions of the ill-housed.

The puzzle as to the differences between United States and European housing and planning policies and interrelationships is much harder to resolve. The absence of immigration and pervasive racism in Europe (situations both of which may be changing in some ways today), different political traditions and views of class and the role of government, different legal structures and attitudes towards the control of land, and even differences in international position, have all been suggested as relevant. But precisely what threads are to be found in common, and which different, in the evolution of housing and planning policies in similarly situated industrialized countries has not been satisfactorily adduced, nor has the effort even seriously been made as yet. It should be a step well worth taking in the international study of the history of city planning. For it may help us not only better to understand city planning, but also to change it.

NOTES

1. The critical comments and suggestions of a number of persons were most useful in the writing of this paper; I would like to acknowledge particularly those of Robert Fitch, Sigurd Grava, Tom Angotti and Gordon Cherry, the editor of this volume.
2. Scott, Mel (1969) *American City Planning Since 1890*. Berkeley: University of California Press, p. 10.
3. *New York Tribune* (December 28, 1884) p. 4, in Jackson, Anthony (1976) *A Place Called Home: A History of Low-Cost Housing in Manhattan*. Cambridge: M.I.T. Press.
4. Campbell, Helen (1891) *Darkness and Daylight: Or Lights and Shadows of New York Life,* in Jackson, Anthony (1976) *A Place Called Home: A History of Low-Cost Housing in Manhattan*. Cambridge: M.I.T. Press, p. 88.
5. Wood, Edith Elmer (1931) *Recent Trends in American Housing*. New York: The Macmillan Company, p. 135.
6. Burns, John, President of the Local Government Board, in Parliamentary Debates on the Housing, Town Planning, etc. Bill, *H.C. Debates,* Vol. 188, May 1908, in Cullingworth, J. B. (1974) *Town and Country Planning in Britain*. London: George Allen and Unwin.
7. Ashworth, William (1954) *The Genesis of Modern British Town Planning*. London: Routledge and Kegan Paul, p. 181. But for a contrary view, just received, capital and land: the history of town planning revisited. *International Journal of Urban and Regional Research,* 3, (3), p. 361.
8. *Proceedings of the Tenth National Conference on Housing,* p. 59.
9. Howe, Frederick C. (1911) The municipal real estate policies of German cities. *Proceedings of the Third National Conference on City Planning,* Philadelphia.
10. Toll, Seymour (1969) *Zoned American*. New York: Grossman, p. 129.
11. U.S. Bureau of the Census (1975) *Statistical Abstract of the United States*. Washington, D.C., p. 711.
12. Jane Morton cites the figures in *Roof,* May 1976, p. 84.
13. Alonso, William (1963) Cities and city planners. *Daedalus,* 92 (4), reprinted in Eldridge (ed.), *Taming Megapolis,* Vol. II. New York: Anchor Books, 1967.
14. Scott, Mel (1969) *American City Planning Since 1890*. Berkeley: University of California Press, p. 33.
15. Adams, John C. What a great city might be—a lesson from the White City. *New England Magazine,* 20 (10), p. 3, in Lubove, Roy (1962) *The Progressives and the Slums: Tenement House Reform in New York City, 1890–1917*. Pittsburgh: University of Pittsburgh Press, p. 217.
16. The origins of the City Beautiful movement are of course more complex; see Peterson, Jon A. (1976) The city beautiful movement: forgotten origins and lost meanings. *Journal of Urban History,* 2, pp. 415–34. Wilson, William H. (1980) The ideology, aesthetics and politics of the City Beautiful movement, in Sutcliffe, Anthony (ed.), *The Rise of Modern Urban Planning, 1800–1914.*

London: Mansell, pp. 165–98, details some of the multiple sources and ideological themes connected with the movement.

17. Robinson, Charles M. (1904) *Modern Civic Art*. New York, p. 29.
18. Marsh, Benjamin C. (1908) City planning in justice to the working population. *Charities,* 19, p. 1514, in Scott, Mel (1969) *American City Planning Since 1890.* Berkeley: University of California Press, p. 82.
19. In the opening address to the Second National Conference on City Planning, for instance, Frederick Law Olmsted, Jr. added a third division to city planning, in addition to Robinson's concerns with circulation and community buildings, public control of lands in private ownership, and listed building codes and tenement house regulations as a subdivision. But they are mentioned as incidental to the overall orderly arrangement of land uses, incidental to the other higher purposes of planning. Introductory Address on City Planning, *Proceedings of the Second National Conference on City Planning, 1910.* Rochester, New York, pp. 15–30.
20. Wilson, William H. (1980) The ideology, aesthetics and politics of the City Beautiful movement, in Sutcliffe, Anthony (ed.), *The Rise of Modern Urban Planning, 1800–1914.* London: Mansell, pp. 165–98. City Beautiful 'schemes often ignored housing and other social problems', is the summary of Roy Lubove, perhaps the leading historian of this aspect of the period. (1967) *The Urban Community: Housing and Planning in the Progressive Era.* Englewood Cliffs, N.J.: Prentice Hall, p.10.
21. Scott, Mel (1969) *American City Planning Since 1890.* Berkeley: University of California Press, p. 108.
22. Lubove, Roy (1967) *The Urban Community: Housing and Planning in the Progressive Era.* Englewood Cliffs, N.J.: Prentice Hall, p. 227.
23. James Ford in 1936 wrote the monumental *Slums and Housing,* a still fascinating description of slums in the United States that included the recommendation of involuntary rural resettlement for incorrigible slum dwellers unable or unwilling to improve their own situation.
24. Ford, George B. (1912) Digging deeper in city planning, an address before the Seventh Annual Convention of the American Civic Association. *American City* (March) p. 558, in Scott, Mel (1969) *American City Planning Since 1890.* Berkeley: University of California Press, p. 121.
25. Ford, George B. (1913) The city scientific. *Proceedings of the Fifth National Conference on City Planning,* p. 32.
26. Scott, Mel (1969) *American City Planning Since 1890.* Berkeley: University of California Press, p. 123.
27. Ford, George B. (1913) The city scientific. *Proceedings of the Fifth National Conference on City Planning,* pp. 37–8.
28. See the discussion of the costs of housing and impacts of the tenement house reforms below. Anthony Jackson (1976) *A Place Called Home: A History of Low-Cost Housing in Manhattan.* Cambridge: M.I.T. Press, gives figures for the rising costs of construction of working-class housing in New York City throughout this period.
29. Details can be found in Scott, Mel (1969) *American City Planning Since 1890.* Berkeley: University of California Press, pp. 163ff., and Lubove, Roy (1967) *The Urban Community: Housing and Planning in the Progressive Era.* Englewood

Cliffs, N.J.: Prentice Hall, pp. 234ff. The point on the significance of the change of name of the Institute is made in Alonso, William (1963) Cities and city planners. *Deadalus,* **92** (4), reprinted in Eldridge (ed.) *Taming Megalopolis,* Vol. II. New York: Anchor Books, 1967, p. 584.

30. Indeed, Veiller's autocratic personality was a factor that in its own right reinforced the tendencies to separation discussed in the text. For a vivid contrast of his views to those of Edith Elmer Wood and other more progressive housers, see Birch, Eugenie (1978) Woman-made America: the case of early public housing. *Journal of the American Institute of Planners,* **44** (2). Lubove, Roy (1976) *The Urban Community: Housing and Planning in the Progressive Era.* Englewood Cliffs, N.J.: Prentice Hall, pp. 144ff.

31. In Warner, Robert A. (1941) *The Planning Function in Government.* Chicago: University of Chicago Press, p. 11.

32. Nolen, John (1911) *Madison: A Model City.* pp. 126–8, in Scott, Mel (1969) *American City Planning Since 1890.* Berkeley: University of California Press, p. 88.

33. Coke, James G. (1968) Antecedents of local planning, in Goodman and Freund (eds.), *Principles and Practice of Urban Planning.* Washington, D.C.: International City Managers Association, p. 22. Content analysis of the first four Conferences on City Planning and Congestion of the Population (the latter phrase was, perhaps significantly despite protestations to the contrary, dropped after the first two conferences), shows the shift away from housing and slums towards more practical issues in this brief but critical period; by the 1912 conference in Boston, a major panel was devoted to 'Paying the Bill for City Planning'.

34. Scott, Mel (1969) *American City Planning Since 1890.* Berkeley: University of California Press, p. 163.

35. Testimony of Bruce Falconer before the Heights of Buildings Commission, Report of the Commission (December, 1913), pp. 52–3, in Makielski, S. J. (1966) *The Politics of Zoning.* New York: Columbia University Press, p. 12.

36. New York City Commission on Building Districts and Restrictions, *Final Report,* p. 213, in Lubove, Roy (1967) *The Urban Community: Housing and Planning in the Progressive Era.* Englewood Cliffs, N.J.: Prentice Hall, p. 243.

37. Lubove, *ibid.,* p. 239.

38. *Ibid.,* p. 240.

39. Scott, Mel (1969) *American Planning Since 1890.* Berkeley: University of California Press, p. 155.

40. The history of zoning in New York City is extensively documented in two well written and illuminating studies: Makielski, S. J. (1966) *The Politics of Zoning.* New York: Columbia University Press, and Toll, Seymour (1969) *Zoned America.* New York: Grossman.

41. *Real Estate Record,* **34** (December 20, 1884), p. 1277, in Jackson, Anthony (1976) *A Place Called Home: A History of Low-Cost Housing in Manhattan.* Cambridge: M.I.T. Press, p. 104.

42. Scott, Mel (1969) *American City Planning Since 1890.* Berkeley: University of California Press, p. 156.

43. See *Hadacheck vs. Sebastian,* 165 Cal. 416, 239 U.S. 394.

44. Scott, Mel (1969) *American City Planning Since 1890.* Berkeley: University of California Press, p. 152.

45. *In re Hang Kie,* 69 Cal. 149 (1886).
46. See Warner, Sam Bass, Jr. (1972) *The Urban Wilderness: A History of the American City.* New York: Harper and Row, p. 28.
47. A good recent comprehensive discussion of these developments is in Danielson, Michael N. (1976) *The Politics of Exclusion.* New York: Columbia University Press.
48. See Lubove, Roy (1967) *The Urban Community: Housing and Planning in the Progressive Era.* Englewood Cliffs, N.J.: Prentice Hall, pp. 231ff., and Scott, Mel (1969) *American City Planning Since 1890.* Berkeley: University of California Press, p. 153.
49. Quoted in Marsh, Benjamin C. (1909) *An Introduction to City Planning: Democracy's Challenge to the American City.* New York: Benjamin Marsh, p. 107.
50. Scott, Mel (1969) *American City Planning Since 1890.* Berkeley: University of California Press, p. 88.
51. *Ibid.,* pp. 130–1.
52. New York City, Commission on Congestion of Population (1911) *Report,* pp. 7, 84, 12.
53. Fitch, Robert (1977) Planning New York, in Alcaly, Roger and Mermelstein, David (eds.), *The Fiscal Crisis of American Cities.* New York: Random House. What follows has been heavily influenced by Fitch's excellent and provocative article, although the conclusions drawn differ in significant particulars from Fitch's.
54. Perloff, Harvey S. (1957) *Education for Planning: City, State and Regional.* Baltimore: Johns Hopkins Press, p. 19.
55. *Regional Plan of New York and Its Environs,* Regional Survey, 1931, Vol. VI, p. 208.
56. *Ibid.,* p. 16.
57. *Ibid.*
58. *Ibid.,* p. 294.
59. *Ibid.,* p. 293.
60. *Ibid.,* p. 17.
61. *Ibid.*
62. Wood, Edith Elmer (1931), *Recent Trends in American Housing.* New York: The Macmillan Company, p. 145.
63. Regional Plan Association (1942) *From Plan to Reality,* Vol. III. New York: p. 1, in Fitch, Robert (1977) Planning New York, in Alcaly, Robert and Mermelstein, David (eds.), *The Fiscal Crisis in American Cities.* New York: Random House, p. 282.
64. The story is told in detail in Caro, Robert A. (1974) *The Power Broker: Robert Moses and the Fall of New York.* New York: Alfred A. Knopf, chapter 37, pp. 850ff. A better perspective on the chain of historical causation is given by Fitch, *ibid.*
65. Marcuse, Peter (1978) Housing policy and the myth of the benevolent state. *Social Policy,* January/February, pp. 21ff.
66. *Ibid.*
67. No exhaustive discussion of these concerns is possible here, nor are the subheadings presented either exclusive or inevitable. The discussion is

confined to the specific forces most influential in the three case studies outlined in this paper, and are presented in outline form, rather than in detail.
Work now in progress will hopefully advance the argument further. Comments
and criticisms on this portion of the paper would therefore be strongly
welcomed.

68. See Jackson, Anthony (1976) *A Place Called Home: A History of Low-Cost
Housing in Manhattan.* Cambridge: M.I.T. Press, p. 26ff., and Lubove, Roy
(1967) *The Urban Community: Housing and Planning in the Progressive Era.*
Englewood Cliffs, N.J.: Prentice Hall, p. 23.

69. Among the best accounts are Lubove, *ibid.,* and Friedman, Lawrence M. (1968)
Government and Slum Housing: A Century of Frustration. Chicago: Rand
McNally.

70. Savenel, Mazyck P. (ed.) (1921) *A Half Century of Public Health.* New York, in
Warner, Sam Bass, Jr. (1972) *The Urban Wilderness: A History of the American
City.* New York: Harper and Row, p. 218.

71. U.S. Bureau of the Census (1975) *Historical Statistics of the United States,
Colonial Times to 1970,* Bicentennial Edition, Part 2. Washington, D.C.

72. Porter, Dwight (1889) *Report Upon a Sanitary Inspection of Certain Tenement-
House Districts of Boston.* Boston, p. 22, in Jackson, Anthony (1976) *A Place
Called Home: A History of Low-Cost Housing in Manhattan.* Cambridge: M.I.T.
Press, p. 74.

73. *Building,* 11 (December 21, 1889), p. 221, in *ibid.*

74. U.S. Labor Bureau (1895) *The Housing of the Working People,* Special Report
No. 8. Washington, D.C., p. 128, in *ibid.*

75. Riis, Jacob A. (1890) *How the Other Half Lives: Studies Among the Tenements of
New York.* New York.

76. *Ibid.,* p. 219.

77. Robinson, Charles M. (1913) *The Improvement of Towns and Cities or the
Practical Basis of Civic Aesthetics.* New York, pp. 211, 200, 292, in Lubove, Roy
(1967) *The Urban Community: Housing and Planning in the Progressive Era.*
Englewood Cliffs, N.J.: Prentice Hall, p. 219.

78. Robinson, Charles M. (1918) *Modern Civic Art, or the City Made Beautiful.* New
York, p. 247, in *ibid.*

79. A City Plan for St. Louis, 1907, in Scott, Mel (1969) *American Planning Since
1890.* Berkeley: University of California Press, p. 74.

80. In Smith, Stephen (1911) *The City That Was.* New York, pp. 99–100, and in
Jackson, Anthony (1976) *A Place Called Home: A History of Low-Cost Housing in
Manhattan.* Cambridge: M.I.T. Press, p. 25.

81. Lubove, Roy (1967) *The Urban Community: Housing and Planning in the
Progressive Era.* Englewood Cliffs, N.J.: Prentice Hall, pp. 247–8.

82. Boyer, Christine (1972) Ph.D. Dissertation, Massachusetts Institute of
Technology, Cambridge, Mass., pp. 88ff.

83. Table 3 in Warner, Robert A. (1941) *The Planning Function in Government.*
Chicago: University of Chicago Press, p. 168.

84. *Ibid.,* p. 171.

85. The resurgence of interest in publicly–assisted housing following the black
ghetto riots of the mid-1960s offers an interesting parallel. Here again housing
proposals, aimed originally at assuaging discontent, seem to have been rapidly

abandoned as the force of that discontent appeared to recede and be brought under control through direct repression and continuing racism in the North.

86. Scott, Mel (1969) *American City Planning Since 1890.* Berkeley: University of California Press, p. 78.

87. Fitch, Robert (1977) Planning New York, in Alcaly, Roger and Mermelstein, David (eds.), *The Fiscal Crisis of American Cities.* New York: Random House, p. 253.

88. Nolen, John (ed.) (1929) *City Planning,* 2nd ed. New York: Appleton, in Coke, James, G. (1968) Antecedents of local planning, in Goodman and Freund (eds.), *Principles and Practice of Urban Planning.* Washington, D.C.: International City Managers Association, p. 22.

89. Scott, Mel (1969) *American City Planning Since 1890.* Berkeley: University of California Press, p. 140.

90. New York Commission on Building Districts and Restrictions (1916) *Final Report.* New York, p. 75, in Lubove, Roy (1967) *The Urban Community: Housing and Planning in the Progressive Era.* Englewood Cliffs, N.J.: Prentice Hall, p. 243.

91. Makielski, S. J. (1966) *The Politics of Zoning.* New York: Columbia University Press, pp. 7–40.

92. Fitch, Robert (1977) Planning New York, in Alcaly, Roger and Mermelstein, David (eds.), *The Fiscal Crisis of American Cities.* New York: Random House, p. 278.

93. Scott, Mel (1969) *American City Planning Since 1890.* Berkeley: University of California Press, p. 155.

94. Warner, Robert A. (1941) *The Planning Function in Government.* Chicago: Chicago University Press, p. 30.

95. Cheney, Charles H., Districting progress and procedures in California. *Proceedings of the Ninth National Conference on City Planning,* p. 185, in Scott, Mel (1969) *American City Planning Since 1890.* Berkeley: University of California Press, p. 161.

96. *Regional Plan of New York and Its Environs,* 1931, Vol. II, p. 400, in Fitch, Robert (1977) Planning New York, in Alcaly, Roger and Mermelstein, David (eds.), *The Fiscal Crisis of American Cities.* New York: Random House, p. 274.

97. Fitch, Robert (1977) *ibid.,* p. 263.

98. *Ibid.,* p. 261.

99. *Ibid.*

100. Howe, Frederick C., The municipal real estate policies of German cities. *Proceedings of the Third National Conference on City Planning,* p. 105, in Scott, Mel (1969) *American City Planning Since 1890.* Berkeley: University of California Press, p. 133.

101. Commission on Building Districts and Restrictions (June 2, 1916) *Final Report,* p. 6, in Lubove, Roy (1967) *The Urban Community: Housing and Planning in the Progressive Era.* Englewood Cliffs, N.J.: Prentice Hall, p. 242.

102. For excellent discussions of similar issues in Italy and Germany within a similar comparative framework, see papers by Giorgio Piccinato (especially at p. 6), Donatella Calabi, and Frank Mancuso (especially at p. 10), presented at the First International Conference on the History of Urban and Regional Planning, London, September 1977, mimeo.

103. Marcuse, Peter (1977) The Political Economy of Rent Control: Theory and Strategy, Conference on Urban Political Economy, Santa Cruz, California.
104. See Wolman, Harold (1971) *Politics of Federal Housing*. New York: Dodd Mead, and Freedman, Leonard (1969) *Public Housing: The Politics of Poverty*. New York: Holt Rinehart.
105. Hofstadter, Richard (1955) *The Age of Reform: From Bryan to F.D.R.* New York: Random House, p. 308.
106. Marsh, Benjamin C. (1953) *Lobbyist for the People: A Record of Fifty Years*. Washington, D.C., p. 35, in Lubove, Roy (1967) *The Urban Community: Housing and Planning in the Progressive Era*. Englewood Cliffs, N.J.: Prentice Hall, p. 231.
107. For an early history of housing by employers in the U.S., see Wood, Edith Elmer (1919) *The Housing of the Unskilled Wage Earner: America's Next Problem*. New York: The Macmillan Company, Chapter IV, pp. 114–28; for a more recent account, see Lubove, Roy (1967) *The Urban Community: Housing and Planning in the Progressive Era*. Englewood Cliffs, N.J.: Prentice Hall, pp. 224ff.
108. *Regional Plan of New York and its Environs,* 1931, Vol. VI, p. 16.
109. See Marcuse, Peter, *The Ideal of Homeownership*. New York: Columbia University, Graduate School of Architecture and Planning, Working Papers Series, forthcoming.

3

Urban planning, the planning profession, and the motor vehicle in early twentieth-century America[1]

BLAINE A. BROWNELL

American city planning was reputedly shaped in the mould of Daniel H. Burnham's famous entreaty to 'make no little plans'. New York City's Central Park, the 'Great White City' of the Chicago World's Fair, the architectural magnificence of civic plazas born of the City Beautiful, and Burnham's plans for San Francisco and Chicago all seemed fitting witnesses to the truth of this injunction. At the least, they conveyed a sense of future possibility, and more than a little flair and audacity. Most of these projects were rooted in a neo-classic past, and rarely responded directly to the deeper social and economic dimensions of urban life; indeed, most were in some sense set apart from the 'real' world. But in the realm of physical design they were hardly timid, and posed some rather dramatic alternatives to the dense, confused, and alienating industrial cities of late nineteenth-century America.

By the 1930s audacity and promise had lost considerable ground to the more modest and acceptable goals of practicality and narrow problem-solving. Even comprehensive plans were often less notable for their breadth than for their technical detail. Many ambitious objectives remained, but these seemed as froth upon waves of statistics, survey results, traffic counts, long lists of street improvements, and zoning maps. And the concerns and aspirations of planners themselves were different. The planners' role had become more typically that of restrained professional consultants than of worldly philosophers or eager reformers bent on reshaping the city.

This shift, usually explained as a transition from the City Beautiful to the City Functional, is easily overdramatized. Burnham himself was well known as a competent organizer and manager, and rather dramatic—if somewhat implausible—solutions to the dilemmas of urban society were put forth during the 1920s and after. Frederick Law Olmsted appealed to the business sense of nineteenth-century New Yorkers and Harland Bartholomew occasionally put renaissance façades alongside curb and median designs in his early twentieth-century plans. Cautious technicians and dynamic futurists are found on both sides of 1900. But changes of emphasis and focus did take place between roughly 1910 and 1930, in both the attitudes of planners and in the substance of planning work—at precisely the same time that the gasoline-powered motor vehicle was transformed in the United States from a curiosity to a mass movement[2].

The purpose here is to fashion one interpretive framework for understanding what impact the arrival of the motor vehicle may have had on city planning in this crucial period, what impetus it may have provided for this transition and how it may have helped, along with many other factors, to shape the emerging profession of planning just as planners doubtless helped to determine what its impact on American cities and their populations would be. Precisely what modern city planning and the present condition of our cities owe to this coincidence is not yet clear, but the debt is probably significant. In short, the automobile and the urban transportation crisis it created and compounded helped to determine the goals, roles, and attitudes of American planners; and the ways in which planners thought about and treated the automobile in their work helped to fashion the modern American city[3]. The motor vehicle and its consequences constitued one important context for the evolution of urban planning in the United States.

The impact of and responses to technology have all too often been considered apart from the larger intellectual and socio-economic setting, implying a much simpler and more linear process than is justified. Attitudes toward technology, and the 'uses' of innovations, are formed within a matrix of economic demands, social expectations and taboos, inclinations toward change, and patterns of opportunity. Thus, the interpretative framework suggested here is very broad indeed, involving no less than the perceived and actual roles of planners in early twentieth-century America, the professionalization of planning, the relationship of planning to established social and economic groups, and the responses of planners to technological innovation and the future.

The year 1909 marked a time when aesthetics and efficiency were held in tenuous balance, under the aegis of a reform spirit. The Municipal Art Commission of Los Angeles published Charles Mulford Robinson's outline of the City Beautiful—an altogether familiar design of stately and decorous boulevards, a system of 'pleasure drives' and carriageways free from congestion and clanging streetcar traffic[4]. In the same year, Daniel H.

Burnham's far more ambitious scheme for Chicago appeared, which surpassed in scope and detail all those that had come before it. While homage to the City Beautiful was obviously paid, largely in neo-baroque architecture and street layouts, the priorities of the City Functional were also evident. The plan covered the entire metropolitan area within a sixty-six mile radius of the city, and included an array of radial and concentric streets, a vast park system (including the proposed twenty mile stretch along Lake Michigan), the redevelopment of the city's railway network and terminals, new harbour projects, improvements in scores of existing city streets, and an impressive new civic centre[5]. And the spirit of urban renaissance through civic reform and greater efficiency which permeated the Chicago Plan also reverberated at the First National Conference on City Planning and Congestion, held in Washington, D.C., in May 1909. Here, however, little attention was devoted to neo-classic design and pleasure parkways. The focus was on relief of social and economic problems to bring health and order to America's often chaotic cities. The participants disagreed significantly on solutions: some railed against land speculators while others worried over the threats of socialism and extremism bred in congestion. The movement away from aesthetics and toward social and economic issues signalled a significant shift from the concerns of the Great White City, and the reformist tone was even more pronounced. The conference also recognized the need, as Robert A. Pope expressed it, for 'a professional equipped to make city planning the social and economic factor it ought to be'[6].

The new emphases on comprehensive planning, on social and economic problems, and on the city's functions as well as its appearance ushered in the era of the City Practical and indicated that planners were expecting more of themselves and expanding the scope and variety of their activities and concerns. They would no longer be content to fashion civic plazas, individual parks, and boulevard systems for sedate residential communities. Through spokesmen like Frederic C. Howe, planning was itself raised to the top of the municipal reform agenda as a means of securing the promise of American life[7].

The rising expectations of planners, so evident in 1909, were frustrated by the events and spirit of the teens and twenties. Though the first official city planning commission was established in Hartford, Connecticut in 1907, the great majority of planners served in a limited consulting capacity prior to 1920—if they were asked to serve at all—and planning functions received at best only minimal appropriations in most cities. Planners understandably lamented the lack of public understanding of their capabilities and contributions, and the proclivity of political leaders to pay them lip service and little else. Their choice seemed increasingly to be between tackling broad social problems from outside the structure of power and decision-making, and working on more modest and less controversial matters from within that structure. They were also buffeted by the huge challenges posed by change.

'Perhaps no other new profession', Mel Scott wrote, 'had to contend with so many rapid technological advances, so many startling changes in urban areas, and so many unfamiliar technical and legal problems as the city planning profession encountered just before and just after its founding'[8].

What was the state of this new profession on the threshold of the 1920s? And how did the professionalization of an occupation affect the roles and self-perceptions of planners themselves[9]? The complex process of professionalization may itself hold some of the keys to these questions. Professionalization, according to one brief definition, is:

> a process by which an organized occupation, usually but not always by virtue of making a claim to special esoteric competence and to concern for the quality of its work and its benefits to society, obtains the exclusive right to perform a particular kind of work, control training for and access to it, and control the right of determining and evaluating the way the work is performed[10].

Rooted in the crafts and guilds of pre-industrial society, professionalization took on the character and velocity of a social movement in the nineteenth and twentieth centuries, as occupations proliferated and work and knowledge became increasingly specialized.[11] The major stages or junctures in the professionalization process, and the attributes and characteristics of professional group behaviour, are especially important— and have understandably drawn the attention of a number of scholars, especially sociologists[12]. In a recent study of American sociologists, for example, George H. Daniels devised a four-stage model of the professionalization process: (1) preemption; (2) institutionalization; (3) legitimation; and (4) the attainment of professional autonomy[13]. Generally, the process proceeds from early efforts to lay claim to a body of knowledge or an area of expertise to attempts at institutionalizing and legitimating these claims. The ultimate goal is to achieve a clearly-defined sphere of activity for a clearly defined group, recognized by the larger society.

These goals, and to some degree the process itself, are reflected in the various attributes with which professions have sought to cloak themselves, especially since the late nineteenth century. Ernest Greenwood identified five such attributes in 1957: (1) a basis of systematic theory; (2) authority recognized by the clientele of the professional group; (3) a broader community sanction and approval of this authority; (4) a code of ethics regulating relations of professional persons with clients and with colleagues; and (5) a professional culture sustained by formal professional associations[14]. B. Barber isolated four 'essential' professional characteristics: (1) a high degree of generalized and systematic knowledge; (2) primary orientation to the community interest rather than to individual self-interest; (3) self-control of behaviour through internalized codes of ethics, fashioned in part through voluntary associations organized and operated by the work specialists themselves; and (4) a system of rewards that is primarily a set of symbols of work achievement[15]. Underlying the professionalization process, and providing the basis for many professional behaviour patterns, according to Talcott Parsons, were certain 'cultural ideals': (1) rationality; (2) universalism; (3) disinterestedness; and (4) specifity of function[16].

Professional concerns and activities are gradually separated from occupational tasks. In this sense, professions are distinctly more than crafts. It is not enough, in other words, for professions to employ certain skills to do a job; skills and expertise must depend, according to many scholars, on a body of systematic knowledge or theory. Since some professions—like planning—do not have a highly developed theoretical base, it can be argued that theory is not a crucial element of professionalization. But most authorities agree that professionalization involves increasing authority over a body of knowlege and range of activities. Various professions have thus tended to define their 'occupational niche' around 'problems of universal, or at least widely experienced, social concern. In each case they encompass specialized areas of knowledge which affect all individuals but where only a few can become expert'[17].

The professions of science, medicine, and the law have received a great deal of scholarly attention, though the professionalization of social work in the United States in the early years of the twentieth century provides a particularly well-documented case. Growing out of the charitable efforts and organizations of the nineteenth century, of which settlement houses were the most dramatic examples, social work was shaped by a variety of factors. 'Group consciousness and professional norms' were used to distinguish 'between social work as a low-prestige occupation and social work as a potential profession'. This development of group identity—an occupational 'subculture'—was facilitated by associations and schools which specified minimal professional standards of training and practice and emphasized qualities of public service (disinterestedness) and objectivity (rationality). Perhaps most important was the effort 'to establish a scientific knowledge base and methodology' which would separate social workers from 'non-professionals' engaged in charitable endeavours. As Roy Lubove wrote in his excellent history of social work, 'The monopoly of a special skill is the essence of any occupational group's claim to professional status'[18].

The planning profession resembles other professions in certain basic ways, though its development is somewhat different, in pace if not in character. A variety of conferences served to bring planners and architects together occasionally before 1910, and these were held at least annually in subsequent years. A professional association—The American City Planning Institute (forerunner of the American Institute of Planners)—did not appear, however, until 1917 and its initial membership was rather small and quite diverse in background and training. Among the fifty-two charter members were landscape architects, engineers, attorneys, architects, realtors, publishers, and public officials[19]. Planning had only a modest place in academic curricula through the late 1920s, and this also made it extremely difficult to develop minimal and uniform professional standards and credentials that would be widely accepted. The only initial membership requirement for American City Planning Institute members, for example, was at least two years of experience in 'some form of city planning activity'[20]. The American City Planning Institute was simply too loosely structured to provide socialization into a new professional culture, though it did doubtless begin this process in a very limited way. But typical of other professions, it did develop a code of ethics and standards of professional behaviour before 1920.

Even when serious attention was devoted to the matter of proper professional training, the results were not very specific. The Conference on Research and Instruction in City and Regional Planning, organized in 1928 by Nicholas Murray Butler, president of Columbia University, and other planners and educators, concluded that planning was inherently inter-disciplinary, involving everything from landscape architecture to law, and that design skills constituted the only basic qualifications for those who would call themselves professional planners. The conference's call for inter-disciplinary and broad-gauged training of planners was quite ahead of its time in many respects, and is perhaps even more relevant to today's planning education; but it did little to advance the profession's sense of its own identity or delimit its precise role and activities. When a School of City Planning opened at Harvard University in 1929, the profession had taken a significant step forward, but no other universities boasted similar programmes at the time[21].

Compared with law and medicine, not to mention less traditional professions such as social work, city planning was a mere foundling. Planners had not, for example, clearly pre-empted a body of knowledge or range of activities for themselves, even though they were moving in this direction. Many of the principal issues in planning—land use, streets, and 'good government'—were widely regarded as the business of elected officials, engineers, chambers of commerce, and civic groups. Planning was only loosely institutionalized, through staffs which served city officials or planning boards. But many more cities had zoning regulations by 1930 than comprehensive plans, and a number of cities did not have official planning departments, a permanent staff for their planning commissions, or continuing relationships with particular planning consultants, even though a good deal of progress had been made in these areas during the 1920s. Planners themselves enunciated many of the 'cultural ideals' attendant to professionalization, but even here there were difficulties. Claims of universalism were supported by growing attention to European experience and models, but since some European societies were often quite different in their attitudes toward the prerogatives of private property such claims threatened to undermine the acceptability of planning as a legitimate and 'practical' function in American capitalist society. Planners stressed their professional rationality and objectivity with little risk, but their claims of distinterestedness were somewhat strained by the fact that so many planners were private consultants engaged in planning for profit. Planning enjoyed wide support as a concept in the 1920s—a handmaiden to good business practice and common sense—but broad public support of planning as a profession did not really exist, primarily because it was not an issue of much interest either to many opinion leaders or to the general populace. Planning was synonymous in the public mind with intelligent forethought, of the sort increasingly expected of businessmen and bureaucrats, rather than with a narrow professional group, a body of theory, or even a set of esoteric skills.

The anxiety of planners over this lack of full public awareness and approval, and their search for a clear professional role and identity, led increasingly toward an emphasis on special skills and, in Parson's phrase, 'specificity of function'. Partly because of the rather varied training and experience of planners and the underdeveloped state of planning education, the movement towards professional identity tended more and more to emphasize what planners actually *did* rather than what they knew or what urban policies they agreed upon. Indeed, the work of planning itself constituted the bulk of shared experience among planners. In short, the emphasis was on professional skills and what these skills could accomplish for society. Theory would have to grow out of practice.

An early advocate of this emphasis was George B. Ford. At a time when Frederick W. Taylor's *Principles of Scientific Management* was the rage among businessmen and many 'reformers', Ford saw many applications for planning. 'This method of work, systematized, standardized, "Taylorized", as it is', he wrote in 1913, 'has most decidedly proved its worth. It appeals strongly to businessmen . . . and convinces everyone that the *experts have real knowledge on which to base their recommendations,* and are not presenting mere dreams, pretty but impractical'[22]. Ford's goal was to guide planning from its status as a 'rather capricious procedure into that *highly respectable* thing known as an exact science'. The ultimate ideal, in Ford's view, was the ability of planners to assess, rationally and objectively, the urban condition, and through a precise set of professional skills arrive at 'one, and only one, logical and convincing solution of the problems involved'[23].

Few other planners were this facile or optimistic in their expectations of the planning profession. But similar ideas and hopes can nevertheless be read in much of the planning literature of the time, and perhaps even more so in the writings of businessmen and editors who supported the concept of planning and called for the rationalization and regularization of the city.

A related phenomenon was the drift of planning away from broad reform goals after 1910, and movement toward more 'practical' activities. A variety of factors help to explain this shift. Since planners were concerned so much with physical arrangements and restructuring, their interests tended to diverge from those calling for social and economic change. The illiberal spirit of World War I may, as Mel Scott suggests, have weakened the reform impulse among planners[24]. The clients of practising planners were almost always among the major established interest groups, and most leading planners were members of the social and economic elite[25]. And a shift from 'reform' to 'functionalism' may have been more or less typical of the professionalization process in the United States, whether in the nineteenth or twentieth centuries[26].

The professional insecurity of planners in the several decades after 1910 almost certainly rendered them more than slightly vulnerable to the vagaries of reform, and thus more susceptible to the call of the particular, the conventional, and the 'practical'. As Mel Scott wrote, as long as planners stuck to the protection of property values and matters of physical readjustment, they 'could gradually win a more secure place for themselves in American life. But let them march too far ahead of the public and they risked loosing much that they had gained by hard work and personal sacrifice'. Beyond that, planners were perhaps too preoccupied with developing techniques, forging legislation, promoting the value of comprehensive plans, and seeking funds for their work to indulge in unconventional and imaginative schemes. In this context, most planners perhaps 'regarded utopian thought as a luxury, and bold schemes for the reorganization of urban areas as futile. Did not many businessmen, politicians, and civic leaders still speak of planners as visionaries?'[27].

During the 1920s the regional planners of New York and the bright 'visionaries' of the Regional Planning Association of America (RPAA)—Lewis Mumford and Clarence Stein among them—advanced the scope of planning activity and only rarely lost sight of the manifold relationships between physical configurations and socio-economic realities, and the role of technology in urban change. But in many respects they went against the professional grain. By the end of the decade, most planners were actively committed to a disciplined, rational, highly functional, and culturally reinforcing conception of planning and professional goals. This increasingly prevalent conception of planning was put forth succinctly by the Los Angeles Regional Planning Commission in 1929:

> It is good business to plan. It is as sound and expedient to plan the development of cities as it is to design and plan the construction of a bridge, a portion of a highway or a water system. Planning is an amplification of those fundamental principles which have always been practised in engineering, namely, the accumulation of data, the reduction to formulae, the application to design, and the accomplishment of predetermined objectives.
>
> These objectives are set forth in definite plans, which are given official recognition, substantiated by statistical information, stabilized by public opinion and supported by methods of procedure consistent with the most modern knowledge of economics.

> Planning is primarily a function of the engineer, but in city and regional planning the engineer must work with the architect, the landscape architect, the attorney and those of other allied professions[28].

Such notions were especially favoured by younger, less well-established planners who aspired to a genuinely professional career, perhaps even in municipal government. Daniel H. Burnham Jr. certainly reflected the stance of a new generation, turning away from his father's great vision and concentrating on practical, limited, strictly functional, and achievable projects.

At this juncture, when city planning was becoming less reform-oriented and more committed to special and rather narrowly focused skills to secure professional identity, the motor vehicle appeared *en masse*. And while its arrival created confusion and indecision within planners' ranks, it also provided the emerging profession with a very real opportunity.

Automobiles swarmed on to downtown streets which were ill-suited by width and condition to accommodate additional vehicles of any kind. Many streets failed to connect with each other in a rational way, and some of the most heavily travelled streets were narrow, poorly-paved, and virtually inaccessible from parallel arteries. Streetcars fought motor cars for space, and disgorged passengers in the middle of clogged thoroughfares. Merchants wrestled with a dilemma: clearing crowded streets of parked cars increased traffic flow and kept the downtown area competitive for customers; but restrictions on parking also kept patrons away. Even early in the decade, jokes appeared in the popular press about the difficulty of finding a place to leave a car in the city's core. Commercial-civic groups endlessly repeated the necessity for efficient urban transportation, but they were not sure how to achieve their goal. They were less concerned about the fate of streetcars or automobiles, as particular modes of transportation, than they were anxious that the transportation system work effectively. Public officials, understandably responsive to the interests of such influential groups, reassured their constituents but were themselves uncertain about what to do. Thus, the transportation crisis created—or at least accelerated—by the motor vehicle demanded immediate attention and some special skills. The key point, as Roy Lubove wrote some years ago, is that 'The transportation challenge enabled planners to exercise their technical skills and demonstrate their usefulness without challenging the institutional status quo'[29]. Indeed, the transportation challenge was eagerly accepted as a means of entrance into that institutional *status quo*. The automobile thus became an excellent vehicle for tansporting planners into a new and more widely-recognized professional status.

The very substance and structure of plans bespoke the new emphasis. While sometimes prefaced with rather grandiose principles and sweeping objectives, most comprehensive plans of the 1920s rested on two major pillars: the major street plan and the zoning plan. Harland Bartholomew, the most active producer of comprehensive plans during the decade, might lace his Memphis, Tennessee, plan with a neo-classical redesign for the entire downtown waterfront, but the emphasis was clearly on a more efficient traffic circulation pattern and the discipline of land-use controls[30]. The comprehensive plan underwent a discernable shift during the 1920s in the direction of greater technical competence, more emphasis upon detail, and the presentation of material in a more 'objective' manner, through charts, tables, and graphs. The proposals of traffic consultants were especially characterized by these features. Engineering diagrams and schematics for street widening and resurfacing projects took up as much as half of many plans, and the conclusions of traffic counts were presented in an array of tables and charts. Certainly, this was a useful way of presenting data, and it was a response in part to the requests of clients; but more and more data were collected on more and more specific items. Consultants like Miller McClintock, head of the Erskine Traffic Bureau at Harvard, and John Beeler, a private transportation consultant, worked on their own and also in concert with Bartholomew and other planners. They brought to comprehensive plans, both as direct participants and through the examples of their detailed engineering studies, a degree of precision and narrow focus quite typical of traffic and engineering reports.

Around the turn of the century, architecture and layout were the planner's stock in trade. By 1910 the planning 'survey' became the most specialized planning tool in general use. By the 1920s the survey technique had been expanded considerably to include data on economic activities and population projections, and began to approach the comprehensive inventories characteristic of modern planning. This was still, however, largely an endeavour of collecting and displaying large amounts of data. Standards regarding recreation, land use, and housing had been developed, though little theory was involved. Transportation, however, provided a new dimension for technique. Not only could large amounts of data be collected—and they were, through innumerable traffic counts and inventories of parking space—but certain 'laws' of traffic movement and street design also evolved. These were not theoretical formulations either, of course, but they were much more esoteric and technical than general surveys and layout designs. and they could be closely tied to specific and detailed recommendations. Traffic engineering would later develop into a virtually separate 'profession', but at this juncture planners fixed upon transportation and the evolving techniques of traffic engineering to bring new dimensions to their work. And the increasingly popular device of zoning enabled them to make connections between transportation and patterns of land use, by relating zoning classifications to traffic patterns and street 'types'.

Transportation studies were fairly common before 1920. They were almost all concerned with streetcar transit, however, and most were prepared for traction companies or municipal transit bureaux. This genre continued into the 1920s, though by then the automobile had to be seriously pondered in an overall transportation plan, and the actual and potential impact of the motor vehicle given at least some consideration in studies focusing only on streetcar systems. Generally, comprehensive plans tended to focus during the 1920s even more on issues of urban transportation than they had before, particularly at the level of local streets. These plans and studies reveal a great deal about how well planners were able to foresee the impact of a dramatic new transportation technology, and how the evolving professional role of planners affected their approach to the motor vehicle.

Planners were generally caught up in the enthusiasm for the automobile prior to World War I[31]. Spokesmen for the industry and assorted auto club leaders often made sweeping predictions of a new age in transportation—predictions which most planners did not dispute. But planners apparently did not take the motor vehicle seriously until roughly the 1920s, when the nature of its impact was more obvious, particularly to client groups, and they continued to maintain a variety of opinions about it. This was due in part to the various interests of clients: streetcar companies, for example, were not inclined to favour a recasting of dominant transportation modes, and they usually seriously underestimated the threat of auto competition. Attitudes toward the automobile also varied according to larger goals and objectives. As Mark S. Foster observes, 'city officials and urban planners failed to develop anything approaching a consensus on what constituted an ideal urban form. They were not only divided over whether to encourage centralization or decentralization, but over what factors actually influenced urban growth in any given direction'[32].

Not surprisingly, planners as a whole were ambiguous about the automobile: a few saw its promise for creating a new urban form and a few believed that its cost of operation and attendant traffic congestion fundamentally limited its mass use. Most planners perceived at least the broad outlines of the motor vehicle's impact, and even the necessity of redesigning the city to accommodate the innovation. Yet they also based most of their actual plans and recommendations on traditional concepts and transit modes. Planners were, in short, not one whit more prescient or deluded in their response to the automobile than businessmen or city officials, and their attitudes often understandably correlated closely with their client interests.

Planners' attitudes toward fixed rail transit provide an excellent case in point. Even by the early years of the 1920s auto registrations were rising precipitously and by the middle of the decade automobility was unquestionably a mass phenomenon. Yet planners generally followed the trolley companies in assuming the absolute necessity of streetcars (though not of subways) as the bulwark of the urban transportation system that was likely to remain basically unchallenged. One consultant, Daniel Turner, informed the 1922 National Conference on City Planning that 'in a modern city, street railways are as essential as the homes of the people and the buildings in which they work'[33]. The typical reasoning behind this belief was that the number of vehicles operating in the downtown sections would eventually reach a saturation point. Consequently, as a transit plan for Los Angeles suggested, 'the total number of vehicles used in the central business district will increase from year to year but at a diminishing rate'. As the saturation point was reached, according to this theory, dependence on public transit would actually grow greater[34]. A number of planners believed, at least in the early years of the decade, that the automobile would actually stimulate streetcar travel by encouraging greater general mobility and more individual trips; and in any event the higher cost and lower safety level of auto operation would blunt any direct threat to rail transit systems[35].

The curious ambivalence toward the motor vehicle was quite apparent. The Pittsburgh transit commissioner, for example, concluded in 1927 that 'This is an automobile age which has brought with it a new type of civilization and we must accept that fact and reconstruct our cities accordingly'. But that sweeping clarion call was succeeded by a report which claimed rising public demands for additional streetcar facilities and the necessity of improving Pittsburgh's rail transit system to keep up in the competition with other cities[36].

'One might have expected city planners', Mark Foster writes, 'with attention riveted upon the dynamics of urban change, to have been more prescient regarding the futures of each element of the transportation networks'. But, as Foster also notes, planners' occupational insecurity and their lack of widespread funding and public support limited their vision: 'During the 1920s city planners were concerned first and foremost with professional recognition, not to mention survival'[37]. They generally did not offer grand prognostications regarding shifting transportation modes and new urban forms—except occasionally during conferences and in informal shop talk—but concentrated on the more limited, and infinitely more detailed, schemes to identify central business district problems, balance conflicting transportation interests, make minor adjustments in the existing mechanism and, perhaps above all, satisfy clients.

Yet the onslaught of the automobile swept inexorably over planners and streetcar companies, and comprehensive plans during the decade showed increasing attention to the motor vehicle. This was especially true in newer, rapidly growing cities without extensive streetcar systems. Los Angeles planners, for example, did a rather abrupt about-face in the early 1920s, moving from support of rail transit to endorsement of population decentralization under the aegis of the automobile[38]. This was in part a practical realization that the city was simply developing in a highly dispersed fashion, to the point that serving the area with fixed rail transit lines—especially elevated or underground—was prohibitively expensive. It was also doubtless due to the support of local business and civic interests for decentralization, and a discernable perference among most of the city's citizens for this option[39]. This then, was less a case of exceptional prescience than the recognition of a different *status quo*.

A number of planners, scattered across the country, advocated decentralization during the 1920s, in a continuing attack on the by-now traditional villain of population congestion and in a new offensive against glutted downtown streets. As Harland Bartholomew put it before the 1920 National City Planning Conference, 'We should decentralize and spread our values over a larger area and automatically by this distribution of business and traffic solve the traffic problem'[40]. Such views were supported by commercial-civic groups, especially in cities like Los Angeles. 'Banking, industry, commercialized recreation, and even retail business are entering upon an era of decentralization', declared the Los Angeles *City Club Bulletin* in 1926. 'Business is pointing the way out of the intolerable congestion situation in downtown areas'[41].

But a number of other planners, like Boston consultant Robert Whitten, questioned the virtues of decentralization, especially as it seemed to imperil existing urban cores and undermine one of planning's major goals during the era—to protect property values. This view found support among a number of business spokesmen as well. The Mayor's Traffic Committee in Pittsburgh pointed out in 1927 that the assessed property values in the two downtown wards constituted one-third of the assessed valuation of the entire city—a situation which called for 'progressive traffic improvements for this District'[42]. Even in Los Angeles, planners and businessmen recognized the dangers in uncontrolled traffic patterns and consequent location shifts. 'Property values are made unstable through the aimless shifting of business centers', a Los Angeles study observed in 1922. 'In time, if the question remains unsolved, financiers, who through their confidence in the future of this city, invested tremendous fortunes in business structures, will hesitate in making additional investments . . .'[43].

Planners were increasingly responsive to the perceived needs of local commercial-civic elites who were their clients and who, in a very real sense, held the keys to a more secure professional status. But commercial-civic groups were themselves often divided on issues of transportation and urban form. In most cities they desired *both* a strong, vital business core and an expanding periphery; *both* continued centralization of many social and economic activities and decentralization of population and economic activities. The overall context for these objectives I have identified as the 'urban ethos', a belief that cities should grow and develop while in their essential social and structural features remaining very much the same[44]. Not surprisingly, many planners attempted to give shape and substance to commercial-civic aspirations, and their plans reflected it. The modern city in short, would be a strong centre surrounded by vital expansion, held together in orderly synergy by rail transit lines and major highways.

The desire to link peripheral growth to a vital centre in a mutually reinforcing fashion led to a concept of major roads and highways that in some ways ignored or de-emphasized the truly revolutionary mobility of the motorcar. Bartholomew supported decentralization as a solution for the traffic problem during the 1920s, for example, yet many of his plans emphasized the central business district as the urban focal point. 'The aim', he noted in a major street plan for New Orleans, 'is to create a series of wide, direct and well paved arteries radiating outward from this primary objective'[45]. The capacity of the motor vehicle for *lateral mobility* was not especially encouraged in most major street plans during the 1920s[46]. Rather, highways were shot out from the urban core in great radial patterns and transportation spines, looking for all the world like roadbeds for rail transit vehicles. The new extensive highway systems could tie together discrete clusters of activity in an orderly and controlled domination of the countryside. Warren H. Manning, a Massachusetts consultant who had served his apprenticeship under Frederick Law Olmsted, proposed 'to establish centers far enough out on the *spokes of the transportation ways* to permit radial roads to again pass off from these secondary centers into the country'[47].

Los Angeles planners, to be sure, were developing a regional highway system that was highly adapted to the new technological potential of the motor vehicle, and equally ambitious concepts were advanced for the New York City region. But Pittsburgh planners were perhaps more typical, using selected major highway routes to stimulate growth and also maintain the viability of the wealthy Triangle[48].

Major exceptions to such notions of transportation and urban form are represented by the New York Regional Plan and the ideas advanced by the Regional Planning Association of America. The New York Regional Plan of 1929, which drew upon a number of concepts contained in previous regional plans, included elaborate highway systems covering a huge territory—with circumvential and radial routes. It posed no break with existing economic arrangements, and no new alternatives, but it recognized the technological potential of the motor vehicle, both for rearranging population patterns and economic activities and for creating chaos in the metropolis. Clarence Stein, Lewis Mumford, and their colleagues in the RPAA were also sensitive to the meaning of the automobile. Their proposals were based on the greater flexibility it brought to intraregional transportation, permitting a wider distribution of population in smaller clusters, and the necessity, as they saw it, to prevent the auto's uncontrolled use in the delicate social fabric of neighbourhoods and small communities. The New York Regional Plan was certainly not typical of most comprehensive plans, and the RPAA, which did pose some alternatives in urban structure, was well outside the mainstream of American planning during the 1920s. These were, then, exceptions which tend to confirm the rule.

Most American planners of this era attempted to find solutions to immediate and specific problems, to satisfy clients who were interested primarily in maintaining the viability of the *status quo*, of adjusting the present to meet the most obvious—and acceptable—demands of the near future. The typical comprehensive plan proposed to protect existing land values in the core and generate new ones of the periphery, largely through more efficient and extensive urban transportation. Fixed rail transit was regarded as the basis of most urban transportation systems, with the automobile serving an increasing and complementary role. Plans devoted more and more emphasis to transportation and zoning, and to the relatively narrow and 'scientific' collection and presentation of information. As planners moved away from broader reform concerns and toward 'practical' proposals and special skills, the future and the past began to shrink toward the present. The long vision of Daniel Burnham had become a period of only five or ten years. The past became yesterday, the future became tomorrow. What should the city do?—'shall it adopt the traffic plan of the city of tomorrow and hope to grow up to it, or shall it continue to be planned or readjusted to meet gradually changing needs and conditions..?[49]. The answer was generally the latter. The successful professionalization of planning depended upon its ability to meet the needs of established interest groups, and the first priority of established interest groups was survival.

History abounds with coincidences and confluences, but giving even the most obviously momentous of these their just due and precise weight is almost impossibly difficult. This paper argues for the significance of one coincidence for American planning, and suggests one interpretative framework for understanding it—an edifice built necessarily of generalizations. A full treatment would do far less violence to the complexity and variety of planning in the early twentieth century. It would take account of those exceptional cases not mentioned here, and deal more subtly with the early beginnings of professional cultures and conflicts between ideals and reality. It would show, among other things, that the greater precision of the plans of the 1920s was in many ways a step forward: these early comprehensive plans and detailed traffic studies provided the foundations for coping with many urban problems in terms public officials could understand, appreciate, and act upon. A trend toward 'objective' social science was underway in planning as in many academic disciplines, of course, and—after all—grand designs were often terribly vague and not particularly relevant to the immediate needs of cities caught in the throes of uncontrolled change. It would also emphasize the many other professions that have developed in similar fashion and that planners, like social workers, physicians, economists, and school teachers, were limited by the constraints and expectations of society in terms of what they could actually achieve.

The coincidence between the emerging professionalization of city planning and the arrival of the automobile in the United States did have an impact on both the profession and the ways in which American cities have been influenced by the motor vehicle. Professionalization obviously does not proceed in a vacuum. It evolves according to the character of society at any given time, within the constraints of economics and values, guided by social and psychological—and technological—incentives in certain directions. Planning was a case in point. Planners were already moving away from broad reform concerns by the 1920s, and were anxious about their role and status, their professional identity, in the larger society. It is argued here that the motor vehicle and the problems it helped to create in urban transportation provided planners with a means of carving out their niche in the professional world, of justifying their work on the basis of 'practical' solutions to tangible problems, of increasing their influence on urban growth patterns, of narrowing and intensifying their focus and thus closing out amateurs. Like many other professions, planning was moulded within the dictates of the *status quo.*

NOTES

1. This paper has benefited from comments and suggestions by Mark S. Foster, David R. Goldfield, and John Hancock.
2. Registered motor vehicles numbered only about 8000 in the United States in 1900, rising to almost 500,000 in the space of a decade. By 1929, a registered motor vehicle existed for about every 4.5 persons in the country.
3. Planners were not, in this era, a clearly defined professional group. A number of private citizens, including business leaders, clergymen, newspaper writers, and civic leaders, were interested in planning and commented on the subject occasionally and when their economic interests were involved. For the purposes of generalization in this essay, the term 'planners' includes only those consultants and public officials who were engaged in 'professional' planning activity, i.e. those for whom planning was a principal source of livelihood or a major element of their work.
4. Robinson, C. M. (1909) *The City Beautiful, Report of the Municipal Art Commission for the City of Los Angeles, California.* Los Angeles: Municipal Art Commission.
5. Burnham, D. H. and Bennett, E. H. (1909) in Moore, C. (ed.) *Plan of Chicago.* Chicago: The Commercial Club. Also see Hines, T. S. (1974) *Burnham of Chicago: Architect and Planner.* New York: Oxford University Press.
6. Scott, M. (1969) *American City Planning Since 1890.* Berkeley: University of California Press, pp. 96–100.
7. Howe's comparisons of English and European town planning efforts with those in the United States were especially important in shaping American planners' concepts of their own potential. See, as examples, Howe, F. C. (1907) *The British City: The Beginnings of Democracy.* New York: Charles Scribner's Sons; (1905) *The City: The Hope of Democracy.* New York: Charles Scribner's Sons; (1913) *European Cities At Work.* New York: Charles Scribner's Sons; (1915) *The Modern City and Its Problems.* New York: Charles Scribner's Sons; and (1925) *The Confessions of a Reformer.* New York: Charles Scribner's Sons. The best full-

length study of Howe is Huff, R. A. (1966) Frederick C. Howe, Progressive. Unpublished Ph.D. thesis, University of Rochester, New York.

8. Scott, M. (1969) *American City Planning Since 1890*. Berkeley: University of California Press, p. 169.
9. Scott's *American City Planning Since 1890* is an excellent narrative history of the planning profession, but more work remains to be done on the professionalization process and its social and conceptual dimensions as they relate to American city planning. An article dealing with the foundations of the modern planning movement largely prior to 1900 is Schultz, S. K. and McShane, C. (1977) To engineer the metropolis: sewers, sanitation, and city planning in late-nineteenth-century America. *Journal of American History,* 65 (2), pp. 389–411.
10. Friedson, E. (1973) Professions and the occupational principle, in Friedson, E. (ed.), *The Professions and Their Prospects*. Beverly Hills and London: Sage Publications p. 22.
11. See Jackson, J. A. (1970) Professions and professionalization—editorial introduction, in Jackson, J. A. (ed.) *Professions and Professionalization*. London: Cambridge University Press, pp. 5–15.
12. It would be quite impossible to cover the extensive sociological literature on professions and professionalization here. Perhaps the most important early systematic analysis of professionalization was Carr-Saunders, A. M. and Wilson, P. A. (1933) *The Professions*. Oxford: Oxford University Press. The various works cited in this essay provide a good introduction to the subject.
13. Daniels, G. H. (1967) The process of professionalization in American science: the emergent period, 1820–1860. *Isis,* 58 (1), p. 151. It should be noted here that some social scientists tend to discount such precise and structured interpretations of professionalization, on the grounds that the process is simply too varied and complex to be usefully categorized in this fashion. See, for example, Veysey. L. (1975) Who's a professional? Who cares? *Reviews in American History,* 3 (4), pp. 419–23.
14. Greenwood, E. (1957) Attributes of a profession. *Social Work,* 2 (3), pp. 44–5.
15. Barber, B. (1963) Some problems in the sociology of the professions. *Daedalus,* 92 (Fall), p. 672.
16. Parsons, T. (1954) The professions and social structure, in Parsons, T., *Essays in Sociological Theory,* revised edition. New York: Free Press, pp. 34–49.
17. Jackson, J. A. (1970) Professions and professionalization—editorial introduction, in Jackson, J. A. (ed.), *Professions and Professionalization*. London: Cambridge University Press, p. 7.
18. Lubove, R. (1965) *The Professional Altruist: The Emergence of Social Work as a Career, 1880-1930*. Cambridge: Harvard University Press, pp. 118, 121–3.
19. Scott, M. (1969) *American City Planning Since 1890*. Berkeley: University of California Press, p. 163.
20. *Ibid.*
21. *Ibid.,* pp. 265–6. It should be noted that some professional planners believed that practical experience and work in the field were quite superior to textbook training in educating planners.
22. (1913) Efficiency in city planning. *American City,* 8 (February), pp. 139–43 (my italics). Though this article was unsigned, Scott concluded that it was almost certainly written by Ford. (Scott, M. (1969) *American City Planning Since 1890*. Berkeley: University of California Press, pp. 122–3).

23. Quoted in Scott, M. (1969) *American City Planning Since 1890.* Berkeley: University of California Press, p. 121 (my italics).
24. *Ibid.,* pp. 117, 181–2.
25. See Brownell, B. A. (1975) The commercial-civic elite and city planning in Atlanta, Memphis, and New Orleans in the 1920s. *Journal of Southern History,* 41(3), pp. 339–68.
26. Lubove, for example, suggests ((1965) *The Professional Altruist: The Emergence of Social Work as a Career, 1880–1930.* Cambridge: Harvard University Press, pp. 157–8) that such a shift accompanied the institutionalization of social work—a shift from 'cause to 'function', from 'charismatic leader' to 'administrator'. 'The movement', according to one scholar, 'was from the broadly political to the narrowly technical, from statesmanship to craftsmanship'. Yeazell, D. C. (1976) Professional lives and the life of a profession. *Reviews in American History,* 4 (4), p. 485. This shift is perhaps especially typical of 'applied' sciences or professions, and has been traced in the history of planning even back into the 'pre-modern' stage (the eighteenth and early nineteenth centuries). See Benevolo, L. (1963) *The Origins of Modern Town Planning.* Cambridge: M.I.T. Press.
27. Scott, M. (1969) *American City Planning Since 1890.* Berkeley: University of California Press, pp. 252, 251.
28. (1929) *The Regional Planning Commission, County of Los Angeles.* Los Angeles: Regional Planning Commission, p. 5.
29. Lubove, R. (1967) *The Urban Community: Housing and Planning in the Progressive Era.* Englewood Cliffs, N.J.: Prentice-Hall, p. 11.
30. Bartholomew, H. (1924) *A Comprehensive City Plan: Memphis, Tennessee.* Memphis: Harlan Bartholomew and Associates. Concern for efficient traffic circulation was by no means new. It had been central in much European planning (in the work of Haussman, for example) and in the plans of Olmsted and Burnham, among others, in the United States.
31. James J. Flink termed this era the 'first stage' of automobile consciousness in Flink, J. J. (1972) Three stages of American automobile consciousness. *American Quarterly,* 25 (4), pp. 451-73.
32. Foster, M. S. (1979) City planners and the evolution of urban transportation in the United States, 1900–1940. *Journal of Urban History,* 5 (3), pp. 365–96. Foster's essay is the best brief survey of the subject, and though we disagree on several points, my indebtedness to his work is substantial.
33. Turner, D. (1922) The fundamentals of transit planning for cities, in *Proceedings of the 14th National Conference on City Planning.* Springfield, Mass.: American City Planning Association, p. 104.
34. Kelker, De Leuw & Company (1925) *Report and Recommendations on a Comprehensive Rapid Transit Plan for the City and County of Los Angeles.* Chicago: Kelker, De Leuw & Company, pp. 35–6.
35. See, as an example, Beeler, J. A. (1924) *Report to the City of Atlanta on a Plan for Local Transportation.* Atlanta: Beeler Organization; and Preston, H. K. (1974) A New Kind of Horizontal City: Automobilty in Atlanta, 1900–1930. Unpublished Ph.D. thesis, Emory University, Georgia, Chapter III.
36. (1927) *Annual Report of the City Transit Commissioner of Pittsburgh.* Pittsburgh: City of Pittsburgh, p. 3 and *passim.*

37. Foster, M. S. (1979) City Planners and the Evolution of urban transportation in the United States, 1900–1940. *Journal of Urban History,* **5** (3), p. 376.
38. Foster, M. S. (1975) The Model-T, the hard-sell, and Los Angeles's urban growth: the decentralization of Los Angeles during the 1920s. *Pacific Historical Review,* **44** (4), pp. 459–84; and Foster, M. S. (1971) The Decentralization of Los Angeles During the 1920s. Unpublished Ph.D. thesis, University of Southern California.
39. See (1926) Report on rapid transit, in Los Angeles *City Club Bulletin* (January 30), which took issue with proposals to provide subways and elevated lines for the city. The report recommended improved public transit, but along existing lines and with accommodations to the automobile.
40. Bartholomew, H. (1920) The urban auto problem, in *Proceedings of the 12th National Conference on City Planning.* Cincinnati, Ohio: American City Planning Association, p. 99. Quoted in Foster, M. S. (1979) City planners and evolution of urban transportation in the United States, 1900–1940. *Journal of Urban History,* **5** (3), p. 376.
41. (1926) Report on rapid transit, in Los Angeles *City Club Bulletin* (January 30), p. 4.
42. (1927) *Report and Recommendations of the Central Business District Street Traffic Survey.* Pittsburgh: City of Pittsburgh, chapter II, p. 3. A similar study of two years earlier noted the need to provide additional street space in the Triangle area 'to develop the full economic limit of its physical possibilities, and thereby to conserve the enormous business interest already located there . . .'. (1925) *Report on a Recommended Subway in the First and Second Wards of Pittsburgh.* Pittsburgh: Pittsburgh Traffic Commission, p. 9.
43. Los Angeles Traffic Commission (1922) *The Los Angeles Plan.* Los Angeles: Los Angeles Traffic Commission, p. 6.
44. Brownell, B. A. (1975) *The Urban Ethos in the South, 1920–1930.* Baton Rouge, Louisiana: Louisiana State University Press.
45. New Orleans Planning and Zoning Commission (1927) *Major Street Report.* New Orleans: New Orleans Planning and Zoning Commission, p. 6.
46. Jackson, K. T., concluded that the 'real significance of the automobile lay in its ability to move laterally and to open up land for settlement not served by the streetcar and railroad'. Jackson, K. T. (1974) Changing spatial patterns of work and residence in the age of the automobile. Unpublished paper delivered to the annual meeting of the Organization of American Historians, Denver, Colorado, pp. 23–4.
47. Manning, W. H. (1922) Atlanta—tomorrow a city of a million. *Atlanta Constitution Magazine,* March 19, p. 9. (My italics.)
48. See, for example, (1921) Development of major street plan promises relief from serious traffic congestion. *Progress,* **1** (January), p. 1. (Published by the Pittsburgh Citizens' Committee on the City Plan.)
49. Shattuck, I. S., *et al.* (1938) Traffic studies in relation to city planning, in James, H. (ed.), *American Planning and Civic Annual.* Harrisburg, Pennsylvania, p. 205. Quoted in Foster, M. S. (1979) City planning and the evolution of urban transportation in the United States, 1900–1940. *Journal of Urban History,* **5** (3), p. 390.

4

Regional planning and its institutional framework: an illustration from the Rhine-Main area, 1890–1945

DIETER REBENTISCH

Today the Rhine-Main area is one of the most densely populated regions of the German Federal Republic and is characterized, above all, by its economic productive strength. Its area occupies only one per cent of the country as a whole, but its population—about four per cent of the total—contributed 5.5 per cent of the gross domestic product in 1966. This contribution was made up of agriculture, 1 per cent; productive industries, 48 per cent; and services, 51 per cent. However, these figures present a problem because the Rhine-Main area cannot be delineated exactly. It includes the plains on both sides of the Main, between Aschaffenburg and its confluence with the Rhine, as well as the area on the right bank of the Rhine between Worms and Mainz. Within the context of the history of civilization, it is an urbanized area, an example of conurbation, the main centre of which—the settlement zone of Frankfurt and Offenbach—is surrounded by a series of economically and culturally independent sub-centres, the towns of Hanau, Aschaffenburg, Darmstadt, Mainz and Wiesbaden[1]. The Rhine-Main area did not develop from the expansion of one major city during the epoch of industrialization and urbanization, but through the progressive integration of various urban centres. It contains those small towns and villages whose populations are dependent on the labour market of the urban centres. Delineation of the area is further complicated because it never constituted either a political or administrative unit, but was always dissected by the borders of several federal states.

Given these problems, to understand the development of regional planning, three groups of questions must be considered. First, why did the Rhine-Main area become an urbanized area and not a city-region as Greater Berlin? Why did Frankfurt not become the single dominating major city, drawing all metropolitan functions to itself? How did the process of industrialization and urbanization take place? Secondly, how did the term 'Rhine-Main' arise, and when did a consciousness of regional unity in the area first manifest itself? How has the Rhine-Main area been distinguished from the surrounding regions at different times? When did the area first achieve sufficient organizational concentration to constitute a planning region, and what form did it take? And finally, what regulative measures were used at various times to direct the process of industrialization and agglomeration, and what socio-political aims were these measures designed to achieve? These questions must be answered in relation to three epochs, the period of the Kaisserreich, of the Weimar Republic and of Nazi Germany.

The main problem, however, is to show how regional planning developed in practice within the framework of the different local, provincial and federal state authorities with administrative powers in region, particularly as these authorities insisted on their individual statutory responsibilities.

THE GROWTH OF REGIONAL UNITY AND THE ADMINISTRATIVE STRUCTURE, 1890-1918

Since the Rhine-Main area is deficient in natural raw materials and energy sources, the phase of high industrialization did not begin until the 1870s and 1880s, when the means of mass communication of the technological age were fully developed. Although the capital market in Frankfurt offered favourable preconditions for the establishment of industrial undertakings, the town did not become the focal point of industrial development. There were several reasons for this.

First, Frankfurt had isolated itself from its surrounding environment in the past both economically, as a town of long-distance trade and of fairs, and politically, as a *Reichsstadt* or *Freie Stadt* (Imperial or Free City). Even after the annexation by Prussia in 1866 it had no political or administrative functions in the new province of Hesse-Nassau[2].

Secondly, the representatives of the ruling classes, wholesale merchants and bankers, clung to the inherited and antiquated economic structure and were opposed to the establishment of industry. Industrial production seemed to them to run counter to the interests of trade. Smoky factories, waste matter and noise disturbed the well-being of the bourgeoisie. The inevitable development of an urban proletariat gave rise to serious social consequences. At an early stage the municipal office responsible for the poor lamented the fact that, as a result of the influx of labour, Frankfurt was becoming 'one of the most desirable and convenient bodies open to exploitation in matters of poor relief '. Where the municipal tax system could be so arranged through the local administration, attempts were made to impede the influx of the poorer classes by high indirect taxes. Frankfurt was to maintain its character as a solid bourgeois refuge and remain, in every respect, a 'beautiful town', the mere sight of which was an enticement to its visitors. Middle-class psychological blocks, political tax restrictions and legal impositions hindered its development into a major industrial city[3]. Only small and, at the most, medium-scale works were permitted in the town. Large-scale enterprises developed outside the town, some at a considerable distance, even though the owners of these firms were citizens of Frankfurt. In so far as the resident bourgeoisie used its capital power to nurture industry, it was, for the most part, the surrounding area that benefited into the 1890s.

Thirdly, the political fragmentation of the Rhine-Main area favoured the development of several urban-industrial centres. The administrative structure of the region remained in existence from 1866, when Prussia advanced to the Main, until the end of the German Reich in 1945. The south of the Rhine-Main area belonged to Hesse, the town of Mainz and its catchment area to the province of Rheinhessen, and the town of Darmstadt and its environs to the province of Starkenburg. The district of Aschaffenburg in the east had been Bavarian territory since the Vienna Congress. The town of Hanau and its hinterland formed a part of the Prussian administrative district of Kassel in the province of Hesse-Nassau. In the north the province of Upper Hesse stretched to the town boundaries of Frankfurt. Frankfurt itself and the entire area to Wiesbaden was administered by the Prussian administrative district of Wiesbaden. Three federal states and seven intermediate authorities shared in the administration of the Rhine-Main area (see figures 4.1 and 4.2).

The Hessian towns of Offenbach, Mainz and Darmstadt, in particular, were thus protected against the radiation of Frankfurt by the state borders and could develop into places with independent, central functions[4]. In expanding their economic power these towns received the eager support of the Hessian state government which pursued a policy of industrial development with a distinct anti-Prussian bias. This development of a series of independent urban centres was facilitated, on the one hand, by the reservoir of labour from the small farms of the Rhine-Main area, and on the other hand, by the economic specialization of the towns. The number of farms was reduced by the division of land between inheritors and, no longer efficient, they forced the rural population to engage in additional forms of commercial activity. Consequently, the introduction of small home industries and the phenomenon of commuting daily between urban work-place and rural domicile occurred very early in the Rhine-Main area. On the other hand, commercial specialization provided a means of support against engulfment by the city of Frankfurt.

HESSEN 1918

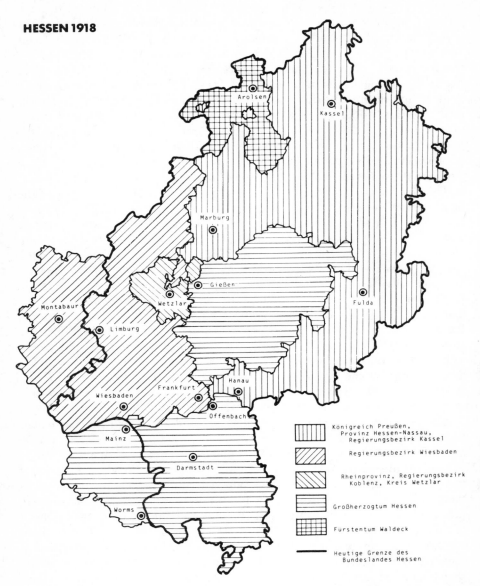

FIGURE 4.1. Provincial and state boundaries in the Rhine–Main area..

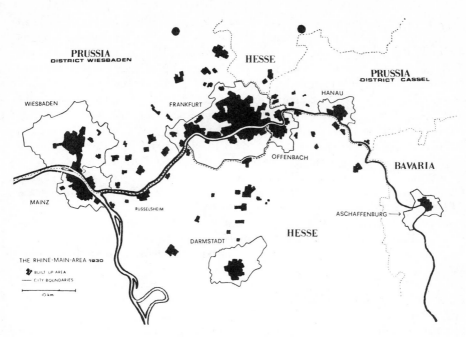

FIGURE 4.2. State boundaries in the Rhine–Main area.

Offenbach was considered a 'provincial manufacturing town' because of its early industrial foundations and its highly skilled craftsmanship especially in the manufacture of leather goods. Mainz was developed as a commercial town and as a centre for the transfer of goods for shipping on the Rhine. Darmstadt retained its character as an administrative and university town. On the Prussian side of the Main economic specialization also helped Hanau, with its goldsmith trade, and Wiesbaden, with its spa, to preserve their independence.

At the same time the developing complexity of the economy also necessitated the introduction of regulative measures that transcended the political borders. As early as 1895 various chambers of commerce in Frankfurt organized a public meeting of the Rhine-Main industrial district. It appears that the term 'Rhine-Main area' was thereby introduced into the political vocabulary for the first time. In 1898 the Rhine-Main League for Adult Education was set up, formed from the public lecturers of the workers' associations and trade unions, and joined by bodies from 185 communities. Its catchment area covered workers who lived within regular rail commuting distance of Frankfurt[5]. This gradual growth in consciousness of regional unity, which at the same time signified an expanding demarcation of the area, with out doubt represents one precondition for modern regional planning.

Before the First World War the term was chiefly used only in Frankfurt and its surroundings. It approximated to the word 'Hesse'; was used in conjunction with it or even as a counter concept.

At the same time a modern idea of planning developed in the towns. In Frankfurt, with the election of Franz Adickes as *Oberbürgermeister* (chief executive official), a fundamental change in the policy of local government occurred. A systematic town development plan was drafted aimed at conscious industrialization and its three phases (1895, 1900 and 1910) led to large incorporations[6]. First, the town needed space for the creation of healthy living conditions at reasonable rents for the rapidly growing population. Secondly, the municipal bureaucracy wanted to obtain new space for the systematic resettlement and expansion of industrial enterprises. Thirdly, the municipal administration wanted to extend the scope of public works, for reasons of profit and to hinder the licensing of private undertakings. Finally, a systematic extension of suburban railway lines took place, since only in this way could the suburban residential districts become attractive.

In the Rhine-Main area, as everywhere, these incorporations were the answer of the municipal bureaucracy to the consequences of industrialization and the growth of population. Moreover, in this way, the leading officials wanted not only to take account of present requirements, but also to create the preconditions for rational urban development in the future. To that extent, an independent conception of large-scale and long-term planning expressed itself in these developments. It was not just a matter of regulating individual technical questions such as the alignment of houses, but of the control of the economic process of industrialization and the social process of urbanization. Even the humanitarian aims of job-creation and house-building for the growing population served ultimately only in the conscious acceleration both processes. Certainly, the Rhine-Main area was not yet conceived of as a unified region. Planning remained on the level of individual acts in isolated towns. The coordination of planning in individual towns did not ensue.

MUNICIPAL ADMINISTRATION IN CONFLICT WITH STATE AUTHORITIES, 1919-32

In the Weimar Republic, the Chambers of Commerce of the Rhine-Main area continued the initial collaboration on questions of economic policy begun before the First World War. This had been intensified as a result of the tendency to centralize the food supply and the production of armaments in the war economy. Above all the Chambers of Commerce in Frankfurt and Mainz wanted to stop the small state of Hesse from restricting their areas. After voting together with Chambers of Trade-handicraft and Agriculture, as well as with employers' organizations and craft unions, they proceeded to establish a *Geschäftsstelle des vorläufigen rhein-mainischen Wirtschaftsrats* (Agency of the Provisional Rhine-Main Economic Council) at the end of 1920. The Hesse state government protested against further measures however, because it considered that the industrial economy was sufficiently represented in the Conference of the Hesse Chambers of Commerce, and it wanted no organizational fusion of Hessian Chambers with Prussian associations.

In Prussian territory the trend towards large-scale economic organization also successfully asserted itself. A fusion of the Frankfurt and Hanau Chambers of Commerce was followed in October 1921 by the foundation, together with the Chambers in Limburg, Dillenburg and Wetzlar, of a Union of Nassau Chambers of Commerce, which Wiesbaden too had to join in 1924, abandoning her opposition to the leadership on Prussian instructions. These organizational experiments indicate that the degree of urbanization and industrial complexity had increased to the extent that the Rhine-Main area was seen as a uniform economic region irrespective of the divisions caused by political boundaries[7].

Even the municipal administrations in the individual towns began to look beyond the confines of their boundaries. Frankfurt demonstrated this most distinctly. In particular the director of the Frankfurt economic department and later *Oberbürgermeister,* Ludwig Landmann (1924-33), were convinced that the economic, social, and technical transport problems of urbanization could only be solved within the framework of regional investment control and control of the trade cycle[8]. Consequently the planning department in the Frankfurt Economic Office became the nucleus of regional planning in the Rhine-Main area. As early as 1922 Landmann had founded a *Verkehrsverband für den Rhein-Mainischen Wirtschaftsbezirk* (Transport Association for the Rhine-Main Economic Region) which was to serve municipalities, boards of trade and private economic associations, as an auxiliary body catering for common transport interests with respect to the Prussian and Hessian state authorities.

The main work of the Economic Office consisted of collecting data relating to the deposit of public funds and to the planning of private investment. Its first general assessment of the economic structure of the region, the communications and transport systems, demographic development and settlement zones was published in 1924. Now, for the first time, data were available which made possible the planning of various resources and services—future increase in industrial development, residential and recreation areas[9], water and energy supply—and created the possibility for the coordination of individual planning arrangements. Even questions of environmental conservation were considered. Thus during an investigation into the urban sewage purification plants and factory waste at the lower course of the Main, it was possible for proposals to be submitted relating both to the inter-municipal organization of waste control and to purification

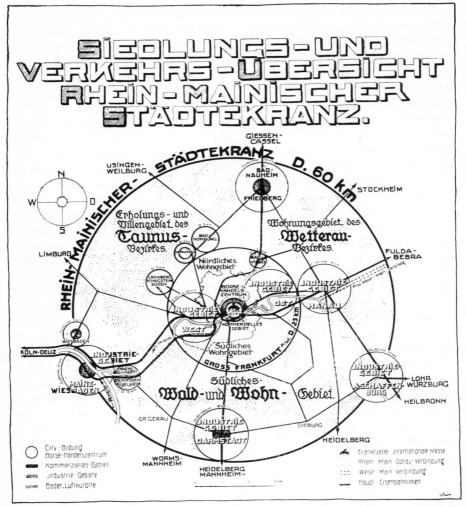

FIGURE 4.3. Plan for the land-use zoning of an area of 60 km radius around Frankfurt.

techniques for industrial waste. The most important result was, however, the submission of a rough plan for the partition of a 60 km zone around Frankfurt. Industrial districts, future settlement areas and recreation grounds were separated from each other (figure 4.3).

The Economic Office assessment defined the Rhine-Main area as 'a ring of towns with the centre, Frankfurt, in the South West German economic area'[9]. This definition corresponded on the one hand to the present situation and contained, on the other hand, an indication of a future political programme. In reality, the towns, by virtue of their independent central functions, formed a conurbation; and through reciprocal interlinkage the region was already an economic unit. But a question as to the future was posed which suggested that the consequences of this reality be realized in the creation of an administrative unit through the union of Prussian, Hessian and Bavarian territory. A purely political idea, indeed even a chimera, was the notion of a South-West German economic province. In this respect the term Rhine-Main area had an expansive tendency: the South-West German economic province was to stretch from Kassel in the north to Mannheim-Ludwigshafen in the south, from Aschaffenburg in the east to Koblenz and Saarbrücken in the west. The supporters of this idea were the towns, the municipal administrations and Chambers of Commerce, which on this issue mainly acted together against the interests of the states and the Reich bureaucracy.

These ideas were the motivating force behind nearly all the municipal-political actions of the Frankfurt *Oberbürgermeister* in the Weimar Republic. He was convinced that the existing common attributes of the Rhine-Main area and the future joint tasks of the towns should be capable of overcoming the growing state particularism of the Weimar Republic. The attraction of Frankfurt as a cultural centre should be strengthened by establishing music and fine arts academies as well as a college for teacher-training. Consultation with the institutions and offices of the Reich administration was to enhance the political significance of the town. The establishment of the main administration of I.G. Farben was only one example of many which confirmed the position of Frankfurt as a major industrial city. These central functions were to make Frankfurt appear to be the natural centre of South-West Germany which, in the course of future territorial reorganization, would develop into a province of the Reich. Basically it was a draft for the internal structural reorganization of the state of the Weimar Republic, as pursued by the Social Democratic Party and Left Liberalism in the wake of Hugo Preuss' constitutional policy[10]. The proposed major economic cities were to become the kernels for the crystallization of a new partition of the Reich in which the self-government of economic provinces would replace the anachronistic states.

The identity of interests led the towns of the Rhine-Main area to adopt a common policy in opposition to the states. This is evident from three examples: first, Frankfurt, Wiesbaden and Hanau aspired to extend their land area. Second, the towns undertook an experiment to coordinate the public gas supply policy and established a common enterprise. Third, they set about organizing a regional planning association.

From the point of view of town planning, the towns needed more space for the creation of dormitory towns and suburban estates in order to relieve the excessive concentration of great masses of people[11]. They could only acquire favourably-priced land for their housing programme outside the old town boundaries. Furthermore, they wanted to release new settlement land for the establishment of industrial manufacturing plants. Finally, because of the municipal finance system of the Weimar Republic which was largely based on indirect and direct taxes, they were able to bring industry back into urban territory, rescuing it from the rural area to which it had 'fled' partly due to lack of space and partly because of the high rates of municipal taxation. Following these main principles, big territorial incorporations took place in 1928 which favoured Wiesbaden, Frankfurt and Hanau. The basis of this growth in territory was a Prussian Law[12]. The Prussian internal administration assumed at that time that a functionally-oriented population, living in a homogeneous community, in the town and in the immediate vicinity, should not be treated differently with regard to local taxes and cultural and social amenities. Financially-weak communities were to be amalgamated with more efficient communities. In this way the distance between the boundaries of the towns of the Rhine-Main area was reduced. The process of urbanization entered a new phase.

The close cooperation of the towns then increased in terms of the public economy. From 1926 there was a danger that a private long-distance gas undertaking of the Ruhr mining industry would compete with the local gas producers. If the towns wanted, on the one hand, to preserve the independence of their gas works, and, on the other hand, to maintain the link with modern technology, they had to find new, rationalized forms of production. In 1929 Offenbach joined the Frankfurt Gas Co. as a share-holder, which in practice meant a fusion of the gasworks of both towns. Both towns, whose boundaries and settlement areas bordered on to one another, from now on acted together. In order to place the protection of the private economy on a broader political and a more solid financial basis, the Frankfurt Gas Co. and the town of Mannheim founded their own long-distance gas undertaking in 1928. Gradually Wiesbaden and Hanau joined, and then eventually the south German towns of Ludwigshafen, Karlsruhe and Pforzheim as well[13]. However, the Hessian towns of Mainz and Darmstadt remained outside the enterprise because the Hessian state government feared defeat by the combined votes of Frankfurt and the Prussian towns, and therefore set up a municipal long-distance gas under-taking of its own.

A similar disposition towards common action was evident in other cases too. Most obvious was close cooperation in road construction (motorways) and in the organization of local rail traffic. Eventually a decision had to be made about the most appropriate position of the Rhine-Main airfield. If Mainz, Wiesbaden, Darmstadt and Frankfurt had continued to pursue their own airfield plans, it would have resulted in the squandering of public funds and created a permanent source of petty jealousies and frictions. Also, there was the possibility of establishing common refuse disposal arrangements and the setting up of joint theatre managements. The reduction of municipal revenue by states and Reich in the Weimar Republic generated a positive compulsion to undertake inter-municipal projects which were beyond the financial strength of individual towns.

Altogether, the number of joint problems facing the towns in the Rhine-Main area had increased to such an extent that occasional conferences of executive officials were no longer sufficient to ensure the coordination of interests. A form of organization had to be found. The ten years experience of the Ruhr towns with the *Siedlungsverband Ruhrkohlenbezirk* (Planning Association of the Ruhr Coal District) played a part in this[14]. Further, regional planning had the attraction of being a novelty. The founding of district planning associations in the industrial area of Middle Germany (1925), in Düsseldorf (1928) and Cologne (1929) also gave the towns of the Rhine-Main area the impulse to follow this example[15].

The initial steps were taken by the Frankfurt Settlement Office which first invited the directors of the technical departments of the Rhine-Main towns to a preliminary discussion on regional planning in the Frankfurt town hall. In April 1929 the chief executive officials of Frankfurt, Bad Homburg, Friedberg, Bad Nauheim, Hanau, Aschaffenburg, Offenbach, Darmstadt and Mainz met in the Frankfurt town hall to set up a regional planning association. They decided that the *Oberbürgermeister* of Frankfurt should preside and the regional planning department of the Frankfurt Settlement Office should be responsible for conducting the business of the association. The Prussian provincial authorities and the Hessian state government were urged to join[16].

The state authorities in Prussia and Hesse were very indignant about the exclusive procedure adopted by the towns. The provincial authorities were of the opinion that it was incompatible with the practice of the Prussian administration not to take over the preparation of an association themselves. The initiative and direction of the planning work must remain with the state agencies. The essence of their argument was that it was their duty to supervise social welfare arrangements for the rural district. They argued that it was not only in the large towns that modern development necessitated the systematic assignment of parts of a larger area. The same was true for the rural areas. In reality, the agrarian sectors of the region still had no interest whatsoever in regional planning. The rural districts with points of contact with urban districts inclined to a municipal rather than a state association. The Hessian state government again feared that the regional planning association was only an embryonic forerunner of future Reich reform which would amount to an 'annexation' of Hesse by Prussia.

Nevertheless, by virtue of 'diplomatic contacts' between Prussia and Hesse the rough plan of a regional planning association was developed under the auspices of the *Oberpräsident* (traditional Agent-General of the Prussian state government in the provinces) in Kassel who, together with the Hessian Minister of the Interior, was to preside over the association on the basis of a two-year rotation. Meanwhile the towns were not to be part of an executive committee, a situation which they could not accept. Also, the participation of Aschaffenburg remained doubtful since, according to Bavarian instructions, it was only allowed to participate in a purely municipal and not in a state association. Thus the foundation of the association stagnated until 1933. Meanwhile, the voluntary association of towns, despite state reservations, had made positive steps by setting up a planning bureau in the Frankfurt Settlement Office and had held a total of eleven meetings of the association by 1933.

According to the decision of the towns the regional planning association was to prepare a plan for dividing up the Rhine-Main area and to establish the guidelines a suitable allocation of traffic areas, green belts, industrial and residential areas. The central bureau was to advise the individual towns in order that their particular plans might be integrated into the overall plan. For them it was a question of applying suitable regulative principles to plan for the future of an industrialized and urbanized area. Starting from the structural data of the economic situation and with a view to economic and technical progress, they wanted to obtain the optimum use of public services. This could not be achieved without interfering with the freedom of the capitalist economy; at the same time, however, local conditions could be improved through control of investment and Rhine-Main industry would obtain advantages in terms of transport. In so far as the aim of regional planning was an ordered and rational increase in industrialization, it strengthened the interests of the industrial economy. Thus the Chambers of Commerce and Industry were able to agree to the planning ideas of the municipal bureaucracy, even though this bureaucracy was dominated by left-liberal and social democratic influences. In the final analysis, these towns were to pursue socio-political aims which favoured the broad masses of the population. Above all the living conditions of the working population were to be raised to a standard which made them politically immune to radical slogans. To that extent it was a plan for deproletarianization.

THE POLITICAL AND INSTITUTIONAL IMPACT OF THE NAZI PARTY, 1933-45

The Nazi seizure of power in 1933 brought no change in the Rhine-Main area with respect to state borders. Through the rise in status of the National Socialist Democratic Workers' Party (NSDAP) to state party and the corresponding eclipse of the state governments, a new element was introduced into regional politics. Apart from the state of Hesse, the *Gau* (Nazi unit of regional organization) of Hesse-Nassau included the Prussian administrative district of Wiesbaden and also the rural districts of Hanau, Gelnhausen and Schlüchtern within the administrative district of Kassel. Ignoring the exclusion of Bavarian Aschaffenburg, the *Gau* of the NSDAP represented an ideal demarcation of the Rhine-Main area. Although the NSDAP maintained that it had taken into account the natural and economic structure of the Rhine-Main area in to *Gau* division, the *Gau* was a rather haphazard and artificial creation, which had developed from two originally separate *Gauen* as a result of internal party rivalries. The area divisions of the NSDAP organizations, Hitler Youth, SA and SS, and even the *Deutsche Arbeitsfront* (German Labour Front), did not follow the *Gau* boundaries.

Nevertheless *Gauleiter* (regional party leader) Sprenger, who was also appointed *Reichsstatthalter* (national governor) in Hesse and after two years took over the provincial government there as well[17], set to work at once in 1933 with great enthusiasm to create institutional links, on the level of associations, unions and the economy, between the Prussian and Hessian parts of his *Gau*. After a year he already allowed himself to be feted as 'the indefatigable conqueror of the Main line'. Under the title 'How the Rhine-Main area developed' the official party newspaper, the *Frankfurter Volksblatt,* enumerated a total of twenty measures for the period June to December 1933 as being 'the most important stages in the work of the *Reichsstatthalter*[18]. A Rhine-Main air transport association and a Rhine-Main district transport association were set up, the Prussian and Hessian Chambers of Commerce were brought together into a Rhine-Main industrial and commercial council and a similar trade-handicraft assembly was called into being (figure 4.4). The retail trade, the wholesale food trade, the newspaper publishers and the house-owners, nearly every professional association and interest group— even the mountain and hiking clubs—acquired their own Rhine-Main district association.

This completely revolutionary regimentation under the banner of Rhine-Main ideology was the *Gauleiter's* preparation for the extension of his personal sphere of power. His immediate aim, pursued with great energy, was the fusion of the Prussian areas of his *Gau* with the state of Hesse. After he established the identity of *Reichsstatthalterschaft* (national governorship) and provincial government in Hesse, he naturally aimed at the acquisition of state power in the Prussian area as well. That he moreover, as a long-term aim, aspired to a Greater Hesse, which was to include the entire province of Hesse-Nassau can be safely assumed[19].

The *Gauleiter* quickly recognized that above all regional planning could be made to serve his desire for an extension of power. He resumed the preparatory work of the Weimar Republic and on 20 September 1933 established a Rhine-Main area Regional Planning Association. The association, the area of which was identical with the *Gau* of the NSDAP, was presided over by the *Reichsstatthalter* in Hesse, his representative being the *Oberpräsident* in Hesse-Nassau. The *Regierungspräsidenten* (heads of district governments) in Wiesbaden and Kassel as well as the *Oberbürgermeister* of the town of Frankfurt were appointed as further members of the executive board. The office remained in the Frankfurt town-hall in the hands of the director of

FIGURE 4.4. The area of the Rhine–Main industrial and trade-handicraft associations.

the department of municipal building construction. In fact all the difficulties of the Weimar Republic seemed eliminated in one go. However, the arrangement between Prussia and Hesse did not last for long. Only two years passed before differences again emerged with undiminished intensity.

Through the law introduced on 29 March 1935, to regulate the land requirements of public bodies, and a Führer decree of 26 June 1935, area planning in Germany was declared to be a supreme task of the Reich, and was centralized, and assigned to the *Reichsstelle für Raumordnung* (Reich office for area planning) for execution. Since in the demarcation of the planning areas the individual regions were to be adapted wherever possible to the state administrative and district arrangements, the *Reichsstatthalter* and, in Prussia, the *Oberpräsidenten* were frequently appointed to the planning authorities irrespective of prevailing regional or economic structures. This too is an example of what has been called 'authoritarian anarchy' in Nazi administrative practice. In executing these legal instructions the *Oberpräsident* in Kassel and the *Reichsstatthalter* in Hesse were quick to dissolve the joint association and again set up separate planning groups for their particular state areas. The Rhine-Main area was thus again split according to the traditional political boundaries.

Naturally, the *Gauleiter* was not prepared to acquiesce in this arrangement. He endeavoured to allow the dissolved association to continue to work with the old office and, after peremptory discussions with the Prussian *Oberpräsident* had led to no result, he established on his own authority a *Arbeitsgemeinschaft der Landesplanungsstellen für das Rhein-Main Gebiet* (Working Party for the Rhine-Main Regional Planning Authorities). The *Oberpräsident,* for his part, protested against this. In the protracted dispute which continued into the war years the Reich Office for Area Planning acted as mediator, with, however, a clear bias in favour of the Hessian *Gauleiter.* By a decree of 25 July 1938 the head of the Reich Office, *Reichsminister* Kerrl, sanctioned the formation of a working party and assigned to it the task of drafting area plans, though its powers were limited in respect of Frankfurt-Offenbach-Hanau and Wiesbaden-Mainz which would cut across political borders. Nevertheless, the working party was not to communicate directly with the offices of the regional planning associations in Kassel and Darmstadt or the Prussian-Hessian authorities, but only via the state channels. Thus, three competing regional planning associations operated in the Rhine-Main area.

Prussian regional planning, which was based in Kassel, concentrated on the north of the province. The responsible town councillor in Frankfurt in 1938 must have been positively astonished to find that the data of the Prussian regional planners were 'extremely scanty'. 'It will probably require the very active collaboration of the Frankfurt offices in the future in order to convey to the men in Kassel and Wiesbaden at least definitive knowledge of our needs.' And a year later he recorded that they were scarcely aware that there was such a thing as Prussian regional planning.

In contrast, the regional planning authorities of the province of Hesse had developed from the administrative departments of the former Ministry of Agriculture. They were mainly interested in agrarian problems. Because of the preference given to the agricultural improvement programme in Hesse on the one hand, and because of the remoteness of the Prussian regional planning authorities on the other, work in the industrial part of the Rhine-Main area had made little progress by 1938. The third institution, the so-called working party, was assigned three tasks by the *Gauleiter* in 1938: an examination of the structure of the Rhine-Main area, the resettlement of industrial towns and the superimposing of a transport system plan. Since, as part of economies necessitated by the war, the regional planning groups were disbanded after two years, the working party had nothing to show for its activity.

During the first two years of Nazi rule regional planning was mainly concerned with the provision of work. The construction of the Reich motor-way system and suburban settlements were given highest priority. Due to scepticism engendered by the world economic crisis with regard to the economic viability of industrial societies, even town and regional planners, who were scarcely influenced by Nazi ideology, hoped 'to make the German worker immune to crisis'. They settled workers in single-family houses and small-holdings on the outskirts of towns in order to achieve a guaranteed livelihood through freedom from the fluctuations of the economy.[20] From the point of view of Nazi economic policy two further motives were important. The small-holding and the financial reorganization of agriculture, through the regrouping of fragmented fields, was to ensure that the German people had sufficient food and were largely independent of food imports. Still more important was an ideological motive. The worker was to be released from the 'tenements alienated from the soil' and brought once again 'into contact with the sod, with the soil and *Lebensraum* of the *völkisch* community'. The idea of 'Blood and Soil' was at the root of regional planning. The living 'sources of new peasant blood', the surplus births of the rural population, would also revitalize the towns. With a view to preserving the German 'peasantry', the regional planning authorities in Darmstadt and the local *Gau* office of the NSDAP and the German Labour Front consequently concen-trated on agricultural improvements and on laying out hereditary farms and new farming villages in the Rodgau and in the Hessian marshland. Hessenaue, Riedrode, Allmendfeld and Rosengarten were considered to be splendid examples of Nazi agricultural policy in the Rhine-Main area.

Special models for the urbanized area, which had been developed in the Weimar Republic, were dispensed with in Nazi regional planning for the Rhine-Main area. Town planning was carried out on the basis of the law of 22 September 1933 relating to the development of residential areas. However, as with the drafting of so-called economic plans, it remained primarily an affair of the individual municipal offices. There was only an initial move towards further industrialization in connection with the autarchy policy of the Four Year Plan. Thus the working of isolated brown coal deposits in the Rhine-Main area was considered as a possible means of preventing, by use of a hydrogenation process, the dependence on the importation of foreign fuels in the name of war preparations. However, this plan was scarcely practicable because of its low profitability. Moreover, it was said that the Rhine-Main area was 'over-industrialized' and therefore did not seem viable, unlike the Ruhr area which had rich mineral resources. Further industrial agglomeration was considered to be an ill-conceived policy of the 'liberalistic' epoch, and was therefore to be avoided.

If one considers the political aims and the practice of Nazi regional planning in the Rhine-Main area a strange contradiction emerges between the promotion of individual areas dictated by the constraints of the territorial structure and an ideologically-motivated re-agrarianization. If the technicians and geographers among the regional planners did not allow themselves to be cramped by the straight-jacket of Nazi ideology and peasant romanticism, they recognized that an unresolvable incongruity existed between the stated aim of directing the movement of population back to the countryside and the socio-economic facts of the Rhine-Main area[21]. There was not only a continued increase in the density of the population in the industrial zones of the Rhine-Main area but also in the neighbouring rural areas. As a result of the division of land between heirs and the fragmentation of estates efficient, big farmers had long ceased to be the dominant element of the population structure. The majority of the population in the rural districts followed dual livelihoods, half industrial, half rural; they were a cross between workers and farmers, hardly suited to be pillars of the Nazi *Volk* order. A study of the commuters in the larger factories of the chemical and machine engine construction industry in Offenbach-Frankfurt-Höchst and Rüsselsheim led to the Rhine-Main area being defined as a region marked by industrial radiation, and as a work and residential area. Only 17 per cent of the employees of the Opel factory in Rüsselsheim lived in the place itself, 83 per cent came from surrounding localities up to a distance of 80 km[22].

If one analyses the growth of population according to the percentage of the municipal population, one sees that an increasingly large proportion of the inhabitants of the Rhine-Main area lived an urban existence. This displacement did not take place as rapidly as in the years 1870-1905 but is unmistakable (see p. 96).

With an urban population of 59.3 per cent in 1939, the Rhine-Main area had achieved a high degree of urbanization, but this figure does not take into account the commuters. In fact the Hesse Statistical Office ascertained that about a quarter of the rural population were commuters. One must therefore conclude that even before the Second World War 70 per cent of the Rhine-Main area was of an urban character.

Year	Large towns	Small towns	Rural population	Urban population as a percentage of total population
1871	270,700	93,400	684,200	34.7
1905	791,400	163,300	835,800	53.3
1939	1,224,700	248,700	1,012,100	59.3

Even in the area of the state of Hesse the forced re-agrarianization policy could not reverse the process of urbanization. In 1933 64.9 per cent of the Hessian population lived in communities with over 2000 inhabitants, in 1939 it was 66.8 per cent. Despite the land improvements and marsh drainage the amount of cultivated arable land in Hesse between 1935 and 1939 fell by 5033 hectares. On the whole Nazi regional planning in the Rhine–Main area was, in methods, aims and results, a failure. In comparison to the plans made during the Weimar Republic, it represented a retrogressive step.

SUMMARY

The Rhine–Main area did not become a homogeneous economic region until the last decade of the nineteenth century, industrialization taking place much later than, for example, in the Ruhr region. The reasons for this are twofold: the lack of natural resources, and the division of the area amongst a number of administrative authorities. Although today the Ruhr and Rhine–Main regions are not dissimilar industrial and urban conurbations, their respective developments were completely different. Urbanization in the Ruhr did not develop from individual settlement centres, but took place regularly throughout the region. The locations of mines and heavy industry were the determining factors; their sites being determined by the geology of the region and not by the historical settlement pattern.

In contrast, the Rhine–Main conurbation comprises a group of towns, whose specialized industrial development led to a close interdependence, particularly through daily commuting. During the process of urbanization, these towns preserved a certain independence because of the existence of the various state borders. This is the main reason why Frankfurt could not become the dominant metropolis as, for example, Berlin or Munich which in fact profited as capitals from the support of the federal authorities.

In the Rhine–Main area the political divisions prevented the development of effective regional planning. In the German governmental system, various statutory obligations are assigned to different administrative units. The communities as the lowest-level units have the full right of self-government, but are subject to state control. All matters of regional importance are the responsibility of the supervisory authorities. During the Weimar Republic, the states therefore considered the association of municipal planning authorities as an offence against superior jurisdiction. The problem grew even worse as the three federal states of Prussia, Hesse and Bavaria saw the delegation of their responsibilities to an association of planning authorities as a loss of their rights of sovereignty. The full implication of their objections only became clear in connection with the question of the 'reform of the Reich'. The acknowledgment of the Rhine-Main area as an economic entity, involving regional planning which crossed the federal state borders, meant either for Prussia the separation of parts of its province, or for Hesse the end of independence and subsequent annexation to Prussia.

These structures did not change even during the Third Reich, although the Rhine-Main area in the territorial organization of the NSDAP was a unit or *Gau*. However, the dualism between party and state, and the ideology of agrarian romanticism worked to hinder the development of regional planning.

NOTES

1. The valid definition of the Rhine-Main area as a conurbation is given in regard to the daily commuting by Krenzlin, A. (1961) Werden und Gefüge des rhein-mainischen Verstädterungsgebietes. *Frankfurter geographische Hefte,* 37, pp. 311-87. The department for Rhine-Main researches, which is a part of the Institute for Geographic Studies at the University of Frankfurt, has published since 1927 a lot of important material showing the relationship of urban growth and regional unity. Very informative is the small book of Hartke, W. (1938) *Das Arbeits- und Wohngebiet im rhein-mainischen Lebensraum.* Frankfurt: Rhein-Mainische Forschungen.

2. For the incorporation of Frankfurt in the Prussian state see Kropat, W. A. (1971) *Frankfurt zwischen Provinzialismus und Nationalismus.* Frankfurt: Waldemar Kramer.

3. The process of industrialization is described in the official history of the Chamber of Commerce, Handelskammer zu Frankfurt (1908) *Geschichte der Handelskammer zu Frankfurt am Main.* Frankfurt: Joseph Baer. A modern interpretation is HInderliter, E. (1978) The Regulation of Industry in Imperial Germany: The Example of Frankfurt: 1867–1914. Ph.D. thesis, Brown University Providence, Rhode Island.

4. For the relations between Hanau and its environment see Klemt, H. (1940) *Die Stadt Hanau und ihr Umland.* Frankfurt: Rhein-Mainische Forschungen. For the economic structure of Darmstadt see Zimmer, W. (1954) *Darmstadt. Grenzen und Möglichkeiten einer Stadt.* Frankfurt: Rhein-Mainische Forschungen. A study of the problems of adjacent cities is Schneider, E. (1962) *Die Stadt Offenbach am Main im Frankfurter Raum.* Frankfurt: Rhein-Mainische Forschungen.

5. A survey of the activities in the first decade after the foundation of the League for Adult Education is given in: (1914) *Zehn Jahre Volksbildungsarbeit 1904-1914*. Frankfurt.

6. For detailed discussion of these incorporations see Rebentisch, D. (1978) Industrialisierung, Bevölkerungswachstum und Eingemeindungen. Das Beispiel Frankfurt am Main 1870-1914, in Reulecke, J. (ed.) *Die deutsche Stadt im Industriezeitalter*. Wuppertal: Peter Hammer, pp. 90-113.

7. Many references to the various plans of economic pressure groups for a new partition of the Rhine-Main area are to be found in Kahlenberg, F. P. (1969) Großhessenpläne und Separatismus. *Geschichtliche Landeskunde,* 5 (2), pp. 355-95. Further information on the political idea of a greater Hesse is given by Struck, W. H. (1970) Zur ideenpolitischen Vorbereitung des Bundeslandes Hessen seit dem 19. Jahrhundert. *Hessisches Jahrbuch für Landesgeschichte,* 20, pp. 282-324.

8. Rebentisch, D. (1975) *Ludwig Landmann. Frankfurter Oberbürgermeister der Weimarer Republik*. Wiesbaden: Franz Steiner, p. 105.

9. Wirtschaftsdeputation Frankfurt am Main (1924) *Der Rhein-mainische Städtekranz und seine Zentrale Frankfurt am Main im südwest-deutschen Wirtschaftsgebiet*. Frankfurt: Selbstverlag.

10. Hugo Preuss, the author of the new constitution of the Weimar Republic, would have liked to abandon the federal system for a unitary one, but the south German states wished to preserve their independence. See Ryder, A. J. (1973) *Twentieth Century Germany: From Bismarck to Brandt*. London: Macmillan, pp. 208-10. The standard information in German is Schulz, G. (1963) *Zwischen Demokratie und Diktatur*. Berlin: de Gruyter.

11. Full details of the political ideas of Ernst May, who was the leader of the municipal planning authority in Frankfurt, are given in an unpublished paper of Nicholas Bullock, Housing in Frankfurt and the New 'Wohnkultur'. University of Cambridge, Department of Architecture. A German translation is printed in *Archiv für Frankfurts Geschichte und Kunst,* 57, 1980. Further information is given in Mullin, J. R. (1977) City planning in Frankfurt, Germany, 1925–1932: A study in practical utopianism. *Journal of Urban History,* 4, pp. 3–28.

12. The parliamentary debates are to be found in Preussischer Landtag (1928) Second period of election. 361st Meeting, pp. 25809. The draft of the law is printed as Drucksache No. 8179.

13. Rebentisch, D. (1976) Städte und Monopol. *Zeitschrift für Stadtgeschichte, Stadtsoziologie und Denkmalpflege,* 3, pp. 38-80.

14. Steinberg, H. G. (1971) Die Geschichte des Siedlungsverbandes Ruhrkohlenbezirk, in Franz, G. (ed.) *Raumordnung und Landesplanung im 20. Jahrhundert*. Hannover: Gebrüder Jaenecke, pp. 5-16.

15. Pfannschmidt, M. (1971) Landesplanung im engreen mitteldeutschen Bezirk, in Franz, G. (ed.) *Raumordnung und Landesplanung im 20. Jahrhundert*. Hannover: Gebrüder Jaenecke.

16. The story of the conflicts between municipal administration and the provincial authorities is outlined in Rebentisch, D. (1975) Anfänge der Raumordnung und Regionalplanung imn Rhein-Main-Gebiet. *Hessiches Jahrbuch für Landesgeschihte,* 25, pp. 307–39.

17. See Orlow, D. (1973) *The History of the Nazi Party, Vol. II: 1933-45.* Pittsburg: University of Pittsburg Press, pp. 52-3.
18. *Frankfurter Volksblatt,* No. 123 from 6 May 1934.
19. The following description is an extract from Rebentisch, D. (1978) Der Gau Hessen-Nassau und die nationalsozialistische Reichsreform. *Nassauische Annalen,* 89, pp. 128-62.
20. See Schoenbaum, D. (1966) *Hitler's Social Revolution.* London: Weidenfeld and Nicolson.
21. Meyer, K. (ed.) (1938) *Volk und Lebensraum.* Heidelberg: Kurt Vowinkel, pp. 504-6.
22. Hartke, W. (1938) *Das Arbeits- und Wohngebiet im rhein-mainischen Lebensraum.* Frankfurt: Rhein-Mainische Forschungen; Weigand, K. (1956) *Rüsselsheim und die Funktion der Stadt im Rhein-Main-Gebiet.* Frankfurt: Waldemar Kramer.

5

Schemata in British
new town planning

W. HOUGHTON-EVANS

Every science works with ideal concepts, like the mathematician's zero and infinity . . . and can do nothing without them[1].

Recent town planning in Britain has eschewed ideal blueprints and architectural modes of thought in favour of analysis, descriptive algebra and a vague populism. Currently, this approaches total disillusionment, and post-war planning is widely regarded as at best a regrettable mistake, at worst a deliberate evil foisted upon an unsuspecting society by arrogant bureaucrats in the service of false gods. The fact that behind the bureaucrats stand their political masters is customarily overlooked and the general public is encouraged to revile an undifferentiated group of professional 'planners' as the cause of all evils.

In truth, many different professions are involved in town planning, each with distinct attitudes, traditions and rôles, and rarely speaking with one voice. Here we shall be concerned with one profession only—architecture—and we shall examine the ideas of those architects who designed our new towns. New towns are chosen not because they typify our present dilemmas—in many ways they are most untypical—but because in them ideas have a freer rein. And it is with the original proposals we shall be concerned, not their implementation which almost always departs from first intentions. Only one aspect will be dealt with—ideas about the overall form of the city—others have been discussed elsewhere[2].

TOWN PLANNING AND ARCHITECTURE

Historically, town planning has been regarded as a department of architecture. Aristotle is the first to write at length about it, and credits the architect Hippodamos with the invention of 'regular' planning. The architects Vitruvius and Alberti provide us with the principal texts on town planning prior to modern times, and it is only with the rise of the modern industrial town that the tradition is interrupted. Those who would now have us believe that it is dead presumably will not mind if we dissect the corpse before we bury it.

The inclusion of town planning in architecture is acceptable if we allow that in essence architecture is the art of designing artefacts to be made by workmen under supervision, and that design in this sense may be held in its fundamental characteristics to transcend differences among its products. Designing is from beginning to end a mental process, and one which comes directly up against the profoundest of human dilemmas—the relation of *concept* to *reality*—but which does so in the opposite way to that which normally concerns philosophy. For the architect, the question is not whether what we understand by order is or is not a property of nature, but what sort of order is it that we should impose upon our natural environment. The answer at one extreme will be: only that which is itself natural—*by obeying Nature we shall master her;* at the other: that which most accords with human reason—*culture is an orthogonal state of mind.*

Aristotle again is the first to discuss some of the rival merits of these two extremes as they affect town planning, and contrasts the obvious orderliness of the Hippodamian grid with the apparent disorder of irregular groupings[3]. His concern is primarily with defence. Alberti takes up the same theme in the fifteenth century. In the more recent past, the contrast between formality and informality assumes political significance in the struggle between ordered monarchy and liberty: the former exemplified by Versailles, the latter by the work of Lancelot Brown, the Romantics, Gothic Revival and Arts and Crafts. In town planning today, it is especially relevant to remind ourselves of the essential difference between the English tradition, with its love of countryside and informality, and the rationalism of much of the continental Modern Movement, with its devotion to straight line and right angle. Today also, the virtues of intelligibility (which demands a measure of recognizable order) competes with the growing awareness that by imposing our limited notion of order upon the world, we disrupt the subtle processes upon which all life depends.

But whether or not the result aimed at appears orderly or not, an orderly approach is an essential ingredient of design—as of all decision-making. And it would seem that an inevitable characteristic of an orderly approach is a broad overall strategic concept—a *schema*—which, in the simplest possible form, encapsulates the total solution. For the architect there is also a further problem. Not only does he have to design within his own conceptual capacity, not only does he have to reckon with the consequences for those who are to use the things he designs, he has also to make clear his intentions to those who are to translate them into reality. To this end, he may make a model. He may even occasionally write an equation or draw a graph. But habitually it is to the drawing board that he will turn to work out and transmit his ideas.

GEOMETRICAL ORDER

It is from this that in large measure arises architecture's traditional association with geometry—especially with its most abstract 'perfect' forms—and the use of grids, axes, regulating lines and the other formulae of draughtsmanship. Both plane and solid geometry are significant, but the former (since it needs no more than the two dimensions of the drawing board) is the more easily handled, and few towns have yet been conceived *ab initio* 'in the round'. Historically we may detect the special significance of the Euclidean elements: *point, line* and *plane* figure or space. Every plan makes some use of all of these. But the emphasis will vary, and one may be taken as the generatrix. Thus the Hippodamian scheme derives from a system of *lines*. It differs significantly from the apparently similar Roman castrum which derives from a rectangular *plane* divided initially into four, and subsequently elaborated in the Greek manner. The Hippodamian colony was thus an irregular totality. It was not necessarily finite, and could grow at its own pace. The Roman, on the other hand, was conceived as a complete whole, to be founded *tout à coup* and developed only by internal subdivision. This is how Vitruvius describes his ideal town, which, although circular, thus conforms to the predilections of its age. The Vitruvian projects of the high renaissance also begin with a total plane figure, Filarete's Sforzinda being perhaps the most eloquent example.

Examples deriving from a single *point* are typical of monarchy and megalomania. We have from Greece the fictional Meton, whose roads radiated from a central place like a star. And again, we have Versailles and its imitators, such as Karlsruhe, with the absolute monarch at the centre of a boundless domain. More common, and infinitely more useful, are those schemata which start from a *multiplicity of points,* each the focus of radiating routes and each linked directly or indirectly to its neighbours. Such a system captures the principle of growth of the strawberry and the buttercup, and combines extensibility with centrality. It finds its best expression in proposals such as that of Wren for London after the Fire.

Examples deriving from a single *line* are not seriously encountered until Soria y Mata's Ciudad Lineal, but this has recently had numerous imitators. Again, there is the advantage of infinite extensibility, but (in the pure form) the lack of focus.

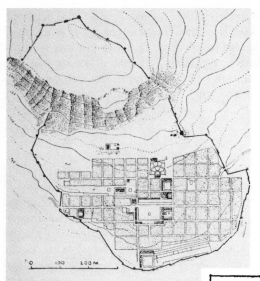

FIGURE 5.1. Priene: the Hippo-damian schema derives from a system of parallel *lines*, and forms an irregular totality.

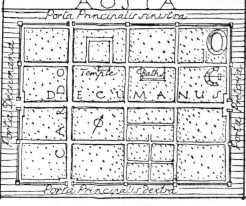

FIGURE 5.2. The Roman castrum derives from a rectangular *plane figure*, and is conceived as a complete whole.

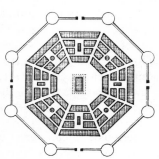

FIGURE 5.3. Vitruvius' ideal town: a regular finite form based on a circle.

FIGURE 5.4. Filarete's *Sforzinda:* typical of the Vitruvian schemes of the high Renaissance. A regular figure elaborated by subdivision.

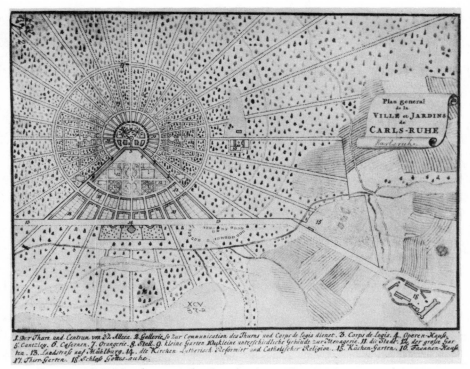

FIGURE 5.5. Karlsruhe: an early plan. A scheme deriving from a *single point*.

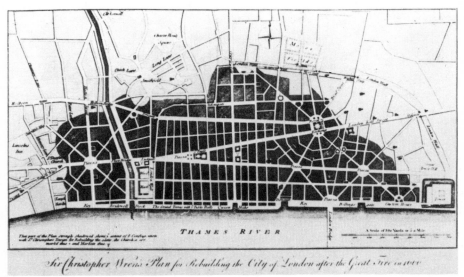

FIGURE 5.6. Wren's London plan: a system of *linked points*, combining extensibility with centrality.

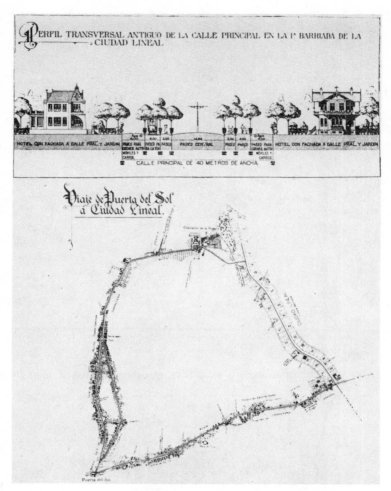

FIGURE 5.7. Soria y Mata's Cuidad Lineal: a scheme deriving from a *single line*.

THE INDUSTRIAL TOWN

Nineteenth-century town planning adopts as its most pervasive idea the notion of the *use zone,* thus conceiving a town as a system of *plane* figures. Again there are some historical precedents. Division into class districts has been discussed since Plato's time, and Alberti suggests some division based upon land use. Suburbs, ghettoes, parishes, wards and similar subdivisions have long been a feature of cities, but there is little evidence prior to modern times of concepts of urban form relying so heavily upon separate *spaces.* Land-use zoning especially assumes significance only with the rise of the industrial town.

Saltaire is an outstanding early example. Howard's Garden City marks an advance in at least one important respect. The larger population necessary to support a variety of industries could not live in one undifferentiated residential zone. Neither could the town grow instantaneously to completion. His city is thus compounded not only of use zones, but of *wards* also. And these two categories deliberately overlap, each ward containing a just proportion of all land uses, so that growth could proceed by balanced stages. The nucleus of each ward was the primary school, placed centrally among the houses, thus also establishing the schoolchild's walking distance as a fundamental dimension in town planning.

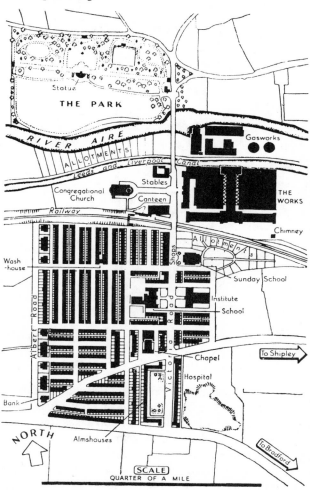

FIGURE 5.8. Saltaire: a town conceived as a system of *plane figures,* each a separate land-use zone.

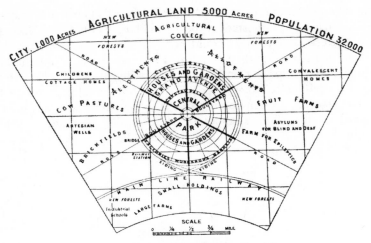

FIGURE 5.9. Howards Garden City.

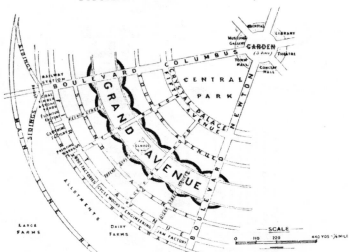

FIGURE 5.10. A ward of the Garden City.

There was little evidence of 'wards' in prewar Letchworth or Welwyn Garden City. Some criticism was levelled at both on the grounds that the division of residential areas was along familiar class lines, and imported unwanted blemishes into the New Jerusalem. Subdivision was however made increasingly desirable because of motor traffic, and Alker Tripp[4] provided a third criterion for conceiving the town as a system of separate spaces. His *precincts* were defined as areas bounded by principal roads from which access was deliberately limited, so that only such traffic as had business within the precinct would enter it.

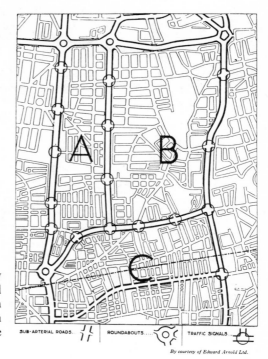

FIGURE 5.11. Tripp's *precincts:* a city remodelled into lightly trafficked areas (A,B and C) skirted by main roads. The part below the broken line shows the city before remodelling.

SUB-ARTERIAL ROADS.   ROUNDABOUTS....   TRAFFIC SIGNALS....

By courtesy of Edward Arnold Ltd.

FINITE HIERARCHICAL CELLULAR

In parallel with these and other influences there gradually came 'neighbour-hood theory'. In postwar town planning the schematic form which emerged for the town as a whole is exemplified by new towns like Harlow. A hierarchy of spaces, starting with a basic dwelling cluster, combine with a primary school and a few shops to form a neighbourhood. Neighbourhoods with district shopping, etc. combine into a district. Districts together with central and industrial areas unite to form a town. To this hierarchy of spaces is married a hierarchy of routes: foot and cycle ways at the lowest level penetrating close to the heart of localities; principal roads at the highest level routed between built-up areas, through the 'green wedges' which kept them apart. As with Howard, growth was to proceed by stages and, as with Howard, it was not intended to exceed the defined maximum of 30,000 or so. Harlow also exemplifies the great English landscape tradition (transmitted via Geddes[5] and Unwin[6] from the days of Capability Brown) which sees town planning not as a matter of the imposition upon the landscape of an artificial preconceived arrangement, but as the modification, hand-in-hand with nature, of given circumstances to make them suitable for habitation with the least possible imposition of alien man-made forms.

The hierarchical cellular principle reaches its extreme form in Gruen's

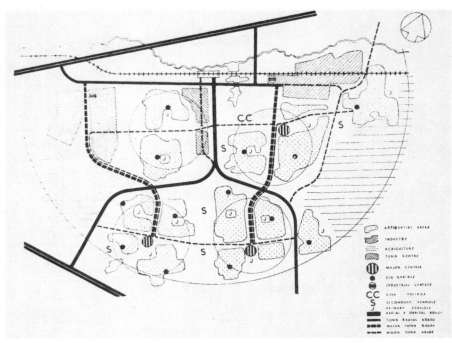

FIGURE 5.12. Harlow: a *finite hierarchical cellular* scheme.

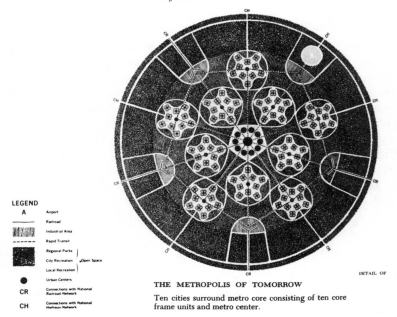

LEGEND
A   Airport

                     Railroad

                     Industrial Area

------   Rapid Transit

                     Regional Parks ⎫
                     City Recreation ⎬ Open Space
                     Local Recreation ⎭

●   Urban Centers

CR   Connections with National
                     Railroad-Network

CH   Connections with National
                     Highway-Network

THE METROPOLIS OF TOMORROW

Ten cities surround metro core consisting of ten core
frame units and metro center.

DETAIL OF

FIGURE 5.13. Gruen's metropolis: the hierarchical cellular principle applied to a
multi-million city.

1965 metropolitan scheme[7]. In Britain, however, it had already been abandoned by the *avant garde* of the later 1950s; a change eventually made manifest in Alexander's article of 1966[8] and in Jane Jacob's *Death and Life of Great American Cities* of 1961[9].

RADBURN MONOCENTRIC

Cumbernauld returns to the unicellular notion of a town, conceived schematically as a compact group of dwellings around a single centre, with only industry separated out from the whole. The idea of the neighbourhood is attacked, and the town is planned entirely on the 'Radburn' principle of total vehicle/pedestrian segregation. To keep the centre within walking distance, high-density housing abuts an elongated multi-storey core, which has roads, service areas and carparks underneath it.

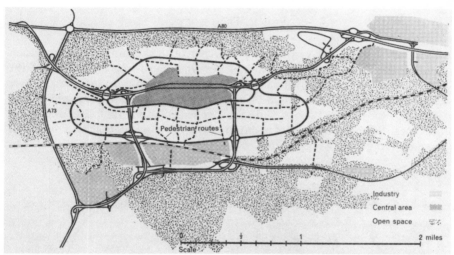

FIGURE 5.14. Cumbernauld: the first new town planned entirely on the Radburn principle of total vehicle/pedestrian segregation, with a single centre surrounded by a residential zone.

The same 'Radburn monocentric' concept underlies the then London County Council's abortive Hook proposals. In both Cumbernauld and Hook it was found necessary to modify the pure form to allow for growth, and the initial requirement for expensive roadworks proved difficult to defend. The published Hook proposals[10], however, raised to a new level a developing debate about urban form, which came to a climax in 1963 with the publication of the Buchanan Report[11].

BUCHANAN REPORT

Although it avoided commitment concerning the social implications of

'neighbourhood', the Buchanan Report approved the established concept of
the city as compounded of cells ('rooms') served by a hierarchy of routes
('corridors') which, except at the lowest levels, are kept outside the cells. The
term 'environmental area' is adopted instead of Tripp's word 'precinct'
(which was beginning to imply a pedestrian-only area) and these are defined
in Buchanan's examples with reference to the catchments of local facilities,
thus acknowledging the spirit (if not the letter) of neighbourhood theory.
Buchanan also tacitly embraces a hierarchical cellular structure by combining environmental areas into environmental 'groupings'. But his most
significant contribution was in the application to town planning as a whole of
the precision and quantitative methods of traffic engineering. Two themes
of subsequent significance emerged. One (from the Leeds study) was public
transport. The other (from Marylebone) was the orthogonal grid.

PUBLIC TRANSPORT

In the light of the large scale and great cost of urban motorways and their
attendant penalties, there was already by 1960 a growing awareness of the
possible alternative of a town based principally upon public transport. There
was revived interest in the Ciudad Lineal of Soria y Mata, in the London plan
of the MARS Group[12], in Miliutin's scheme from the 1930s and other
prototypes. Schematically, this resulted in the development of the concept of
a town deriving from a single *line*.

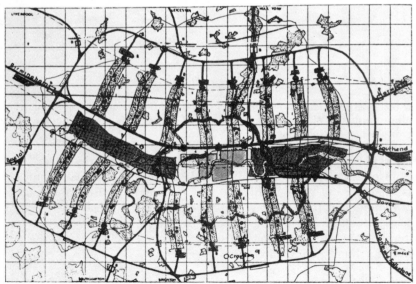

FIGURE 5.15. MARS plan for London: a wartime proposal based on total
reconstruction around a hierarchical railway network.

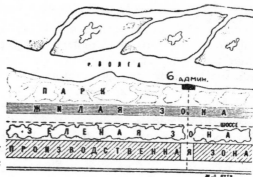

FIGURE 5.16. Miliutin's proposal for a linear city with parallel land-use zones.

UNIFORM CIRCUIT LINEAR

In 1964, Cullen and Matthews produced proposals for a 'circuit linear' town[13]. Here, to improve public transport efficiency, the line is transformed into a loop, along which all development is distributed in a narrow band. The 'line' comprises a roadway as well as an elevated mono-rail. Expansion is possible only by replication of the total form, and a series of circuit-linear towns is proposed, linked by a motorway weaving between them.

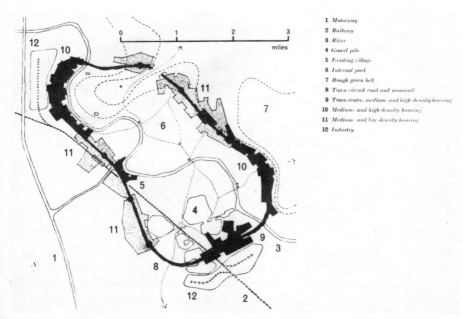

1 Motorway
2 Railway
3 River
4 Gravel pits
5 Existing village
6 Internal park
7 Rough green belt
8 Town circuit road and monorail
9 Town centre, medium- and high-density housing
10 Medium- and high-density housing
11 Medium- and low-density housing
12 Industry

FIGURE 5.17. *Uniform circuit linear:* a proposal from the early 1960s.

EXTENSIBLE CELLULAR CIRCUIT LINEAR

A considerable advance comes with Pooley and Berret's 1962 proposals for a 250,000 city in North Buckinghamshire (Bletchley)[14]. Here, several loops connect residential 'townships' with a central area at one extreme, and an industrial zone at the other. Automobiles and public transport are widely separated, each township having a 'Radburn' layout, with footpaths leading inwards to the public transport stop and township centre, and roads leading outwards to a peripheral motorway. The town is capable of infinite expansion, one loop at a time, and (as with the previous example) the space within the loops is public open space, safely accessible by walking below the elevated mono-rail. The most significant innovation is in the nucleation of settlement around the mono-rail stops, thus combining *linear* with *cellular* concepts.

The separation of public transport from other traffic may be urged for many reasons, and the duplication of route systems which is implied gains considerable support from the concept of a public transport stop as a nucleus. Buchanan had emphasized the desirability of routing heavy streams of traffic away from the centres of high pedestrian activity, and in his Leeds study had uncritically (and misleadingly) routed public transport similarly. The Hook proposals also envisage buses on all-purpose roads, which they leave and rejoin at every stop, thus requiring the impossibility of ramped junctions every few hundred yards. With 'North Bucks', we have a separate public transport route linking nodes on the pedestrian system, but still kept to one side of the built-up area.

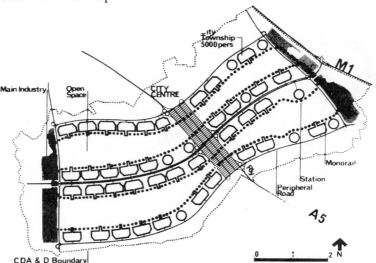

FIGURE 5.18. *Extensible cellular circuit linear:* proposal for a city based on public transport, with residential areas grouped around public transport stops. Parallel zoning permits extension by the addition of more loops.

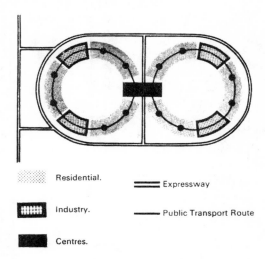

Residential.

Industry.

Centres.

Expressway

Public Transport Route

FIGURE 5.19. Runcorn: a new town near Liverpool based on a segregated bus-way.

FINITE CELLULAR CIRCUIT LINEAR

At Runcorn, we again have a cellular structure nucleated around public transport stops, and again the circuit linear form. But here, development *straddles* the loop, and the stop thus becomes the centre of a notionally circular (instead of semi-circular) catchment area. This is expedient, of course, in terms of public transport efficiency (for a given density, each stop serves twice the number of potential passengers) but it begins also to acknowledge that urban public transport is, by its very nature, intimately associated with pedestrian movement and should be routed *through the middle* of the urban cells, and not (as should most other traffic) peripherally. The peculiar 'figure-of-eight' form chosen gives emphasis to the centre but sets a definite limit to the size of the town.

CELLULAR TRIPLE STRAND

Arthur Ling, the architect of Runcorn, published in 1967[15] his own account of schematic urban form, based on a lifetime's involvement since the days of the MARS Group and the Abercrombie County of London Plan. The architect of Cumbernauld (Sir Hugh Wilson) was throughout the 1960s also exploring the theme as a consequence of numerous town planning commissions. The first of these was concerned with the same area as Pooley and Berrett, but with a more extensive brief[16]. After Cumbernauld, Wilson especially was aware of the consequences of neglecting public transport and he quite deliberately sets out to explore its influence upon urban form. He arrives at the idea of cities built up from basic cells, each nucleated around bus stops spaced at appropriate intervals, with private transport routed tangentially alongside. To avoid the necessity (as at Runcorn) for local distributor roads to cross the bus route, *two* tangential roads are proposed, and

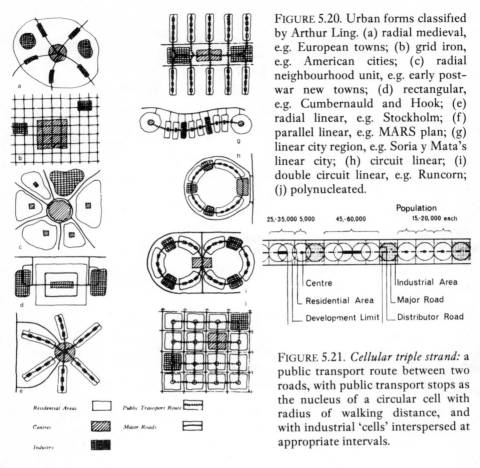

FIGURE 5.20. Urban forms classified by Arthur Ling. (a) radial medieval, e.g. European towns; (b) grid iron, e.g. American cities; (c) radial neighbourhood unit, e.g. early post-war new towns; (d) rectangular, e.g. Cumbernauld and Hook; (e) radial linear, e.g. Stockholm; (f) parallel linear, e.g. MARS plan; (g) linear city region, e.g. Soria y Mata's linear city; (h) circuit linear; (i) double circuit linear, e.g. Runcorn; (j) polynucleated.

FIGURE 5.21. *Cellular triple strand:* a public transport route between two roads, with public transport stops as the nucleus of a circular cell with radius of walking distance, and with industrial 'cells' interspersed at appropriate intervals.

there thus emerges *'cellular triple strand'*. The basic cells are elaborated principally in terms of residential areas, but the possibility is explored of having interpersed industrial cells of a similar size (i.e. with a radius of acceptable walking distance) and at a frequency determined by the ratio of the areas of industrial to residential land.

INCREMENTAL MODULAR

At Redditch, Wilson develops the concept of a cell based upon public transport, using the analogy of a 'bead' on a 'string'[17]. The public transport stops and their associated footpaths become the focus of all social facilities within a Radburn residential cell, whose dimensions and other characteristics are well defined. The concept is elaborated and applied to other projects, the most notable being Irvine, near Kilmarnock in Scotland[18]. Wilson emphasizes the dynamic potential of his scheme, arguing that development

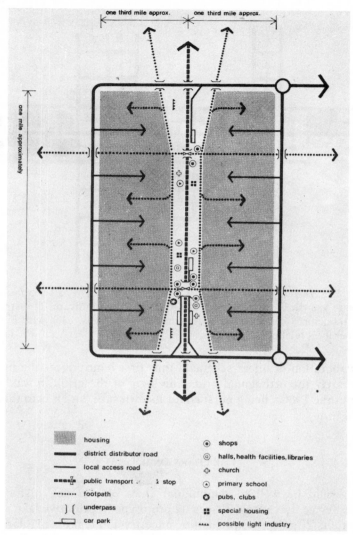

one third mile approx.   one third mile approx.

one mile approximately

housing	shops
district distributor road	halls, health facilities, libraries
local access road	church
public transport · ½ stop	primary school
footpath	pubs, clubs
underpass	special housing
car park	possible light industry

FIGURE 5.22. A residential cell ('bead') based on a segregated public transport route.

may commence along an all-purpose route (such as an existing country lane) which at first will cope adequately with all traffic. Later, everything other than public transport may be diverted onto new tangential routes alongside, thus allowing the original lane to continue as the *community* route, linking the urban cells. The 'triple strand' may also be developed eventually to provide a 'tartan grid' of alternating routes capable of infinite extension by finite 'modular' stages.

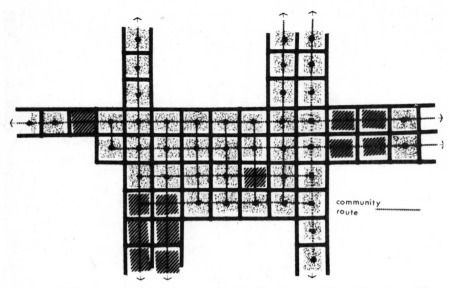

FIGURE 5.23. *Incremental modular with extensible 'tartan' grid:* a schema capable
of infinite growth by finite stages. Diagonal hatching indicates industry. The
public transport ('community') routes link modular cells, each with bus stop
and other local facilities as nucleus.

The elaboration of linear schemata thus first reintroduces the urban cell,
and ultimately the orthogonal grid. The logic of the gridiron was however,
throughout the 1960s, being pursued for its own sake, and it is to this that we
must now turn.

THE OTHOGONAL GRID

First, it would be well to remind ourselves of the long history of this
venerable device. Lavedan[19] sees its prototype in primitive lake dwellings.
Axel Boethius[20] disputes prehistoric ancestry and regards regular planning
as the hallmark of civilization. For von Gerkan[21], the Hippodamian plan
derives from a system of parallel terraces alongside streets in one direction,
intersected by minor alleys at right angles. Haverfield[22] emphasizes the
link in Roman ritual with divination and orientation. Tunnard[23] charac-
terizes the gridiron as the 'trader's town' and throughout history it has
remained the chosen form for pioneer, colonist, speculator and military man.
In the recent past, we again find the contrast between the continental
modernists, typified by Le Corbusier, for whom the right angle was
rational, Cartesian and French; and the British Arts and Crafts tradition, for
which rectangularity and straight lines were anathema. Tripp and others had

in the 1930s attacked cross-roads on the grounds of traffic safety, and official planning at the time of the first new towns preferred informality and the 'staggered' junction.

In *Traffic in Towns,* Buchanan had briefly explored the problems of inserting a motorway network into London, and had suggested that an orthogonal grid might best distribute the inevitably heavy flows of metropolitan traffic. The underlying assumption was that the best device for distributing traffic evenly over an area was a uniform grid, in much the same way as a space frame or similar lattice may distribute forces in a structure. High local concentrations are avoided, and there is always an alternative path. Buchanan's investigation was largely concerned with finding the optimum relationship between land use and traffic generation, a key consideration being the spacing of roads and the area of the insula they bounded. Within the insula, a variety of land uses was always possible, provided that development was controlled in such a way that the volume of traffic generated did not exceed the capacity of junctions giving access to and from the road grid.

Some new town planners in the 1960s thus came to look favourably on the gridiron. Instead of channelling heavy traffic flows along a few roads, lighter loads and smaller roads were possible. Instead of deciding in advance every detail of land use, the future could largely be left to itself, and options kept open.

POLYCELLULAR UNIFORM GRID

Livingston, in Scotland, was the first new town to explore the form. At Washington[24], a new town in the declining Durham coalfield, the virtues of

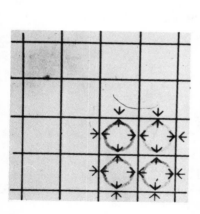

FIGURE 5.24. *Polycellular uniform grid:* each insula contains a 'village' of 4500 people, and the road grid spreads the traffic load evenly.

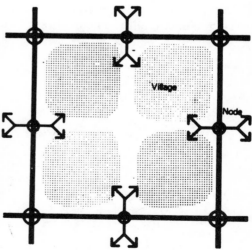

FIGURE 5.25. A modified scheme eventually adopted for Washington.

the grid are systematically explored. The intention originally was a uniform half-mile spacing of roads, each insula containing a 'village' of 4500 people, and major 'traffic generators' spread throughout the whole to avoid local build-up of traffic. It later became apparent that the half-mile spacing was too close, and the revised plan has roads one mile apart, with four 'villages' per insula (or fewer villages plus some other land use). Within each insula, the local roads are designed to prevent 'through' traffic. Today, 'bus-only links' allow public transport to penetrate more freely.

POLYFOCAL UNIFORM GRID

The designers of Washington later moved on to design Milton Keynes, a new town of 250,000[25]. By this time, uncertainty about the future and the slogan 'freedom of choice' were dominant. Throughout architecture, solutions were being sought through the divorce of the basic 'infrastructure' (in buildings, an open-plan skeleton, lifts and service ducts; in towns, a road and services network) from a 'superstructure' left largely to the future and capable of modification as circumstances might require. The expression 'plug-in' was borrowed from contemporary industry to describe a city devised on principles analogous to those of modern electronic equipment where 'sub-assemblies' are plugged-in or unplugged at will from a basic 'chassis'.

At Milton Keynes a uniform grid of roads, one kilometre apart, serves several square miles of low-density development. There is no deliberate subdivision, and each insula is connected to its neighbours by footpaths passing under the road grid. With these underpasses are sited bus stops and such local facilities as may be required in uniformly spread 'activity centres', so placed that freedom of choice prevails. There are some industrial zones and a city centre, but in general the intention is to avoid concentration and an over-structured totality. The roadways run through ample 'reservations', the

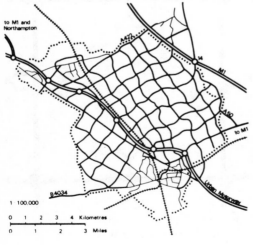

FIGURE 5.26. *Polyfocal uniform grid:* roads 1 km apart. No deliberate subdivision, but 'activity centres' with pedestrian underpasses midway between cross-roads provide focal points for overlapping catchment areas straddled by road grid.

expectation being that, although no more than conventional dual carriageways with 'roundabouts' should be needed, the provision is there for any form of transport the future might demand. No separate provision is made *ab initio* for public transport, which it is claimed (with unconscious irony) will 'compare favourably' with that in other towns of similar size.

INFINITE HIERARCHICAL DIRECTIONAL GRID

In 1966, Buchanan was commissioned to make a study of South Hampshire[26], which he begins with an enterprising excursion into 'systems analysis'. He shows that within a city there are various 'sub-systems' with internal linkages requiring a systematic network of communications. He explores three categories of network—the radial-concentric, the linear, and

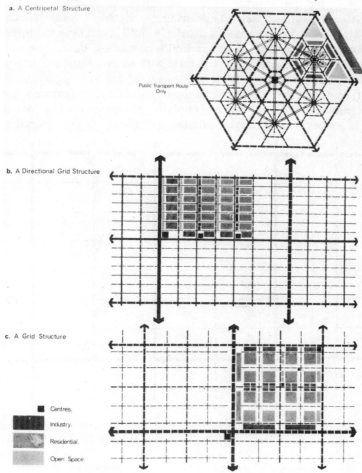

FIGURE 5.27. Basic urban structures compared.

the grid—and chooses a 'directional grid' which combines the virtues of the line and the lattice.

The essential and novel feature of this scheme is in the hierarchical arrangement of routes. At the highest level, there are the national routes. At right angles to these are those carrying regional traffic, which moves in the principal direction of the grid. At right angles to the regional routes, and more closely spaced, come district routes. At right angles again, a lower category—and the system continues down to the lowest level of closely spaced footpaths.

The cross-roads formed by routes of adjacent categories are conceived as 'nodes' in the system, and it is here that appropriate land uses are to be situated. Thus a factory, which draws its workers from the region and distributes its goods nation-wide would stand near the junction of a regional and a national route. A school, drawing pupils from local housing, and teachers and services from a larger district, would stand near the intersection of local and district routes. In his preliminary studies, Buchanan recognizes the desirability of segregating public transport on to a separate network, and in his 'directional grid' goes some way towards this by suggesting an alternation of routes within the same category, providing separately for rapid 'through' movements and slower 'random' movements. The whole, it is claimed, is adaptable and capable of indefinite growth at any desired rate.

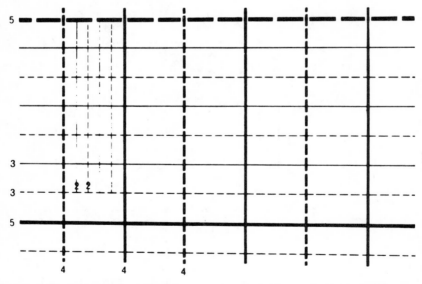

FIGURE 5.28. *Infinite hierarchical directional grid:* the lower the route category, the closer the spacing. Each category intersects at right angles with those above and below. At intersections ('nodes') are sited appropriate focal activities. Routes within the same category may alternately serve 'through' and 'random' movement.

SHAPE

Much of what we have so far discussed has been concerned with *lines*—something which eloquently reflects recent pre-occupation with route systems and traffic in towns. But we should not lose sight of some equally significant considerations reflected in other geometrical concepts.

The city conceived as a finite whole will tend, as we have seen, to exploit the geometry of *plane* figures. History again has much to show, especially prior to modern times, when defensive works dictated the total form of the town. Although the first new towns followed Unwin in allowing the lie of the land to dictate the total form, this was nonetheless schematically circular, with the central area appropriately at the centre. Such a form readily expresses the finite unity and common purpose at which they aimed. Cumbernauld and Hook are essentially similar, their elongated form being a consequence of extending the central point to a line with everyone living within easy walking distance of it. Hook does however leave the centre open at one end and free to grow, and thus points the way to what was to become the dominant solution for the shape of the town as a whole: amorphousness, and all that this may imply in terms of uncertain purpose and disunity. The linear towns, however, with their reliance upon public transport, retain definition in one dimension at least, in that walking distance from the stops is precisely prescribed.

BOUNDARY

Nowhere (except perhaps in South Hampshire) is the idea of a boundary or edge to the town completely abandoned. On the contrary, most schemes still call for a distinct break between town and country as a primary aim. Robert Owen, it will be remembered, placed fields and allotments around his model industrial village. Howard's 'agricultural belt' with its farms and sanitoria is as much a part of his scheme as the Garden City itself. Unwin still looked to the city wall and gateway to bring back the definition characteristic of the historic town. For the early propagandists of the Garden City, an essential ingredient was a boundary which would give distinction 'without conveying any idea of antagonism'[27]. Geddes conceived the fully developed city as a flower, with green wedges between its petals. Gibberd wanted a distinctive profile with a dominating crown cementing the unity of the whole[28]. Hook revived Howard's intention that the city should be surrounded by a green zone in urban ownership and for the use of the citizenry. The universally adopted device to secure a boundary for the town has long been the 'green belt', and no one yet proposes to abandon the 'urban fence' in favour of modest deceptions like the ha-ha—still less for the boundless perspectives of Versailles. But many of the schemata we have reviewed stand in no real need of boundaries and tacitly accept the possibility of the town-without-end.

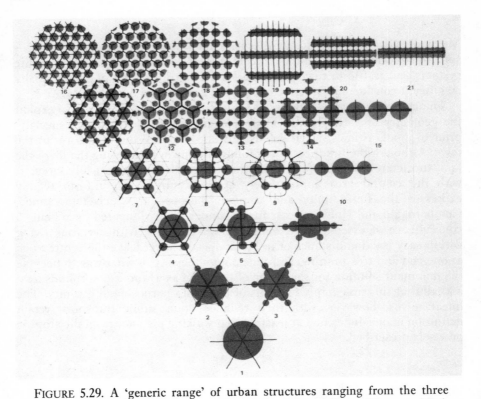

FIGURE 5.29. A 'generic range' of urban structures ranging from the three extremes of 'centralized', 'dispersed' and 'linear' as follows: (1) centralized; (2) linked radial; (3) radial; (4) web; (5) figure-of-eight; (6) radial linear; (7) centripetal net; (8) centripetal grid; (9) ringed spine; (10) spine; (11) triangular net; (12) hexagonal net; (13) regular grid; (14) directional grid; (15) nucleated corridor; (16) dispersed; (17) honeycomb; (18) uniform grid; (19) canalized grid; (20) linear grid; (21) linear.

CONCLUSION

The burst of creative thinking about the form of the city which we have described was slowed by the onset of the present 'recession'. But it continued unabated into the last decade. Just before 1970, Sheffield Corporation published a proposal for a new settlement at Mosborough[29] which begins with a comparative analysis of urban forms. 1974 saw the publication of work at Cambridge by Lionel March and others[30] exploring similar and related themes.

It is difficult at this stage to draw conclusions without extending the discussion into other aspects of design, but the following is a summary of the most significant ideas which emerge.

ROUTE SYSTEMS

Recent concern for transport in general is reflected in concepts of urban form deriving from *lines* and systems of *lines*. Of the three concepts considered— *radial, linear* and *gridiron*—the *radial* is rejected as inappropriate to the needs of traffic and growth. The *linear* form tends to commitment and precision in detail; the *gridiron* to uncertainty and *laisser faire*.

There is growing recognition of the need to route public transport *through* the centres of pedestrian activity, and not *around* them as with automobiles. This leads to proposals embodying an *alternation of routes,* tending, (with linear schemata) to 'triple-strand', and, (with the gridiron) to a 'tartan grid'.

NUCLEUS

Schemata based on focal *points* are in general less consciously pursued— something which probably reflects the lack of unifying purpose once characterized by agora, temple or town hall. With the public transport *stop,* however, the idea of a focus reappears, and is exploited as the *nucleus* of a *cell* having acceptable *walking distance* as its radius. Even plans like Milton Keynes which begin by explicitly rejecting cellular structure, find local 'activity centres' becoming the nucleus of local catchments, inappropriately straddled by a main road. Where footpaths converge upon focal points, the radial form reasserts itself in detail.

ZONES, INSULAE AND NEIGHBOURHOODS

In spite of the emphasis placed upon linear concepts, there persists through all modern town planning the notion of a city subdivided into separate *spaces*. Fundamental in this regard is the notion of the land-use *zone,* and especially the separation of 'living' from 'working' areas. Urged throughout the nineteenth century on sanitary grounds, this separation is now debated in terms mainly of traffic generation (which argues its continuation) and the social damage implicit in dividing life from work. In spite of misgivings, employment zones are still set aside, but the tendency is to disperse them throughout the city. The greater significance of office employment is acknowledged and finds some reflection in the design of the *central area,* which tends also to be regarded as distinct, primarily as a zone catering for retail trade. The inclusion within most central areas of some housing and other land uses—as well as its social purpose—raises an unanswered question concerning its categorization as a land-use zone.

In addition to land-use zones, two other types of subdivision are employed: *insulae* and *neighbourhoods*. There is some confusion in the use of all three of these categories, and their respective peculiarities are imperfectly appreciated. Only the land-use zone is used in every instance. The *insula* is conceived primarily as a consequence of the orthogonal grid. Its dimensional and other characteristics are explored mainly from the point of view of traffic engineering, confirming its historic rôle as little more than a technically convenient device. The *neighbourhood,* although largely rejected in name, continually reasserts itself in the detailed design of local catchment areas—especially in those schemes based on public transport. It is in these also that the Garden City tradition, with its ideal of healthy community life, is most apparent.

INCREMENTAL MODULAR DESIGN

Undoubtedly the most significant concept to emerge is that of the residential cell as an *incremental module,* adapted to the achievement of *infinite* growth by *finite* stages. At the same time, concepts of the city as a whole have tended to weaken, while hierarchical arrangements *within* the residential cell, extending downwards to the level of a cluster of houses, have been strengthened.

In place of a definite city, conceived as a totality and subsequently elaborated in detail, we see the beginnings of an alternative procedure: an *indefinite and adaptable aggregation of parts.* Again architecture provides historical parallels and precedents: witness the difference between cathedrals such as renaissance architects wanted, conceived as perfect wholes; and those of the

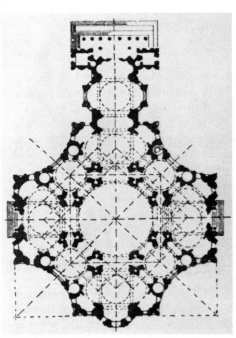

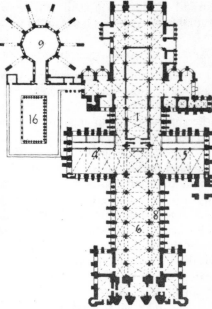

FIGURE 5.30. Finite perfection: Wren's proposal for the rebuilding of St. Paul's.

FIGURE 5.31. Incremental modular design: Lincoln, a typical medieval cathedral based on a repeated 'module' of a vaulting bay, and always extensible.

FIGURE 5.32. Howard's vision of a group of settlements.

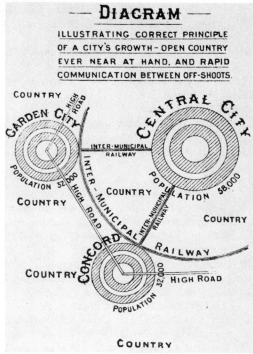

Middle Ages, based upon the module of a vaulting bay, and always extensible.

There is confirmation here of the idea of the city region as a *'constellation of neighbourhoods'* a notion first given currency at the U.N. symposium on the planning of new towns in 1964. There is confirmation also of Howard's vision of a group of settlements, each distinct and restricted in size, linked by a variety of transport systems and by a degree of social and economic interdependence. And in the detail of the residential module there is the reaffirmation, to be expected from architecture, of the overriding significance of the *human scale,* which, if it may no longer be achieved in the infinity that the city has become, might yet be recovered in its parts.

NOTES

1. Geddes, P. (1915) *Cities in Evolution,* 3rd ed. London: Ernest Benn.
2. Houghton-Evans, W. (1978) *Architecture and Urban Design.* Lancaster: Construction Press.
3. Aristotle, *Politics* VII.ii.
4. Tripp, H. A. (1944) *Town Planning and Road Traffic.* London: Arnold.
5. Geddes, P. (1915) *Cities in Evolution,* 3rd ed. London: Ernest Benn.
6. Unwin, R. (1909) *Town Planning in Practice.* London: Unwin.
7. Gruen, V. (1965) *The Heart of our Cities.* London: Thames and Hudson.

8. Alexander, C. (1966) A city is not a tree. *Design* (February).
9. Jacobs, Jane (1961) *The Death and Life of Great American Cities*. New York: Random House.
10. Bennett, H. *et al.* (1961) *The Planning of a New Town*. London: London County Council.
11. Ministry of Transport (1963) *Traffic in Towns*. London: HMSO.
12. Korn, A. and Samuely, F. (1942) A master plan for London. *Architectural Review* (June), pp. 143ff.
13. Cullen, G. and Matthews, R. (1964) *A Town Called Alcan*. London: Alcan Industries Ltd.
14. Pooley, F. (1966) *North Buckinghamshire New City*. Aylesbury: Buckinghamshire County Council.
15. Ling, A. (1969) Urban form, in Sharp, D. (ed.), *Planning and Architecture*. London: Barrie and Rockcliffe.
16. Ministry of Housing and Local Government (1965) *Northampton, Bedford and North Buckinghamshire Study*. London: HMSO.
17. Wilson, L. H. and Womersley, L. (1966) *Redditch New Town*. Redditch: Development Corporation.
18. Irvine Development Corporation (1971) *Irvine New Town Plan*. Irvine.
19. Lavedan, P. (1926) *Histoire de l'Urbanisme I*. Paris: Laurens.
20. Boethius, A. (1960) *The Golden House of Nero*. Ann Arbor, Michigan: University of Michigan Press.
21. von Gerkan, A. (1924) *Greichische Stadteanlagen*. Berlin.
22. Haverfield, F. (1913) *Ancient Town Planning*. Oxford: Oxford University Press.
23. Tunnard, C. (1953) *The City of Man*. New York: Scribner.
24. Llewellyn-Davies, R. *et al.* (1966) *Washington New Town Master Plan*. Washington: Development Corporation.
25. Llewellyn-Davies, R. *et al.* (1970) *The Plan for Milton Keynes* (2 vols.). Milton Keynes: Development Corporation.
26. Ministry of Housing and Local Government (1966) *South Hampshire Study* (3 vols.). London: HMSO.
27. Purdom, C. D. *et al.* (1921) *Town Theory and Practice*. London: Ernest Benn.
28. Gibberd, F. (1955) *Town Design*. London: Architectural Press.
29. Culpin, C. *et al.* (1969) *Mosborough Master Plan*. Sheffield: Sheffield Corporation.
30. March, L. M. (1974) History of regional and urban models, in Perraton, J. and Baxter, R. (eds.), *Models, Evaluations and Information Systems for Planners*. Lancaster: Construction Press.

6

Garden city Japanese style: the case of Den-en Toshi Company Ltd., 1918–28[1]

SHUN-ICHI J. WATANABE

About 12 km south-west of downtown Tokyo, or half an hour's ride from Ginza station is a suburban railway station named Den-en Chofu. The area around it is generally known as one of the best residential areas in Tokyo (figure 6.1). In front of the west gate of the station, there is a comfortable semi-circular plaza decorated with beautiful rose bushes and a tiny carp pond. Visitors to the plaza will notice there a metal monument, which reads

> The 131 hectare area around this plaza is the place which old Mr. Eiichi Shibusawa, one of the leading cultural spirits of the Meiji Era, chose as a site for a model residential area which would improve the living standard of the people by combining the advantages of town and countryside—namely, a 'garden city', which was then emerging in Britain and the United States. He did this by personally visiting the site after his retirement from public life and in spite of his old age.
>
> For this purpose, Den-en Toshi Company Ltd. was created in 1918, which then sold land in lots to those who accepted old Shibusawa's idea. Thus, there has emerged here the first great urban planning in our country . . .[2]

Den-en Chofu is well known for its superb physical environment and prestigeous residential character. But few people know that it was built as part of a Japanese 'garden city' more than half a century ago.

This century has witnessed Ebenezer Howard's Garden City idea attaining international reputation. Various forms of urban settlement have emerged in many quarters of the world under the name of 'garden city', *cité jardin*, *'Gartenstadt'* or, in the case of Japan, *'den-en toshi'*[3]. But this does not

129

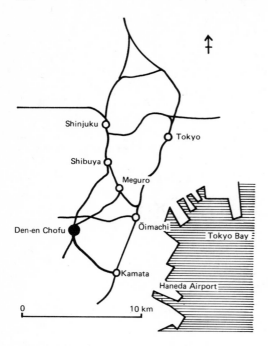

FIGURE 6.1. The location of Den-en Chofu.

necessarily mean that the British Garden City idea has been correctly under-stood and sincerely accepted by the planners and the people of the world.

History shows that the international exchange of planning ideas which has enriched modern urban planning does include cases of misunderstanding of the original idea or even mere borrowing of a planning jargon. The study of such a reality would reveal some of the hidden dimensions of the socio-historical background behind the planning systems of each country.

This paper is devoted to a case study of Den-en Toshi Company Ltd. (hereafter, the Company), which built a 'garden city' during its existence between 1918 and 1928. This is more or less the only development in Japan to which the British Garden City idea has given an impact to any meaningful degree[4].

EIICHI SHIBUSAWA

Eiichi Shibusawa (1840–1931) was one of the most successful and public-spirited business leaders since the Meiji Restoration of 1868[5]. He was basically a designer of various new social institutions for modernizing Japan, often following Western models. During his ninety-one-year life, Shibusawa created or was associated with hundreds of enterprises including banking, paper manufacturing, textiles, and shipping. He was the founder of Japan's first stock company and its Chamber of Commerce. Shibusawa was also active in public affairs and philanthropic works, for which he was later made a viscount.

In 1915, Viscount Shibusawa made his fourth trip abroad to attend the San Francisco Exposition commemorating the opening of the Panama Canal. On his return early the next year, this seventy-seven-year-old man decided to retire from business and to devote the rest of his life to public service. Den-en Toshi Company was to become the only exception to this decision.

Viscount Shibusawa is often believed to be the initiator of the whole enterprise, but the existing records indicate he was more the organizer than the initiator[6]. In March 1915, a group of agricultural landlords in rural Ebara-gun led by Yaemon Hatake visited Shibusawa. They proposed an idea for developing their land and asked Shibusawa for his assistance. Two months later, Shibusawa referred to the 'garden city' for the first time in his diary[7].

It was a time when modern industry and commerce were rapidly becoming concentrated in the Tokyo City area as a result of the boom due to World War I. The newly emerging middle class was spilling out of crowded central Tokyo into the adjoining areas. Yet local authorities outside the city area had insufficient financial capacity and little regulatory power. Random suburban developments were taking place and land values began to rise in these areas.

The areas further from the city, however, remained as rural as before, since they were not within commuting distance of central Tokyo. Most of the landowners visiting Shibusawa were those whose holdings were located in these areas. They wanted to know how they could share in the astonishingly high prices which land owners in urban fringe areas were receiving. It is interesting to note that the whole enterprise was initiated by these speculation-minded landlords rather than by reform-minded social activists such as Ebenezer Howard.

Old Shibusawa had many unrivalled talents. First, he had insight into the nature of suburban life from his observations abroad. He believed that the separation of job and home was inevitable and that suburban housing had a potentially large market. Second, he knew how to organize a company which would develop suburbia possibly with a good rate of return. In fact, this enterprise was to be another challenging social 'invention'. Third, his prestige commanded trust and cooperation, especially from the land owners, in the Company's land acquisition.

In short, Shibusawa played a pivotal role in combining the interests of landlords, investors, company managers, and, later, of *den-en toshi* dwellers.

PROSPECTUS

The promoters spent three years defining the nature of the company, finding investors and, above all, negotiating informally with landowners. Then in

January 1918, the eight promoters of Den-en Toshi Company Ltd., including old Shibusawa, announced their 'Prospectus for the Company'[8].

It denounced the overcrowding of cities and the decaying of agriculture as the crucial problem of the time. One of the most basic and long lasting solutions to this problem, the prospectus claimed, was the 'restoration of country life'. This would be done by means of moving the excess urban population back to rural areas, which would eliminate various potential urban problems and would promote healthy rural life.

The garden city *(den-en toshi)* idea, according to the prospectus, was on this line. Den-en Toshi would be the ideal place to live for middle-class families, who were then suffering from inconvenient living, unhealthy conditions and moral threat in the overcrowded and dusty capital city. Here would be a suburb of fresh air and healthy and convenient homes with sufficient facilities and services, the prospectus emphasized.

Thus, the promoters defined the Company's nature as property business and its clients as middle- (but in fact, upper-middle-) class people to whom suburban life was a dream.

The Company planned to develop a garden city of approximately 138.6 ha (420,000 tsubo) in Ebara-gun outside Tokyo City, and had already applied for a licence for a new suburban railway line connecting Den-en Toshi with Tokyo. In the initial stage, the Company was to build 500 houses for middle-class residents which were to be first rented for a reasonable price. The lot and house would be eventually owned by the occupants upon payment of all the annual instalments.

The prospectus pointed out the public nature of this private company and stressed its investment potential. The company hoped that rising suburban land values would make a 7–9 per cent annual dividend possible within a few years. This marks quite a contrast with the British Garden City movement, which from the beginning intended to limit the dividend rate at 5 per cent per annum.

FOUNDATION

On 2 September 1918, the Company was formally founded with the capital of half a million yen. The capital was soon increased to one million yen and then, in January 1920, to five million yen. The Company originally had eleven stockholders, mostly gentleman-businessmen who warmheartedly responded to Shibusawa's vision. Six of them became board members.

It is interesting to note that the Company's initial capital of half a million yen, or £50,000, amounts to two and a half times that of Garden City Pioneer Company, which was founded to develop the first Garden City of Letchworth in 1903.

Viscount Shibusawa, one of the largest stockholders, did not sit on the board of directors but was involved in all the important decisions. He later sent his son Hideo Shibusawa to make a nine-month trip abroad to investigate garden cities. Upon coming home, young Shibusawa joined the board.

According to the original Articles of Incorporation[9], the Company aimed at:

(1) managing the urban area it would develop;
(2) buying, selling and renting real properties and acting as an agent for them;
(3) designing, performing and supervising construction and engineering works; and
(4) undertaking, or investing in, related businesses in order to fulfil the above purposes.

In short, the Company intended to build a 'garden city' in the Tokyo suburbs, and to sell the land to owner-occupants. This was a very new kind of real estate business. In fact, the Company was more a developer than a real estate agent. It had to develop not only residential areas which were to be subdivided for sale, but also various urban facilities and services which were needed for suburban living.

The land the Company was to develop was agricultural countryside away from the built-up areas. There were hardly any facilities and services which the urban middle class would require. Thus, the development had to be carried out with a significant amount of investment and careful management. This was exactly why those Ebara landlords had solicited Viscount Shibusawa's leadership.

The Company had to arrange for various services. It asked the government to provide police, telephone and postal services, and a water company to supply water. The Company later amended its original articles of incorporation to take responsibility for providing electricity. Power companies were reluctant to serve Den-en Toshi, located as it was so far away from the built-up area. The Company bought electricity from them and 'retailed' it to the inhabitants. Later, it turned out to be a profitable business as the number of inhabitants increased.

The most crucial problem was to make it possible to commute from Den-en Toshi to central Tokyo. To do this the Company created its subsidiary, Meguro-Kamata Electric Railway Company Ltd. in 1922, which will be discussed in detail later. In May 1928, when most of the land had been sold and Den-en Toshi was taking fairly clear shape, the railway took over its parent company.

LAND AQUISITION

The Company's promoters were fully aware that the success of such an enterprise depended upon land acquisition. Its establishment seems to have been delayed until land in sufficient quantity was available at reasonable prices and in desirable locations.

On 17 May 1918, the viscount and his followers paid a visit in rickshas to the site of the future 'garden city'. This was a happy ritual demonstrating that everything was going well, and is inscribed on the Den-en Chofu monument.

Four months later, Den-en Toshi Company Ltd. was formed and it started energetically signing land contracts. The Company originally planned to acquire some 130 ha (about 400,000 tsubo) including areas somewhat nearer to the already developing urban fringe. But land values there were rising so rapidly that they exceeded the Company's expectations. Therefore, the board members of this eighty-eight-day-old company decided to give up some of the land close to the city and buy other land away from the urban areas[10]. They also decided to pay the extra premium in some areas in order to secure the total amount of land as originally envisaged.

It is noted that Den-en Toshi, as planned, had no population figure as the British Garden City had. The Company's concern was land itself, not population or living patterns upon the land.

Thus the Company worked hard to buy as much land as quickly and cheaply as possible. On Christmas Day, the first 100,000 yen was given to the group of land owners. During its first nine months, the Company paid nearly a million yen for about 90 ha (270,915 tsubo)—nearly 56 per cent of the total eventually acquired. This figure grew to 70 per cent six months later, and to 87 per cent a year later. At the end of November 1921, the Company owned slightly less than 150 ha (452,578 tsubo), nearly 98 per cent of which had been agricultural or wooded land.

The Company had originally hoped to pay about 7000 yen/ha (2.33 yen/tsubo). But in some cases, it had to pay more than three times as much. Thus, the average cost was about 12,000 yen/ha (3.73 yen/tsubo, or £480/acre) at the end of the first nine months, which was nearly fourteen times the amount Howard paid for the second Garden City of Welwyn in 1919. The book value per net land acquired at the end of November 1921 was about 18,000 yen/ha (5.94 yen/tsubo)[11].

The Company did not succeed in obtaining a neatly-shaped parcel of land. The land it obtained was more or less an irregular belt about 3.4 km long and 0.2 to 1.2 km wide. It stretched over six rural jurisdictions, and its nearest corner was about 2 km away from the fringe of urban Tokyo.

Overall, however, the land acquisition was extremely successful. The Company obtained much more land than originally planned. The higher acquisition costs were later balanced off by the higher sales price of sub-divided lots. The remote location and irregular shape of the site were not a problem because the Company could freely decide the location of railway lines and stations to serve Den-en Toshi. In fact, the Company did not stick to the idea that the garden city should be an independent and identifiable entity, thus parting from the British Garden City idea.

DEVELOPMENT WORKS

When the Company was established in 1918, the country did not have the City Planning Act. Although passed the next year, the Act was primarily concerned with the improvement of streets in the built-up area. Developing suburbs were largely ignored. However landowners could get public assistance for organized land improvement under the Arable Land Re-Plotting Act of 1899. The original purpose of this Act was to raise agricultural productivity by physically improving arable land, but it was often used merely to subdivide agricultural areas for residential purposes. It was mostly under the terms of this Act that Den-en Toshi was developed.

The Company had chosen high and well-drained agricultural land with practically no buildings. Application of the Re-Plotting Act would easily turn this into residential areas for sale. Besides installing electricity, the Company had only to lay out lots, open spaces, streets, railway lines and stations.

Lacking statutory zoning, the company designated most individual lots as residential and the rest as neighbourhood commercial. The ownership of land remained in the hands of the Company until all payments were made, which enabled it to enforce rather detailed and strict building controls. It should be noted that Den-en Toshi was developed almost completely as a private enterprise and without statutory planning.

LAND DISPOSAL

Out of some 150 ha (nearly 460,000 tsubo) net, the Den-en Toshi Company sold about 106 ha (321,000 tsubo) during its ten-year operation. The rest was partly streets, parks, and other public space, and partly land used by the Company and its subsidiary companies.

The areas the Company disposed of are roughly grouped into three separate areas[12].

(1) the Senzoku area—19.3 ha (58,500 tsubo) in Hibusuma-mura, Hiratsuka-mura, and Magome-mura;
(2) the Ooka-yama area—30.0 ha (91,000 tsubo) in Hibusuma-mura, Magome-mura, and Ikegami-mura; and
(3) the Tamagawa-dai area—56.6 ha (171,530 tsubo) in Chofu-mura and Tamagawa-mura.

The Company called the entire development Den-en Toshi, so it follows that this Japanese 'garden city' was composed of three islands of development.

THE SENZOKU AREA

The Company first undertook development of the Senzoku area. It submitted its first application for replotting work to the prefectural government for approval in February 1922. The business report for the period between December 1921 and May 1922 reads:

> Because such works as sewer and street pavement need some more time, all the works in the area will not be completed before the coming October. But some of those who are applying for the purchase of lots eagerly wish to sign contracts as soon as possible even before the completion of the works. Therefore, the Company plans to start selling lots in the near future.[13]

Similarly as the viscount's son Hideo Shibusawa, wrote.

> ... As soon as the site plan for Senzoku was completed, it was printed, and 'lots' were put up for sales. It was even before the first train ran and, I think, was around May 1922. We had only had strips of land dug for streets according to the plan. The other part remained a field with green wheat plants and white potato flowers. There the potential purchasers wandered around with the site plan in their hands and sought the lot they wanted to buy.[14]

At the first sale, residential lots were sold for 17 to 56 yen/tsubo and commercial lots for 36 to 80 yen/tsubo—roughly ten times their original cost. The size of residential lots ranged between 182 and 3700 m² (55 and 1121 tsubo), averaging about 660 m² (200 tsubo). Commercial lots were one-quarter to one-fifth of residential ones in size. About 80 per cent of the total lots were contracted for within the first ten days, and the rest mostly by the end of November[15].

Sales at the Senzoku area clearly demonstrated the appeal of suburban living to the middle class. The Company's instalment plan was particularly innovative for its time. A purchaser of a lot could deposit 20 per cent in cash and pay the rest in instalments at 10 per cent interest.

THE OOKA-YAMA AREA

The Company originally planned to develop and sell the Ooka-yama area in lots. It first applied for the government's approval for replotting work there in July 1922, but further actions were not taken for unknown reasons. The next year, an extraordinary thing happened—the Tokyo earthquake of 1 September 1923. The Kuramae Technical High School (presently Tokyo Institute of Technology) was one of those severely damaged in central Tokyo, and it was looking for a new campus site in the suburbs.

In January 1924, the Company agreed to give the entire Ooka-yama area (91,000 tsubo) to the school in exchange for its former campus (12,000 tsubo). This it sold to the Earthquake Reconstruction Agency for 1.8 million yen, nearly seven times what it had paid for the Ooka-yama land[16]. These enormous profits led to stock-holding and were the beginnings of the present mammoth Tokyu Corporation.

THE TAMAGAWA-DAI AREA

The Company attached a special importance to the development of this area. It was the largest and best shaped tract, mostly located on beautiful hills

FIGURE 6.2. The plan for the Tamagawa-dai area.

FIGURE 6.3. Present-day Den-en Chofu which consists of most of the Tamagawa-dai area.

looking towards Mount Fuji and the Tama River (figure 6.2). A Company pamphlet described it as 'the future centre of Den-en Toshi'[17].

The layout of this area was started late in 1922, and the first replotting application submitted in August 1923. The earthquake struck the next month, and by October the first 10.7 ha (some 32,000 tsubo) were on sale[18]. The price ranged from 13 to 55 yen/tsubo, and averaged 40 to 50 yen/tsubo, eight to ten times the acquisition cost. The minimum lot size was 175 m² (53 tsubo), and one could purchase lots up to 1650 m² (500 tsubo).

The next April, the first family moved in, and about forty-two houses were occupied at the end of the year.

The Tamagawa-dai area was subdivided and sold at eight different times. In spite of its incremental development, the layout remained coherent and gave the residents a sense of identity. The present Den-en Chofu consists of most of the Tamagawa-dai area, which grew into one of the most prestigeous suburbs (figure 6.3).

Briefly, Senzoku gave the Company encouragement, Ooka-yama profit, and Tamagawa-dai fame.

THE RAILWAY

Railway transportation was the key to the whole enterprise. The promoters of the Company wisely started their actions even before its creation. In January 1918, they applied to the government for a railway licence in the name of the promoters for a dummy company named Ebara Electric Railway Company Ltd.

In March 1920, they finally obtained a licence to build a railway line between Oi-machi and Chofu-mura (the Oi-machi Line). This was to run through three areas of Den-en Toshi and connect them with the government's Tokaido Line at its Oi-machi Station. As soon as the licence was granted, the promoters decided to give it free to Den-en Toshi Company, of which most of them were also board members.

In March 1922, the Company began to build a branch line between the Senzoku area and Meguro Station on the government's Yamanote Line.

FIGURE 6.4. The railway company managers with one of the first trains.

During construction the subsidiary Meguro-Kamata Electric Railway Company was created. The initial capital was 3.5 million yen, of which 3.4 million yen was invested by Den-en Toshi Company. The board members of both companies were nearly the same. They were almost one company, managed under a single decision-making body.

On 11 March 1923, the railway company opened the first portion between Meguro and Maruko Stations, and the rest of the line to Kamata Station on the Tokaido Line eight months later. The first trains consisted of a single car for sixty-four passengers. They ran at an average speed of 30 km per hour, at approximately quarter-hour intervals. An executive living in Den-en Toshi could expect to be at his down town office in an hour or less.

This railway was a lifeline for most of the residents. Five months after its inception an average of over 10,000 people rode the line each day.

BUSINESS PROGRESS AND TERMINATION

When Den-en Toshi Company was founded in 1918, the nation's economy was in a boom due to World War I, but soon came a severe postwar depression. The years 1925 to 1927 were the worst; the bank moratorium took place in April 1927.

Since its establishment, the Company had been paying the stockholders an 'interest dividend' of 5 per cent per annum, and since its first land sale in 1922, it began to pay the 10 per cent dividend. The Company retained this dividend level all through its business life, when many others paid no dividend, and some even went bankrupt. In 1927, the Company paid an additional 20 per cent special dividend. In the middle of the nation's hardest depression, Den-en Toshi Company was a miracle.

This high level of dividend reveals the nature of the Company as property business rather than as social movement. In the case of Letchworth, the Garden City Pioneer Company needed eleven years to pay the first dividend of 1 per cent, and another eight years for the 4 per cent dividend. In other words, the Japanese company started with the dividend level which it took the British company nearly twenty years to attain.

Shibusawa deserves the credit for recognizing the potential for suburban living, but one cannot overlook the impact of a 'lucky' happening—the Tokyo earthquake. At lunchtime on 1 September 1923, an earthquake of magnitude 7.9 on the Richter scale devastated Japan's capital and its environs. Over 100,000 persons were killed or lost (0.9 per cent of the region's population). Nearly half a million homes were destroyed (20.4 per cent of the housing units). The earthquake and the fire it spawned levelled most of central Tokyo.

However, the Company and the Den-en Toshi inhabitants suffered very little damage. There had been about forty houses built in the Senzoku area, which at worst suffered cracked walls. Shibusawa's son, who walked through the destroyed capital to Den-en Toshi, recalls: 'In contrast to the hell-like tragedies and miseries in the City area, how beautiful Senzoku area was! Here the sun is shining over the green forest, and the birds are singing peacefully. This is heaven and that, hell'[19].

The Tokyo earthquake accelerated the suburban exodus of the upper-middle class. Suburbia became a heaven for all who could afford it. It was at this time that Den-en Toshi was on sale.

The earthquake firmly convinced the Company that the Garden City concept had been proved valid. In fact, the Company took full advantage of the time, and bought such a newspaper advertisement as:

> This formidable earthquake has proved Den-en Toshi is a safe place. From the central city to Den-en Toshi! It means to move from a cinema without an emergency exit to a huge park. It is now that we should secure the land for peaceful life which is the most important property.[20]

Business success, however, shortened the life of the Company. It was neither a developer whose activity was not limited by location nor a land-owner which rented its property. Rather it was a land subdivider of a specific place. Once all of its land in stock was sold, it had no longer had a *raison d'être;* it had obviously attained its goal. Thus, the capital of the Company was reduced from 5 to 3 million yen in January 1927, and further to 1.5 million yen in December. The Company was finally merged to its subsidiary railway Company in May 1928. In this process, the stocks of the Company were changed into those of Meguro-Kamata and Musashi Railway Companies. Thus, Japan's first and only 'garden city' company ended its ten-year life under the ever-watchful eyes of Viscount Shibusawa, then eighty-eight years old.

CONCLUSION

In concluding the story of Den-en Toshi Company Ltd., we wish to ask an important question: 'was our Den-en Toshi really a garden city in Howard's sense?' The answer is obviously 'No'.

The three areas were not three separate garden cities nor, as a whole, a single garden city. Senzoku was an ordinary subdivision estate and Ooka-yama a campus. Tamagawa-dai was an extraordinary development, but was, at most, a garden suburb. None of them was a functionally independent town, but heavily dependent upon Tokyo as the social, cultural and employment centre. Although they were all surrounded by agricultural areas, these were by no means green belts owned by the 'communities', but potential urban areas. It was this expectation which motivated landlords to sell part of their land to the Company. Thus, sprawl around Den-en Toshi was inevitable.

This development was just in accordance with landowners' 'planning'. To the Company and residents it meant an increase in the value of their land and, to the Railway Company, an increase in passengers. Everybody was happy about this sprawl.

It should be noted that the Company never intended to create a garden city in Howard's line. Shibusawa envisaged a garden city as suburban Tokyo, where rural character was still preserved. He never dreamt of an independent country town when he wrote: 'The garden city is, in short, a city with plenty of nature in it, and a town which has, by blending rural and urban characteristics, the charm of country'[21].

During his investigative trip to the United States and Europe, Shibusawa's son visited Letchworth late in 1919. He wrote: 'As it was not yet completed, there were few houses built and few people walking around. Broad front yards on both sides of the streets were covered with dead leaves. It was a lonely place where I would not dare to live'[22]. He had read such British classics as Howard's *Garden Cities of Tomorrow* and Unwin's *Town Planning in Practice,* but the actual garden city was a disappointment to him. Instead, what impressed him most were residential areas in Honolulu and San Francisco's St. Francis Wood. To young Shibusawa, the Garden City was the American suburbia of the late 1910s.

This suggests that the whole idea of 'garden city' was taken very loosely by many people, especially by those outside Britain, so that it was used to describe almost anything. This ambiguity seems to be one of the reasons why the Garden City idea became well known all over the world. In other words, what was transmitted from Britain to other countries was often the *word,* not the *concept,* of the Garden City. The original idea was often misunderstood and sometimes intentionally misunderstood by developers who knew 'garden city' was an attractive catchword in the suburban market.

While this private business was going on, the City Planning Act was enacted in 1919. But it provided the Company hardly any planning control or public assistance. Public planning was basically concerned with providing urban centres with streets and other infrastructures, while in the suburbs a private company was building a 'garden city' with an environmental quality that the statutory planning could not attain. The two are totally unrelated. It was ironic that the absence of public planning, complemented by private business, resulted in the far better environment.

There were, however, several limitations to what the Company was doing. First, it never became a social movement for a better urban environment like Howard's Garden City Association. Instead, it remained as a self-help movement by the upper-middle class. Second, it demonstrated and, indeed, popularized suburban living, but it never questioned the problem of continuous metropolitan growth. It was concerned about how to solve housing and environmental problems and not about the social and political problems which caused those problems. Third, it demonstrated that cheap land away from the urban areas could be turned into an expensive commodity, especially if a new railway was built. This combination of land development and railway business has become a typical large-scale suburban development pattern in Japan. Thus, the increase in land value, or British 'betterment', often goes into the hands of developer-railway companies, and not of the government.

It would be unfair to ask so much of Den-en Toshi Co., which was after all a private enterprise. This company was one of the cases which raised the question of residential environment for the first time in our planning history. Its 'garden city', which was in fact a garden suburb by the British definition, was hardly rivalled except possibly by the 'new towns' of Japan in the 1960s onwards.

Den-en Toshi has been submerged in the urban texture of a huge Tokyo-Yokohama metropolis, just like Hampstead Garden Suburb in London and Forest Hills Gardens in New York City. Yet the unique street pattern of Den-en Chofu remains a witness to the forgotten story of Den-en Toshi Company Ltd. (figure 6.3).

NOTES

1. A slightly different Japanese version of this paper is: Watanabe, Shun-ichi (1977) 'Nihonteki Den-en Toshi Ron no Kenkyu (1): Den-en Toshi Kabushiki Gaisha (1918–28) no Baai. *Nihon Toshi Keikaku Gakkai Gakujutsu Kenkyu Happyokai Ronbunshu* (City Planning Institute of Japan), No. 12 pp. 151–156 (in Japanese).

2. Yano, Ichiro, President of Den-en Chofu Kai (1959) Den-en Chofu no Yurai (The Origin of Den-en Chofu).

3. *Den-en Toshi,* literally 'countryside city' has been established as a Japanese term for 'garden city'.

4. The first time the phrase 'garden city' was used was Tamagawa Den-en Toshi Project (16 ha) (developed by Tokyo Shintaku Co. on the outskirts of Tokyo in 1913) which was merely a subdivision development.

5. Eiichi Shibusawa's writings are collected in Shibusawa Eiichi Denki Shiryo Kanko-kai (ed.) (1955–65) *Shibusawa Eiichi Denki Shiryo.* (68 vols), Tokyo: Shibusawa Eiichi Denki Shiryo Kanko-kai. A huge collection of the materials related to his activities are preserved at Ryumon-sha (Shibusawa Seien Memorial Foundation), Nishigahara 2-16-37, Kita-ku, Tokyo.

6. Shibusawa, Eiichi, (1937) *Shibusawa Eiichi Jiden.* Tokyo, p. 953, pp. 966–7.

7. Shibusawa Eiichi Denki Shiryo Kanko-kai (ed.) (1955–65) *Shibusawa Eiichi Denki Shiryo,* Vol. 53. Tokyo, p. 352; 'Diary' dated May 12, 1915.

8. Sugimoto, Kan-ichi (ed.) (1942) *Tokyo-Yokohama Dentetsu Enkaku-shi* Tokyo: Tokyu Dentetsu Co., pp. 5–9.

9. Articles of Incorporation, Article 3, as reconstructed from Shibusawa Eiichi Denki Shiryo Kanko-kai (ed.) (1955–65) *Shibusawa Eiichi Denki Shiryo, op. cit.,* Vol. 53. Tokyo, pp. 360–2.

10. Sugimoto, Kan-ichi (ed.) (1942) *Tokyo-Yokohama Dentetsu Enkaku-shi.* Tokyo: Tokyu Dentetsu Co., pp. 10–12.

11. Calculated from *ibid.*, pp. 12–13, and *Den-en Toshi Kabushiki Gaisha Eigyo Hokoku-sho* (Business Report of Den-en Toshi Co., Ltd.), No. 1 (September 1918 to May 1919) to No. 6 (June to November 1921).

12. *Ibid.*, pp. 25–26. In addition to these three areas, some 54,400 tsubo (18 ha) of land in Shinmaruko and Hiyoshidai Areas in Kanagawa Prefecture was developed jointly with Tokyu Dentetsu Company and sold in the name of Den-en Toshi Company.

13. *Den-en Toshi Kabushiki Gaisha Eigyo Hokoku-sho,* No. 7 (December 1921 to May 1922), p. 7.

14. Shibusawa, Hideo (1971) *Waga Machi.* Tokyo: Ensen Shinbun-sha, p. 24.

15. Tokyu Fudosan Co. (ed.) (1973) *Machi Zukuri 50 Nen.* Tokyo: Tokyu Fudosan Co., p. 23.

16. Miki, Yonosuke (1955) *Goto Keita.* Tokyo: Toyo Shokan, p. 58.

17. (1923) *Den-en Toshi Annai.* Tokyo: Den-en Toshi Co., p. 11.

18. These dates, though having some ambiguity, are based upon Tokyu Fudosan Company (ed.) (1973) *Machi Zukuri 50 Nen.* Tokyo: Tokyu Fudosan Co., p. 24.

19. Shibusawa, Hideo (1971) *Waga Machi.* Tokyo: Ensen Shinbun-sha, p. 25.

20. The Company's advertisement in *Jiji Shimpo* 28 October 1923, as shown in Tokyu Fudosan Company (ed.) (1973) *Machi Zukuri 50 Nen.* Tokyo: Tokyu Fudosan Co., p. 30.

21. Shibusawa, Eiichi (1937) *Shibusawa Eiichi Jiden.* Tokyo, p. 952 as quoted in Sugimoto, Kan-ichi (ed.) (1942) *Tokyo-Yokohama Dentetsu Enkaku-shi.* Tokyo: Tokyu Dentetsu Co., pp. 3–4.

22. Shibusawa, Hideo (1971) *Waga Machi.* Tokyo: Ensen Shinbun-sha, p. 6.

7

Town planning in Germany: change and continuity under conditions of political turbulence[1]

GERD ALBERS

Leonardo Benevolo sees the beginning of modern town planning—that is to say town planning in the industrial society—between 1830 and 1850 in Britain and France, the industrially most advanced countries of that time[2]. In Germany, industrial development was somewhat retarded, but here, too, the year 1840 was considered by the German historian Heinrich von Treitschke as a turning point:

> Around 1840, along with factories and stock exchanges, railroads and newspapers, life in Germany began to be affected by the class struggles, the unrest and the enterprising spirit of modern economics. Until then, the majority of the people had been residing in the small-town customs of the first peaceful years, settled on inherited ground, quietly busy in traditional crafts, contented with the modest comfort of the unadorned home[3].

an idyllic picture indeed not unlike the scenes of a romanticist painter.

Germany in 1840 was a politically-diversified landscape: the German Federation, founded in 1815 and comprising nearly forty member states of different types and sizes. In 1866, with the Prussian-Austrian war, that Federation broke apart and five years later, the German Reich—without Austria—was founded. By that time, the first problems arising from rapid urbanization had made themselves felt. The town planning competition of 1857 for the area of the former fortifications in Vienna had received much attention in Germany. In the rapidly growing Prussian capital, Berlin, a street plan had been drawn up, between 1858 and 1862, under the auspices of the

145

police president, designed to accommodate four million people—compared with less than half a million inhabitants at that time[4]. That this should have been a task for the police was more logical than we would think today; if there was, in the liberal state, a justification for interfering with the rights of private property, it was the need to avert danger from the general public— fire hazards, inadequate access, lack of sanitation—and this was traditionally seen as the responsibility of the police.

Consequently, town planning was a matter of the building police authority being a part of the state administration, until, around 1870, several German states transferred the responsibility for statutory planning of streets and building lines to local authorities, while retaining the right to regulate all matters of building.

The 1870s also saw the first important publications referring to town planning: a sophisticated criticism of the Berlin plan by the statistician Bruch (1870); an ardent plea for more open space and better housing for workers, indeed for more social responsibility in town development, by the Countess Dohna-Poninski under the *nom de plume* 'Arminius' (1874); and the first expert's book on urban extension and town planning by Baumeister (1876), Professor of Civil Engineering at Karlsruhe[5].

At the same time, rapid economic and demographic expansion made for increased urbanization with an aggravation of housing problems which had been deplored and criticized ever since the 1850s. So, it was tendencies toward improved housing on the one hand, the engineering tasks of street building, sanitation and the provision of public utilities on the other, which constituted the first motivations for town planning, soon to be supplemented by the architect's concern with urban form. Among local authority officials, there was a growing recognition that the obvious deficiencies of expanding cities—lack of open space, mixture of incompatible uses, exaggerated residential densities—called for better planning instruments. So, in the 1880s and 1890s, the tool of zoning was developed—the differentiation of use areas by local statutes based on state enabling legislation.

The books by Sitte (1889) and Stübben (1890) established the term *'Städtebau'* (town building) for what had been called before somewhat narrowly *'Stadterweiterung'* (town extension), and promoted the development of general principles in town planning[6]. Fritsch (1896) published the first structural concept of a new town[7].

The first decade of the twentieth century brought a number of important new developments in town planning: the establishment of a 'Deutsche Gartenstadtgesellschaft' in 1902 under the impact of Howard's ideas; the foundation of the first periodical—*Der Städtebau*—by Sitte and Goecke (1904); the first exhibitions referring to town planning (Dresden 1903, Berlin 1910). Developments in Britain were observed with close attention; Howard's *Garden Cities* was published in translation in 1907, Unwin's *Town Planning in Practice* in 1910, only one year after its appearance in Britain, with a title revealingly mistranslated as *Grundlagen des Städtebaues*[8]. In fact, the interest was a mutual one; in 1904 Horsfall published *The Example of Germany* with special regard to the role of German municipalities in town planning, and personalities like Geddes and Nettlefold visited German cities for more detailed information[9]. It was also in 1910 that the term *'Planung'* was used for the first time in the title of a German publication—shortly after 'planning' had come into general use in the English language[10].

Most of the initiatives of this time did not bear fruit until after the First World War in an atmosphere which was characterized by a strange combination of political instability and economic scarcity on the one hand, and the promise of a new beginning in the recently created republic on the other. The early 1920s saw a considerable number of town planning publications; the Weimar Republic did much to promote a progressive housing policy, and in a number of major cities we find remarkable planning and housing achievements, which won international recognition.

Most of this was achieved with rather modest legal tools; preparations for transforming the new approach to planning into law led to very few palpable results—probably due to the political instability and the hectic succession of cabinets. Some of these preparations, however, influenced the few laws and ordinances enacted under National Socialist rule. Although, at that time, planning and building activities experienced a revival after the nearly complete stagnation during the Great Depression, actual results were rather ambiguous and heterogeneous due to many divergent forces; at least in the field of town planning, the Third Reich had no consistent policy. National planning in the sense of coordinated space allocation on supra-regional scale made some headway by the establishment of a Reich Office, which was created mainly to coordinate space demands for public, especially military, purposes but came to serve also more general goals.

After the war, shortage of materials and lack of any long-range perspective obstructed planning and development for the first few years. Because of urgent reconstruction problems, the states enacted Reconstruction Laws around 1949 which were largely based on considerations developed between the wars. Most of the rebuilding followed the lines established before 1933, embodying the tenets of the Athens Charter, and it was not until 1960 that a revaluation of these principles took place. By that time, the main lines for reconstruction of city centres and other built-up areas had been fixed, and many additional developments on virgin ground had been added at the outskirts of the cities. In 1960, the Federal Town and Country Planning Act (*Bundesbaugesetz*) superseded the state laws; soon enough, problems of urban renewal made themselves felt, which called for additional legal instruments and, in 1971, led to the enactment of a law on urban renewal and development[11].

The 1960s were characterized by a new situation: planning had come to be accepted as an important tool to guide development, whereas before it had been considered by most people as just a necessary evil for the period of rebuilding. Along with this came a new excitement with the dense and lively urban atmosphere and a somewhat naive extrapolation of economic growth and technological progress toward the fascinating year 2000. Meanwhile, the crest of this wave has passed; we find ourselves confronted with new problems of restricted economic development, of a shrinking population, and of a widespread scepticism with respect to change, with concomitant changes in planning priorities.

IDEOLOGICAL BACKGROUND AND GOALS OF PLANNING

This rough sketch of the general development is meant to serve as a frame of reference for the subsequent discussion of three special aspects. First of all, it seems necessary to look behind the events presented so far, to search into what we might call the climate of planning, the ideological background by which it was influenced, as well as the goals and objectives which were pursued in any given period.

As in other European countries, so also in Germany was the rise of the industrial city and of what Louis Wirth later called 'the urban way of life' observed with some scepticism. To be sure, the town had a good reputation since the time of the 'free imperial cities' of the Middle Ages, which was seen as a period of a flourishing urban civilization characterized by common faith, successful communal efforts, and remarkable cultural achievements. But on the other hand, there was also a strong current of thought favouring country life and regarding the city, especially the large city, as the source of many evils. The cultural historian Wilhelm Heinrich Riehl had warned against city growth around the middle of the century: 'Europe is sickened by the bigness of her big cities[12]'. Bismarck did not like the cities where he 'did not find the genuine Prussian people'[13], and the sociologist Simmel described and analysed, around the turn of the century, the urban scene and the specific behaviour of the urbanite in a very critical way[14]. But Simmel's essay was a contribution to a book which was published in connection with a city exhibition and contained many other articles in praise of the city—'paving the way toward an ascending, truly social, cultural development', as the editor called them[15].

Indeed, the climate of town planning had been strongly influenced by the belief in continuing progress, with only minor frictions to be solved by planning, or 'town regulation', as one used to say. But slowly, the confidence in the positive results of unbridled development, in progress through *laissez-faire,* was shrinking; the arguments of critics and reformers received more and more attention. By the turn of the century, the emphasis in town planning had shifted from technical matters to questions of urban design, under the impact of Camillo Sitte's book, and to the social side of planning which manifested itself mainly in problems of housing. 'Order' came to be an important goal, and obviously a correspondence was seen between visual and functional order of the city on the one hand, and its social order on the other. The planner was supposed to be concerned with both aspects; even if his tools were directed merely toward spatial objectives, they were to be applied with a sense of social responsibility. This was clearly expressed by Fritz Schumacher, an outstanding German town planner of the first half of this century who, in summarizing retrospectively, remarked that in this first decade of the twentieth century, town planning in the eyes of architects and planners won a new dimension: 'before it could be considered in terms of art, it had to be considered in terms of decency[16]'.

Here, too, we find some parallels to, perhaps direct influences of, British and North American developments. In his report on the 1910 town planning exhibition in Berlin—in the same year as the famous London exhibition— Werner Hegemann, who had been exposed for some time to the American approach to city planning, gave special emphasis to a quotation from the American Benjamin Marsh: 'No city is more healthy than the highest death rate in any ward or block, no city is more beautiful than its most unsightly tenement. The back yard of a city and not its front lawn is the real criterion for its standard and its efficiency'[17]. And five years later, Martin Wagner—in the 1920s to become chief planner for Berlin and still later professor at M.I.T.—chose as the motto for his doctoral dissertation a quotation from Muirhead (unfortunately without exact indication of the source): 'The problem of the generation was to provide gas and water; the problem of the next is to provide light and air'[18].

At the beginning of the new century, the first results of what might be called urban science reached the consciousness of the planners; demographic research, sociological interpretations, economic studies of the city contributed to a new understanding of the town which could offer a point of departure for planning. Socio-economic developments as a basis for urban growth or change came to be more clearly envisaged and forecast; planning was expected to provide a framework in which the forces of society and economy could be accommodated.

In contrast to the rather passive attitude towards urban growth prevalent in the nineteenth century, we observe now the aspiration to influence not only the pattern of urban extension but also the settlement structure as a whole— up to the idea of the complete dissolution of the big city. It may be that this thought has been advocated in Germany with more zeal than elsewhere; the aversion to the big city and the plea for 'resettlement' in small towns had a certain tradition in Germany, but only after Hitler's rise to power did it receive some official sanction, although one cannot really speak of something like a consistent National Socialist settlement policy to this end[19].

After the last war, we find a mixture of ideological elements in German planning—even when leaving the development in the Soviet zone out of consideration. In the Federal Republic, the aversion to the big city persisted; deglomeration—*Entballung*—was still an important word in the vocabulary of regional and national planning. The family home, considered as the ideal form of residential accommodation by the reformists of the nineteenth century, by progressive planners of the 1920s like Ernst May, as well as by the National Socialists, received special attention in legal and financial provisions; its promotion was one of the very few substantive goals expressly mentioned in the Federal Town Planning Act of 1960.

Most other goal formulations are very general and lend themselves to a broad range of interpretations. Taken as a whole, the 1960 Act stands at the end of the period indicated above: a period marked by the notion that planning has to provide for the spatial requirements of society and economy, the evolution of which is seen largely as an autonomous process.

Meanwhile, this notion has given way to the conviction that planning should not be limited to purely spatial or physical matters but that it should encompass other aspects of society and economy which are open to goal-oriented human action. Thus, whereas the goal of planning in the first half of the century could be defined as *Daseinsvorsorge* (verbatim, provision for existence), it shifted after 1960 to a more complex group of goals intricately interwoven with political decision-making. So, it is no accident that the amendment to the Federal Planning Act restates the central goals of planning in a specific way[20]. Besides the 'ordered development' of the environment which had been mentioned already in the 1960 Act, two more points were added: a land use consistent with social justice, and an environment in keeping with human dignity. Both terms are very general, but they do indicate a basic change in planning philosophy: from a restrictive action of local government directed solely toward the property-owners—who were seen as the only partners of the authority, since they alone seemed directly concerned—we have now arrived at the notion of a public responsibility to shape the environment to the benefit of all citizens, property-owners or not. And to identify such benefit is no longer seen as the task of the expert, the administrator, the planner; instead, public participation both in goal definition and in the procedure of realization is considered indispensable. To be sure, this change was not an abrupt one; it has been prepared slowly, by small steps, through modifications in the general understanding of planning, modifications which seem to occur more or less contemporaneously in a number of industrially-advanced countries.

A final observation on ideological change: for the planner, at least since the turn of the century, 'new development' had been associated with better development, better architecture, better planning, and after the middle of the century, the term 'change' had assumed the status of a panacea—change being considered naturally change to the better. But for the last few years, environmental change has been received with scepticism, if not open antagonism. Conservation has won considerable public support through this phenomenon, and the success of Architectural Heritage Year 1975 is hardly understandable unless we assume that there was already a strong disposition in that direction. This has, of course, to do with immediate energy shortage, imminent exhaustion of natural resources and wide-spread economic problems—but there may be a more basic and lasting tendency behind it. This will be for the researchers of the next generation to find out.

LEGAL DEVELOPMENT

At the root of legal aspects, we find the question as to what degree the property-owner can be expected to restrict his choice as to the utilization of his land, and has to conform to decisions by the local authority on that matter. The general attitude prevalent in the nineteenth century is well expressed by a paragraph in a Prussian law of 1794:

> As a rule, every owner is entitled to erect buildings on his ground or to modify his buildings. But to the detriment or to the unsafety of the common weal or to the defacement of town and public places, no buildings and no modification shall be undertaken.[21]

Averting 'detriment and unsafety' was the task of the police which were under the direction of the state, and one could say that planning legislation in the present sense of the word started around the year 1870 with a number of building lines Acts (*Fluchtliniengesetze*) in several German states. These regulations enabled local authorities at the city and community level to fix building lines and thus to determine the location of streets and building sites, then largely synonymous with public and private land.

At that time, and for most of the rest of the century, the use of the land was determined by the market, and the case for public intervention into this process seemed to be very small. But by the turn of the century, the institution of local zoning ordinances (*Staffelbauordnungen*) had come to be an accepted tool of planning. At about the same time, the need became apparent for a plan which was to be more comprehensive in spatial terms as well as more flexible in legal terms than the statutory plan. Thus, the concept of a general land-use plan was born, similar to the 'master plan' concept in Britain and in the United States.

While generally—but not in all German states—town planning, by state enabling legislation, had come to be a matter of local responsibility, the density of land use—lot coverage, floor space index, distance between buildings—continued to be regulated by state building ordinances. They allowed, during most of the nineteenth century, a very high degree of exploitation—up to a floor-space index of 5 and to net population densities of more than 1000 inhabitants per hectare. Beginning with the last decades of the nineteenth century, however, these upper limits were gradually reduced in the different states by amendments of building ordinances, mainly for hygienic and social reasons. In Prussia, instruments for planning were considerably improved by the *Preußisches Wohnungsgesetz* (Habitation Act) of 1918; enacted during the war and thus under the monarchy, it was a law beyond which the Prussian republic of the Weimar years did not advance.

In the 1920s, the control of land was achieved partly by local statutory plans and partly by the more general state ordinances with the consequence of an uneasy dualism of local and state powers. Another dualism existed between state and Reich (later federal) competences to establish the legal framework of town planning. Since planning legislation, for a long time, had been considered to be an outgrowth of building legislation, it was vested originally in the states and was handled with varying degrees of efficiency; the best coordinated and most progressive planning act of its time was that of Saxony (then kingdom) of 1900. In the 1920s, the need for comprehensive legal regulations was apparent, but neither in Prussia nor in the Reich were the drafts for planning laws enacted. Under National Socialist rule, with legislative powers centralized at the level of the Reich, work on legislation continued and a draft was finished in the early 1940s, but was not enacted due to the war situation. It is known, moreover, that Hitler did not care for such a law but tended to rely much more on *ad hoc* decisions. It is interesting to note that this 1940s draft is almost a direct continuation of the predictatorship legal developments. Indications of National Socialist ideology are hardly discernible apart from a more or less decorative use of current phraseology in the more general statements.

Some of this preparatory work entered into the reconstruction laws (*Aufbaugesetze*) of the postwar *Länder* (in the majority newly created), most of which were based on a model law cooperatively drafted by experts from different states. In general, these laws display an obvious continuity with former legal regulations, the main difference being a stronger emphasis on instruments for land assembly, for example through the right of pre–emption. This was due to the urgent need for reconstruction and the desire to achieve a more rational subdivision of land for that purpose.

Already in 1950, the first draft for a federal law was published, but deliberations took ten years, partly because more legal clarification of the competences vested in the Federation and the States was required, so that the law was not enacted until 1960. In its main points, it follows closely the lines which had been developed over roughly one hundred years. Again it was the local community which had the right to draw up plans, subject only to legal control by the state. The two kinds of plans, developed around the turn of the century, appeared again: the land-use plan indicating the intentions of the local authority for the future use of land, and the development plan (*Bebauungsplan*) as a legally binding statute. It should be made clear to British readers that the German statutory plan was stricter than the British one; building and planning permission was nothing more than the statement of the public authority that public law contains no obstacles to the realization of the project. That is to say that the range of discretion was very limited; once a certain development was indicated in a plan, any project complying with legal regulations was bound to be permitted. This led to less flexibility compared with Britain in that statutory planning manifests itself in the first place as the distribution of rights and restrictions which establish a legal position for the owner and are therefore rather difficult to change.

This fairly elaborate law does not offer any provision for the solution of the problem of compensation and betterment, although the first draft did contain a scheme not unlike that of the 1947 Act in Britain (since partly repealed). But it had been dropped during the deliberations—obviously also under the impression of what appeared as a failure of that system in Britain. A first attempt towards the solution of this problem is contained in the Urban Renewal Act of 1971 which excludes rises in value based solely on the expectation of renewal or development. This Act offers a number of tools to facilitate more positive planning, and most of them have been taken over into the amendment of the Federal Town and Country Planning Act of 1976. Whereas the 1960 Act really did not go very far beyond the state of thinking achieved around 1930, both the 1976 amendment and the Renewal Act of 1971 represent a somewhat new approach to planning law—in line with the changes in the ideological climate of planning discussed in the preceding section.

PRINCIPLES OF PLANNING

Turning now to the evolution of planning principles, we might distinguish between those referring to planning procedure and those concerned with the content of planning, with the actual concepts of physical development, which again could be divided into concepts for land-use patterns and those for the shape and the arrangement of buildings; we might speak of urban structure and of urban form, respectively. Both these physical aspects received early attention in German literature: Baumeister saw the future city composed of three main elements differentiated by land use: the business centre, the residential area and the industrial area, and he discussed at length the possible systems for street networks, but mainly under the aspect of function, without consideration of aesthetic components[22]. Sitte concentrated on design, especially on the qualities of urban space in streets and squares, and his formal preferences are clearly opposed to the then current street patterns which were still vaguely reminiscent of the system developed in Haussmann's Paris. Nevertheless, there is an important similarity: both approaches put space first and regarded the buildings basically under the aspect of limiting and defining space. Stübben can be said to occupy an intermediate position, although he is closer in approach and outlook to Baumeister than to Sitte[23].

The first concept of an organized land-use structure in the form of an abstract model was published by Theodor Fritsch in 1896, two years before Howard's Garden City diagram in *To-morrow*. There are similarities, although—as it seems to be accepted today—both authors worked independently of each other. Both start from a concentric arrangement of the town with a spacious, representative central area and the places of employment at the periphery. Fritsch, in contrast to Howard's more egalitarian concept, advocated a use pattern mirroring the class society. But he gave much thought to the arrangement of open space for public use[24].

It is probably safe to say that the provision of open spaces was the first generally accepted structural goal for town planning in the late nineteenth century on both sides of the Atlantic, as the park system of Chicago and other American cities show. In contrast to the concept of green belts common in Britain, most German contributions to land-use patterns were characterized by the introduction of green wedges between building areas, forming these into ribbons extended along either side of a public transport line and/or traffic artery.

Such a system obviously allowed for more flexibility in growth, and one might consider the linear city as a concept in which this principle is carried to the extreme. But notwithstanding some interest in such new solutions both rational and radical, the centre of attention in actual planning was the development and the transformation of the existing city. The need for transformation was undisputed after the experiences with what .Mumford later called the paleotechnic city, and unchallenged also were some mutually supporting goals of such a transformation:

A more even distribution of densities, suppressing the multi-storey tenement building with narrow backyards—the rental barrack, as the literal translation of the derogatory German term would run—and promoting the two-storey house, mainly in terraced form to save ground.

A higher proportion of open space penetrating from the open landscape right to the heart of the built-up area.

A visual as well as functional separation of clearly discernible urban quarters which, at the same time, was considered as a precondition for better social coherence, counteracting the 'anonymity' in the big city.

A clear separation of different uses, in the first place a separation of industrial from residential quarters.

This might be considered as the basic consensus arrived at during the 1920s (its close relationship to the tenets of the Athens Charter is obvious) which in practice was not changed in any important sense during National Socialist rule. The neighbourhood unit played an important part in structural considerations, and it is not without irony that this concept seemed to lend itself to the objectives of totalitarian systems because it offered a clear hierarchy and facilitated control on each level, while in the United States the neighbourhood unit was advocated as the basis for face-to-face interaction among citizens, protecting them against totalitarian temptations[25].

These principles, with the neighbourhood unit given particular attention due to the emphasis attributed to it in American planning, also guided the main considerations for reconstruction after World War II. Up to the end of the 1950s, a widespread consensus in this respect persisted, and if some critic felt that the opportunities provided by wartime destruction had not been sufficiently utilized, he would have liked to see rather a more stringent application of these principles instead of the many compromises which property rights and the legal and financial obstacles forced upon planners.

And what about urban form in this period? Sitte's followers made some inroads into the prevailing mode of the 'surveyor's plan' and—at least in theory—dominated the scene well beyond the turn of the century with what Le Corbusier later termed sneeringly 'the religion of the donkeys' path'[26], i.e. with curved streets, closed vistas, small-scale building elements conjuring up the spatial sequences of medieval towns. All this blended very nicely with eclecticism and its predilection for what was believed to be the German Middle Ages, although there were also counter-forces favouring the 'grand design' elements of baroque and classicism[27]. But regardless of such differences, aesthetic considerations soon took second place after a growing social concern in planning, as explained before. It was no longer street and square only that counted, it was the backyard as well and it was the building with its ground plan and its orientation.

Influences from Britain worked in the same sense: the principles of garden city or garden suburb layout received much attention as well as the advantages of the English country house advocated by Muthesius[28]. Through the *Jugendstil* (the German version of Art Nouveau), the *Deutscher Werkbund* and other influences, the ground was prepared for a radical change in design concepts. This change came into the open after World War I—with the *Bauhaus* and the *'Neues Bauen'* (the German term consciously avoids the word 'architecture' for its aesthetic connotation; it could probably be best translated by 'new way of building'). The corridor street was dissolved; parallel rows of buildings (*Zeilenbau*) with access streets at right-angles came to dominate the scene. What later appeared as the loss of the street as enclosed space was at that time obviously seen as an aesthetic enrichment. On the other hand, to quite a number of opponents, the *Neues Bauen* appeared bolshevist, the *Zeilenbau* with its egalitarian element—all dwellings to share the same orientation—was considered leftist. No wonder that these opinions gained ground with Hitler's rise to power, but their influence was stronger in architecture than in city planning, and even in architecture had some loopholes since industrial architecture was somehow exempt from ideological influences. But otherwise, the flat roof was tabooed, and although in residential planning the open plan was still pursued (no closed blocks or squares), the restriction to parallel rows were generally avoided. There was a return to courtyards, although still composed of disconnected linear buildings, and to a more outspoken definition of space. In marked contrast to the modest residential developments which in their simplest form were groups of cottages in what came to be called 'blood-and-soil' style, concepts for the transformation of some German cities under Hitler had the air of an arid classicist monumentalism on a very ambitious and extravagant scale, but remained mostly on paper.

Postwar planning in Germany, of course, turned away from such attempts to demonstrate power, and even developed what might be called an allergy to axial symmetry. Rather, it sought to establish ties with the time before 1933, although the stern geometrical rigidity of some prominent designs around 1930 was no longer aimed at. Instead, we find the tendency to achieve some impressions of at least partly enclosed space by an arrangement of building rows at oblique- or right-angles. This was still in keeping with the structural goals of low density and more open space while trying to recapture some elements of what was believed to constitute an urban atmosphere.

This may roughly serve to indicate the situation around 1960 when suddenly the accepted concepts were seriously challenged. It is somewhat surprising but nevertheless true that one of the most powerful influences backing this challenge was Jane Jacobs' book, *Death and Life of Great American Cities*[29]. After all, town planning in Germany—and even more so urban renewal in Germany—was both in its achievements and in its shortcomings different from that in the United States, and although the author's analysis has its definite merits, most of her proposals for remedy are rather dubious. Obviously, there was a latent discontent which was set free by this publication.

What followed was a tendency towards much higher and more complex buildings, based on the notion that all previous planning had been basically anti-urban and had in its antithesis to the evils of the early industrial city tended to discard also the positive side of the 'urban way of life'. Higher density seemed to promise a more diversified and active urban life, more communication, and more 'urbanity', as the slogan went; the separation of functions was seen as an error depriving the city of its richness in interactions. Along with this went an added interest in new modes of transportation—the electronically-directed cabin offering door-to-door service without traffic jams, and many other promising prospects.

In urban design, this led to an additional diversity of heterogeneous forms. In the 1920s and 1930s, the only available element, besides terrace houses, had been the three- to five-storey apartment building with a depth of around 10 metres; in the 1950s, we experienced a differentiation in height, which brought together groups of buildings with a different number of storeys—eight, four and two was the common combination—whereas the 1960s confronted us with the full reaction to the geometric clarity of Mies van der Rohe and the curtain wall: an arbitrary mixture of building heights, a somewhat artificial craving for variety of forms and interesting detail.

In the meantime, most of this has proved to be a very temporary fascination. The complex structures with a delicate mixture of functions have demonstrated their weaknesses, the euphoric prospects of growth both in demographic and economic terms had to be reassessed, and planning was forced to 'bake smaller rolls'—to use a German colloquialism. High buildings, especially point blocks, have fallen from grace, and the shrinking housing market is dominated by the family home. The optimism of the 1960s belongs to the past.

If we look finally at the questions of procedure in planning, we find that they received little attention during the nineteenth century. Sitte gives a few hints in this respect, and in the first decade of this century, the planning survey was recognized as an important part of the planning process, analogous to and possibly influenced by Geddes' insistence on 'survey before plan'. The planning process, then, was seen as a sequence of survey, design of plans, and realization, which seemed to have a simple and linear relation like a mathematical equation. Not much before the 1960s, planning came to be interpreted as a process of choice among alternatives—certainly under the influence of the extended discussions on this topic in American planning theory[30]. This shed new light on the planning process: a choice among alternatives must be based on goals and values which can only be of a political nature. And the growing recognition of the complex reality with which planning interferes, leads to the search for better scientific buttressing of planning decisions. Thus, the improvement of the planning process— hopefully leading to an improvement of its results—has become a central topic of planning literature. In this context, two tendencies are visible which run, in a way, counter to each other: the hope to improve decisions through more political transparency, more public participation, more involvement of politicians, and the expectation to benefit from scientific methods, quantifi- cation, and the systems approach for better decisions. In this field, trends are clearly transgressing national borders.

CONCLUSION

We have set out to discover elements of change and of continuity in the planning history of Germany, and one might assume that the somewhat turbulent political history of that country should be reflected in such changes. But what we have seen, does not quite bear out this assumption. Of the changes affecting town planning in Germany within the time of our study, only very few can be attributed to the rather violent changes in German government structure and in political outlook. This refers, for example, to the National Socialist tendency for centralization, their (ineffective) ideology to dissolve the big cities into small towns, their predilection for large-scale, ambitious 'grand design' schemes.

In most other matters, especially in legislation, we find a high degree of continuity in spite of political changes. Where there are obvious breaks in continuous development, they have more or less exact parallels in other countries, especially in Britain and the United States, with a political history widely divergent from the German.

Are we therefore to conclude that planning is not so closely tied to politics, after all, as we have come to believe? The answer cannot be a simple yes or no—it has to be differentiated. Planning in the nineteenth and well up to the middle of the twentieth century was generally considered as a professional activity, as an art and a science dominated by the expert. The political implications, already recognized by the more perspicacious planners between the wars, were realized neither by the politicians nor by the general public at that time. This may explain that, during this period, international contacts among experts could exercise a stronger influence on prevailing concepts of planning than national political characteristics.

Moreover, socio-economic development in west and central European countries as well as in the United States showed many parallels in the last hundred years. It is understandable that, around the turn of the century, disillusionment with urban development of the nineteenth century led to quite similar reactions in countries with comparable cultural background and equal state of technological and industrial development; and it is no less understandable that the disturbing impact of the Great Depression paved the way in most countries affected to more State intervention into the free interplay of market forces and thus to more planning.

Since then, with the strengthening of political ties, intellectual exchange in the Western World has also been intensified. It is therefore not surprising that developments in the second half of this century show a high degree of interrelation between Western countries: the heavy politization—some speak already of overpolitization—of planning, the successive waves of planning euphoria and of planning misery, the quest for public participation, the faith put in scientific methods, and the trend toward conservatism and, seemingly, immobility—they all have their counterparts in other countries, although sometimes with different phasing in time. But here I am transgressing the borders of my topic—these are ongoing changes, still too close for a perspective of historical evaluation: a harvest to be reaped by future researchers.

NOTES

1. This paper has appeared in German as: Wandel und Kontinuität im deutchen Städtebau, *Städtebauwelt*, 69, 1978, pp. 426-33.
2. Benevolo, L. (1964) *Geschichte der Architektur des 19. und 20. Jahrhunderts*. München: Callwey, p. 107.
3. 'Erst um das Jahr 1840 begannen mit den Fabriken und den Börsen, den Eisenbahnen und den Zeitungen auch die Klassenkämpfe, die unstete Hast und das wagelustige Selbstgefühl der modernen Volkswirtschaft in das deutsche

Leben einzudringen. Bis dahin verharrte die Mehrheit des Volkes noch in den kleinstädtischen Gewohnheiten der ersten Friedenszeiten, seßhaft auf der väterlichen Scholle, im hergebrachten Handwerk still geschäftig, zufrieden mit den bescheidenen Genüssen des ungeschmückten Hauses'. Von Treitschke, H. *Deutsche Geschichte im 19. Jahrhundert,* as quoted by Schumacher, F. (1935) *Strömungen in deutscher Baukunst seit 1800.* Leipzig: Seemann, p. 55.

4. Hegemann, W. (1963) *Das steinerne Berlin.* Berlin, Frankfurt, Wien: Ullstein, p. 207. (First edition, 1930.)
5. Bruch, E. (1870) Berlins bauliche Zukunft und der Bebauungsplan. *Deutsche Bauzeitung,* 4, p. 71; Arminius (Adelheid Gräfin Dohna-Poninski) (1874) *Die Großstädte in ihrer Wohnungsnot und die Grundlagen einer durchgreifenden Abhilfe.* Leipzig: Duncker und Humblot; Baumeister, R. (1876) *Stadterweiterungen in technischer, baupolizeilicher und wirtschaftlicher Beziehung,* Berlin: Ernst & Korn.
6. Sitte, C. (1889) *Der Städte-Bau nach seinen künstlerischen Grundsätzen.* Wien: Graeser; Stübben, J. (1890) *Der Städtebau.* Darmstadt: Bergstraesser..
7. Fritsch, Th. (1896) *Die Stadt der Zukunft.* Leipzig: Fritsch.
8. Howard, E. (1907) *Gartenstädte in Sicht,* Jena: Diederichs; Unwin, R. (1910) *Grundlagen des Städtebaues.* Berlin: Baumgärtel.
9. Horsfall, T. C. (1904) *The Improvement of the Dwellings and Surroundings of the People: The Example of Germany.* Manchester; Geddes, P. (1950) German organization, in *Cities in Evolution.* New York: Oxford University Press (1st ed. 1915). As to Nettlefold, see Cherry, G. E. (1975) *Factors in the Origin of Town Planning in Britain: The Example of Birmingham 1905-14,* Working Paper No. 36, History of Planning Group.
10. Eberstadt, R., B. Möhring and R. Petersen (1910) *Groß-Berlin, ein Programm für die Planung der neuzeitlichen Großstadt.* Berlin.
11. Bundesbaugesetz (BBauG) 23.6.1960, *Bundesgesetzblatt* I, p. 341; Gesetz über städtebauliche Sanierungs- und Entwicklungsmaßnahmen in den Gemeinden (Städtebauförderungsgesetz – StBauFG), 27.7.1971, *Bundesgesetzblatt* I, p. 1125.
12. 'Europa wird krank an der Größe seiner Großstädte'. Riehl, W. H. (1891) *Die Naturgeschichte des deutschen Volkes als Grundlage einer deutschen Sozialpolitik,* Vol. 2. Stuttgart: Cotta, p. 102. (First edition, 1861.)
13. '... daß auch ich allerdings der Bevölkerung der großen Städte mißtraue, solange sie sich von ehrgeizigen und lügenhaften Demagogen leiten läßt, daß ich aber dort das wahre preußische Volk nicht finde'. Büchmann, G. (undated) *Geflügelte Worte und Zitatenschatz,* new ed. Zürich: Classen, p. 316.
14. Simmel, G. (1903) Die Großstädte und das Geistesleben, in Petermann, T. (ed.) *Die Großstadt.* Dresden: v. Zahn & Jaensch.
15. '... Bahnbrecher auf dem Wege einer aufwärts strebenden, wahrhaft sozialen Kulturentwicklung'. Bücher, K. (1903) Die Großstädte in Gegenwart und Vergangenheit, in *Die Großstadt, Vorträge und Aufsätze zur Städteausstellung.* Dresden: v. Zahn & Jaensch, p. 31.
16. 'Ehe es sich um Kunst handeln konnte, handelte es sich um Anstand'. Schumacher, F. (1951) *Vom Städtebau zur Landesplanung und Fragen städtebaulicher Gestaltung.* Tübingen: Wasmuth, p. 10.
17. Marsh, B. C. (1909) *An Introduction to City Planning.* New York: Marsh, p. 27. Quoted in German translation by Hegemann, W. (1911) *Der Städtebau nach den*

Ergebnissen der allgemeinen Städtebau-Ausstellung in Berlin, Vol. 1. Berlin: Wasmuth, p. 114.

18. Wagner, M. (1915) *Städtische Freiflächenpolitik.* Berlin: Heymanns.
19. See Langen, G. (1927) *Stadtplan und Wohnungsplan.* Leipzig: Hirzel; and, for a semi-official National-Socialist publication, Feder, G. (1939) *Die neue Stadt.* Berlin: Ernst & Sohn. For comparable objectives, see William Morris, Ebenezer Howard, and Frank Lloyd Wright.
20. Bundesbaugesetz (BBauG), 18.8.1976, *Bundesgesetzblatt* I, p. 2256.
21. 'In der Regel ist jeder Eigentümer, seinen Grund und Boden mit Gebäuden zu besetzen oder seine Gebäude zu verändern, wohl befugt. Doch soll zum Schaden oder zur Unsicherheit des gemeinen Wesens oder zur Verunstaltung der Städte und öffentlichen Plätze kein Bau und keine Veränderung vorgenommen werden'. *Allgemeines Landrecht für die preußischen Staaten,* 5.2. 1794, §§ 65 and 66 I 8.
22. Baumeister, R. (1876) *Stadterweiterungen in technischer, baupolizeilicher und wirtschaftlicher Beziehung.* Berlin: Ernst & Korn, p. 83.
23. Sitte, C. (1889) *Der Städte-Bau nach seinen künstlerischen Grundsätzen.* Wien: Graeser; Stübben, J. (1890) *Städtebau.* Darmstadt: Bergstraesser.
24. Fritsch, Th. (1896) *Die Stadt der Zukunft.* Leipzig: Fritsch.
25. See Dahir, J. (1947) *The Neighborhood Unit Plan.* New York: Russell Sage Foundation.
26. Le Corbusier (1929) *Der Städtebau.* Stuttgart: Deutsche Verlagsanstalt, p. 9. (Translation of (1924) *Urbanisme.* Paris: Crès.))
27. See Ostendorf, F. (1922) *Sechs Bücher vom Bauen.* Berlin: Ernst.
28. Muthesius, H. (1904/5) *Das englische Haus,* 3 vols. Berlin: Wasmuth.
29. Jacobs, J. (1961) *Death and Life of Great American Cities,* New York: Random House.
30. See Davidoff, P. and Th. Reiner (1962) A Choice Theory of Planning. *Journal of the American Institute of Planners,* 28 (2), p. 103.

8

The place of Neville Chamberlain in British town planning

GORDON E. CHERRY

By the end of the nineteenth century an influential body of opinion held to the view that social, housing and land reforms were pressing requirements for urban Britain. As part of a comprehensive programme, a sustained attack was necessary upon overcrowding, high residential densities and insanitary conditions then prevalent in major towns and cities. Out of the context of a liberal, environmentally-minded reform movement, which addressed itself to the late-Victorian and Edwardian urban crisis, town planning itself emerged and proceeded to assume a recognizable identity of its own[1]. The main influences on both the rise and subsequent development of British town planning has been sketched in general terms, but the detailed understanding of particular events, or contributions of certain individuals, often remains to be more fully examined.

In this paper I examine the place of, and the part played by, one of the lesser recognized contributors to town planning in Britain: Neville Chamberlain. The son of Joseph Chamberlain who made his mark first in Birmingham politics (crowned by a successful mayoralty of municipal reform), next in national affairs (much concerned with housing and social matters), he had a distinctive background, highly conducive to questions which the twentieth century identified as 'town planning'. He was closely associated with the powerful development of town planning practice in Birmingham just before the outbreak of World War I. He entered national politics and carried his concern for housing reform, social questions, town planning and local administration to Westminster; he became a very successful Minister of Health (then the relevant Minister for town planning affairs).

Neville Chamberlain is today largely remembered for his Prime Ministership, 1937–40, and the events leading to the onset of World War II. Although his importance obviously extends to other fields, it is still perhaps a matter of surprise to reflect that the planning historian can find him a figure of significance. But this is indeed so: full recognition of his place in town planning has been neglected. In fact he kept alive and enhanced a particularly Birmingham view of land planning and housing reform; in national circles he was a powerful advocate of the principles of environmental improvement and dispersal of city functions at a regional scale; he significantly placed 'statutory' town planning within a local authority setting of sound, orderly administration; and as Minister of Health he was a notable reforming influence.

THE BIRMINGHAM PERIOD

Chamberlain's first business involvement was in the Bahamas when he directed a sisal-growing experiment. Over a period of seven years (1890–97) this failed, after which he returned to Birmingham. He became chairman of Elliotts, manufacturers of copper, brass and yellow metal at Selly Oak, and joined Hoskins, a manufacturer of cabin berths in Bordesley. In Birmingham at this time, the city's housing and social problems were acute. The central districts had high sickness and mortality rates; the quality of the housing stock was poor; overcrowding rates were high; sanitary problems were accentuated; and environmental living conditions were deplorable. There were 40,000 back-to-back houses and 6000 courts. Ten per cent of the city's inhabitants lived more than two to a room. Until Welsh water reached Birmingham in 1904, night soil had to be carted from many thousand closets. In 1911 there were 5000 recorded cases of tuberculosis. The city of half a million people had barely 300 acres of open space. No wonder when Bishop Gore, the first Anglican Bishop of the city, and popular for his reforming drive, left the city in that year he spoke of 'a profound social discontent'[2].

But Birmingham was by no means the worst of British cities and matters were already improving. The worst of the overcrowding and high density rates had begun to decline. A recognizable process of decentralization had begun, and over 60,000 people migrated from the inner wards to the periphery in the first decade of the century. Districts in the adjoining counties of Staffordshire, Warwickshire and Worcestershire gained population, and the city's territorial expansion was inevitable. In 1891 Saltley, Balsall Heath and Harborne were added to the city, and in 1909 Quinton was incorporated. Birmingham proceeded with a major Extension Bill and in 1910 Chamberlain gave evidence at three stages of its legislative process. He favoured the idea of a Greater Birmingham, arguing that economically it was one region, that it was centralized by its University and the Education Act of 1902, and that the city and its suburbs formed one area for drainage, water, light and communications. The Bill passed through the House and received the Royal Assent: in June 1911 an area totalling more than 30,000 acres was added to a city which formerly totalled less than 13,500. Birmingham's rateable value nearly doubled, its population rose to 840,000 and its Council expanded from 72 to 120 members. Chamberlain declared his interest in serving on this new Council and, as a Liberal Unionist, was duly elected as second of three councillors for All Saints Ward. His election address dwelt on town planning and open spaces, the need for more technical education and the redevelopment of canals.

At local election meetings his policies ran on these lines:

> Those who advocated the extension of the city boundaries did not do so because it would be wiser to be bigger ... it was better government and not bigness that they were after ...
> They wanted a forward and progressive policy. They wanted to tackle some of those social problems on which the happiness of the people so largely depended ... What they had to do to distinguish themselves from other towns was to set a new example in town planning. In that word he included for the moment housing, because although the improvement of houses in the old city was in one sense not a part of a town planning scheme, the great objects were the same, the health and happiness of the people.[3]

Chamberlain became an alderman within three years, and by the time he was lord mayor (within four) he had made his first distinctive town planning contribution. His immediate concerns were with regard to health, housing and town planning—and their interrelationships—and he was a natural incumbent of the chair of the city's first Town Planning Committee in November 1911. This was the successor to the prototype Town Planning Committee of the General Purposes Committee, set up in February 1910. He immediately appointed three subcommittees, two of which allowed for the continuation of the work begun by his cousin John Nettlefold as chairman of the City's first Housing Committee in respect of town expansion plans; the other was to develop a new and wider town planning remit. Councillor George Cadbury (Jr.) chaired the subcommittee for the Quinton and Harborne Scheme and Alderman Aston chaired that for East Birmingham; Councillor James chaired the General Survey Subcommittee.

The idea of town expansion plans had been Nettlefold's[4]. He had been particularly impressed by what he had seen in Germany and by T. C. Horsfall's advocacy for town extension plans as prepared for German municipalities. The Housing, Town Planning etc. Act, 1909, gave permissive powers to local authorities to prepare town planning schemes, and Birmingham, first under Nettlefold's and then Chamberlain's enthusiastic embrace, proceeded to prepare them in greater number than any other local authority in the country. Nettlefold's philosophy was that the function of the local authority was to facilitate land assembly through these plans, to provide the main services and lines of communication, to harmonize an acceptable form of low-density building operations, and to provide cheap public transport. It was argued that this approach would materially contribute to meeting the city's housing problem. Chamberlain's policy was to embark on a vigorous programme of scheme preparation in support of this philosophy. In this way a number of very important suburban expansions were directed in ways not previously attempted: the alignments and widths of main roads were safeguarded; land was reserved for open spaces; land uses were reserved for particular purposes; the number of houses per acre was restricted; and building plans were carefully controlled.

Four principal schemes were prepared under Chamberlain. The Quinton, Harborne and Edgbaston Scheme covered 2320 acres in the west of the city. The first scheme in the country to receive the approval of the then Local Government Board, it provided for residential development, without factories, but with open spaces, the whole unified and tied in with adjoining areas with ring and radial roads. The East Birmingham Scheme on the other hand provided for an industrial area of 1673 acres, traversed by three main railway lines. The North Yardley Scheme also in the east of the city covered 3164 acres in a completely rural area, isolated by lack of good road communications. The South Birmingham Scheme was a mixed area of 8400 acres, largely residential but with a northern industrial zone and some factories in the south-west. All this was excellent progress and gave confidence to those who saw the statutory device of the town planning scheme as a most useful form of suburban land management whereby orderly urban expansion might be obtained.

But Chamberlain's own views on the emergent field of town planning did not stop with statutory regulation. In his eyes, town planning came to represent a convenient, pragmatic framework for wider action in respect of housing improvement and environmental management by a munificent local council, namely Birmingham. As he remarked on his election as lord mayor, he hoped that

he might bring the influence and authority of the Lord Mayoralty to bear upon that noble and fascinating ideal, the transference of the working classes from their hideous and depressing surroundings to cleaner, brighter and more wholesome dwellings in the still uncontaminated country which lay within our boundaries ... Among the many crimes which lay heavy on the head of the German Emperor and his advisers not the least was that by their wicked ambitions they had stayed the march of progress and had set back for an indefinite period reforms that might have bettered the lot of generations to come.[5]

Through town planning those reforms might still be achieved.

His grasp of the situation led him to adopt positions beyond those of most of his contemporaries, advancing the frontiers of local government initiatives. Take for example the question of land acquisition. In Birmingham the Calthorpe Estate at Edgbaston and Cadbury at Bournville had shown the unique benefits of common landownership for satisfactory harmony of development. Chamberlain acknowledged this (although he finally drew back from the logic of municipal land ownership):

A great many of the difficulties and much of the expense which is at present involved in town planning would be avoided if the land belonged to the Corporation. The allocation of sites, the direction of streets, the density of houses to the acre—all these points are often thwarted and checked in town planning, because we find that what would be best for the community would involve injustice or hardship to individuals.[6]

The Town Planning Committee's General Survey Sub-Committee promoted Chamberlain's wider vision. It soon recommended town planning for the whole of the extended city: one 'skeleton plan' which gave 'a general settled policy with regard to open spaces, radial roads, and ring roads and the division of districts into residential, business and factory areas'[7]. In fact this one plan had to be approached piecemeal through the schemes mentioned above, but it was rapid conceptual progress, which no other local authority in Britain could begin to match. Early in 1912, the city surveyor reported a complement of seventeen staff engaged on town planning work, and the growth of activity necessitated the appointment of a plans sub-committee in October 1913 to deal with plans deposited for buildings in areas covered by schemes.

But in the meantime, the housing problem in the older parts of the city was slow to ease. In 1913, Chamberlain himself took on the chairmanship of a committee appointed to investigate the housing conditions of the city's poor and to review past policies in administering the Housing Acts. This was work which revealed him at his best: a patient collector of evidence, a sharp, succinct report writer, realistic in policy, incremental but determined in reform. The evidence showed that the quality of the city's housing stock was depressingly poor: there were 43,366 back-to-back houses, and 27,518 dwellings situated in courtyards; 42,000 properties had no water supply inside the dwelling and 58,028 had no separate toilet facilities. Chamberlain's report laconically commented in the language of the time, that 'a large proportion of the poor in Birmingham are living under conditions of housing detrimental both to their health and morals'[8].

The report went on to illustrate the way in which the device of town planning might be a framework within which housing and environmental improvement might be effected. Chamberlain urged 'a gradual reconstruction of the old city on better lines' done to a 'prearranged and carefully thought out plan'. He explained:

it must be remembered that the process of demolition and reconstruction of all kinds of buildings, factories, offices, shops and warehouses, as well as dwelling houses, is going on continually, and even now without any compulsory powers it would often be possible to induce owners to modify their schemes if there were such a plan of a reconstructed City in existence. Such a plan would not only show amended street lines, but would also differentiate the quarters which should be allocated to various classes of buildings and should make proper provision for the requisite open spaces. It would only be an ideal plan, and would doubtless have to be modified from time to time, yet it would be an ideal to which we might generally draw nearer and it would serve as a guide to the Council in many of the problems of transit, street widening, provision of public buildings and other matters with which they now have to deal separately and without regard to the City as a whole.

In the evolution of the rudiments of comprehensive city land-use planning this resolve in 1914 must be seen as a remarkable advance, building as it did on the virtually single-handed experience of town extension schemes. Ten years of pioneering effort, far ahead of the field, had put Birmingham into a notable position of planning thought and practice. The report concluded: 'The Committee attach considerable importance to the preparation of a Town Plan to include the whole built-up area of the city, and they recommend the Council to give instructions to the Town Planning Committee to put the work in hand immediately'.

Chamberlain was a tireless spokesman for town planning. Amongst his astonishing range of other commitments, ranging from housing reform to inland waterways and the ultimate development of the Birmingham Municipal Bank (the first Municipal Savings Bank in the country), opened in 1916, he successfully promoted Birmingham's name in town planning affairs of the day. His list of speeches on town planning matters from 1911 to the time he became Lord Mayor in 1915 testifies to this[9].

The next three or four years need only brief mention. In December 1916 Lloyd George formed his Government and Chamberlain was offered the directorship of a new department of National Service. He had no seat in Parliament and after nine unhappy, disillusioned months he resigned (August 1917), returning to Birmingham, the City Council and the Town Planning Committee. He plunged into health matters, workers' leisure and cooperation between management and labour. He was instrumental in the appointment of welfare supervisors at the Council House; he induced his own firm, Elliotts, to buy land for housing; he pleaded for more adequate pensions for the disabled; and he experimented in sending women from the city's slums to the Welsh coast—an early example of 'social tourism'. All this was in the tradition of the late Victorian social reformer, bearer of a family tradition in a city alive to the expectancy of beneficent paternalism.

THE UNHEALTHY AREAS COMMITTEE

Chamberlain's life was to change dramatically. In 1919 he was elected to Parliament; making his maiden speech (on rent restrictions) at the age of fifty, he was a late entrant to the House, but for the next two decades he strode the national political scene, finally to capture the highest office, Prime Minister, in 1937.

Under the Reform Act of 1918, Birmingham was redivided into twelve constituencies instead of seven. Chamberlain was elected for Ladywood. His election address captured the mood of the time: 'we could best show our gratitude to those who have fought and died for England by making it a better place to live in'[10]. His general sympathy for wide social objectives was reflected in his hopes for ample pensions, minimum wages, shorter hours, protection of key industries, increased provision for health and welfare, assistance to widows with young children and Exchequer support for house building by the State.

In his first year as an MP, he was appointed by Christopher Addison, Minister of Health, as Chairman of the newly established Unhealthy Areas Committee. The terms of reference, broadly, were to consider the principles to be adopted in the clearance of slum areas, the actual rubric reading 'to consider and advise on the principles to be followed in dealing with unhealthy areas, including the circumstances in which schemes of reconstruction, as distinct from clearance, may be adopted, and as regards cleared areas, the extent to which rehousing on the site should be required, the kind of housing which should be permitted, and the use of the site for factory or other purposes than housing'. The composition of the committee was:

N. Chamberlain, MP, Chairman
Mrs. E. Barton, Sheffield City Council, Women's Cooperative Guild
E. J. Brown, Federated Institute of Builders
C. W. Bowerman, MP
Dr. W. J. Howarth, Medical Officer of Health, Corporation of London
R. C. Maxwell, Ministry of Health
G. L. Pepler, Ministry of Health
Capt. R. L. Reiss, Chairman, Garden Cities and Town Planning Association
H. Jennings, Secretary

(In due time Pepler was to be President of the Town Planning Institute on two occasions; Maxwell was also to serve as President.)

The committee worked expeditiously and submitted its interim report in March 1920[11]. This related to London in particular. Three main impressions were recorded:

(a) the vast size and complexity of the London problem;
(b) the intimate connection between housing, transport and the ultimate distribution of land uses of all kinds, residential, commercial and industrial, so that the housing question 'can only be successfully attacked by the simultaneous consideration of all these aspects over a wide area';
(c) the impossibility of carrying out any large schemes of reconstruction because of the acute shortage of houses.

The interim report considered that there were only two alternative methods of relieving the congestion of London: either by vertical expansion in multi-storey buildings or by removal of part of the population elsewhere in order to achieve lower densities and larger open spaces. It favoured the second, to be achieved through the imposition of restrictions on the use of congested areas and, at the same time, the encouragement of factory relocation to new centres of population. The report recommended therefore that local authorities should have power to declare, by resolution, that any part of their area was congested and that thereafter no demolition of houses or erection of buildings other than dwelling houses should take place in the area without a licence from the local authority. Side by side with these recommended restrictions on factories in London, the report advocated the establishment of garden cities surrounding London to which industry might be moved: 'there should be encouraged the starting of new industries and the removal of existing factories to garden cities which should be founded in the country where the inhabitants will live close to their work under the best possible conditions'. A population size in the range 30–50,000 was suggested, the town to be surrounded by a belt of agricultural land for the purposes of health, recreation and local food production.

It is difficult to overestimate the importance of this report in the history of strategic land-use planning. It was the first Government Committee Report to advocate dispersal and decentralization on a comprehensive scale, and hence was the obvious forerunner of the lesser known Marley Report of 1935[12] and the better known Barlow Report of 1940[13], itself the guiding light for much of postwar planning policy, particularly for the regions. No doubt it was strongly affected by the influence of the Garden City movement and Ebenezer Howard's seminal work *Garden Cities of Tomorrow* (1902), but Chamberlain had no need simply to be the mouthpiece of a propagandist body, for the report's recommendations represented the logical extension of his own views based on experience in Birmingham. Indeed, he was always prepared to go further and present the next step in the argument. The report acknowledged that 'intervention of the State' was necessary to achieve the dispersal and restriction policies recommended. This tentative step forward in the extension of central and local powers over land allocations and processes of development proved to be the developing pattern of British planning both in the interwar years, and subsequently.

The report went further, recommending the preparation of a general plan for the reconstruction of London and for a new authority covering an area larger than that of the London County Council. Chamberlain's hope for a plan for the whole of Birmingham, built-up areas as well as undeveloped suburban periphery, was now expressed more firmly and in respect of a larger, more complex metropolis. The necessity for a general plan was argued in typically administrative terms. In the area of Greater London, i.e. the metropolitan and city police districts, there were 122 local authorities which were also housing authorities under the Housing Acts. Coordination of their developments was impossible and in order that London's reconstruction might be planned as a whole, 'A plan should be prepared now which should broadly assign to the various districts in and about London their respective functions in the future, so that every reconstruction scheme may conform to such a plan in its main details'. This sort of advocacy could not fail to encourage the tender growth of strategic, land-use planning and the constancy of Chamberlain's approach succeeded in persuading the London authorities to action of the kind recommended.

An Addendum to the interim report by Mrs. Barton and Capt. Reiss agreed that the General Plan was essential. They went on to argue, however, that this would result in 'an enormous transference of land values', a problem which could only be overcome by land nationalization or purchase by the LCC. But compensation and betterment was another problem, for deeper analysis and solution at a much later time.

Mrs. Barton and E. J. Brown resigned from the committee in April 1920 (due in no way to differences of view). There were no new appointments and the committee proceeded to make visits to such centres as Birmingham, Leeds, Liverpool and Cardiff to see the common factors of haphazard growth, indiscriminate mixture of land uses and inequality in provision of open spaces and parks. The final report was submitted in April 1921[14]. Once again it was very much Chamberlain's: as he wrote to his sister Hilda, 'I had a very successful meeting of my Unhealthy Areas Committee on Wednesday; I had spent a lot of time going through the report, re-drafting and adding to it, and the Committee simply opened its mouth and swallowed everything at a gulp'[15].

The final report was of less consequence than the interim, although it repeated and confirmed the recommendations of the first. It touched on at least three further important questions. The first was the problem of compensation payable for unfit housing. It acknowledged that S9 of the 1919 Act was not working well, and it put forward new suggestions to remove inequality and injustice; the details need not concern us here. The second was the recognition that delays in slum clearance were inevitable and therefore it was important to achieve improvements of older houses. There was little confidence in private owners doing this, and hence local authority acquisition was envisaged. The third had a more direct bearing on town planning, the report recommending extension of planning powers to land already built upon. This proposal was some years in advance of its time as far as statutory powers were concerned, but it represented the further extension of Chamberlain's ideas about planning in both Birmingham and London. 'It is not necessary to introduce any complex conditions or procedure, but local authorities should have the power in the public interest to prescribe the lines of main traffic routes and also to arrange for "zoning" in a built up area'.

So ended his work on the Unhealthy Areas Committee. It was another five years before he himself could take on another step forward on this incremental path. Again it was in respect of the replanning of London. In October 1926, this time in his new position of Minister of Health, he received a deputation from the LCC (at his request) to discuss the question of provision of playing fields in Greater London. He took the initiative of calling a conference of the LCC and surrounding county councils and boroughs to consider their collaboration on the preparation of a Greater London Regional Plan. From this meeting, representative of 130 local authorities, sprang the Greater London Regional Planning Committee, the appointment of Raymond Unwin as Director, and his preparation for the London green girdle, playing field provision, dispersal of activities and general strategic planning matters.

MINISTER OF HEALTH

We now turn to Chamberlain as Minister of Health and his direct contribution to local government, housing and planning. In the general election of 1922 he was again returned for his Birmingham constituency of Ladywood, and became Postmaster General. In 1923 he became Minister of Health. In the general election of 1924 Ladywood was won again and he became Chancellor of the Exchequer. With yet another general election he returned this time to Health, for the second time and remained there throughout the second Baldwin administration until 1929. Here he proved himself to be a conspicuously successful reformer.

There is little to detain us in his first short Ministry. The chief matter to note was that he inherited a Housing Bill in which he felt committed to a principle of subsidy. £6 a year for 20 years was payable, but the houses which benefited were severely limited in size: they had to be 'non-parlour' houses and the dimensions of the rooms were strictly regulated. He was attacked for lowering the living standards of working people, but he countered this with the argument that it was only by concentrating subsidy on the cheaper houses that houses for the working class could be built at all.

The Housing etc. Act, 1923 (which included four sections relating to town planning) was the principal of five enactments which Chamberlain piloted through a few short months. It was a forerunner to a vigorous legislative session subsequently between 1925 and 1929 when thirty Acts reached the Statute Book from his Ministry. He was assisted by a noteworthy team: Kingley Wood as Parliamentary Secretary, Arthur Robinson as Permanent Secretary, and George Newman as Principal Medical Officer. Amongst his officers concerned with town planning were George Pepler and Raymond Unwin. The team was a sound one, but there is little doubt that behind the strategy and the incessant progress lay Chamberlain's own vigour and philosophy. It is reputed[16] that on 17 November 1925 he set his office to work on a four-year plan. On 19 November he presented to the Cabinet a list of twenty-five desirable measures; of these, twenty-one became law before he left the Ministry and the remainder were incorporated in later legislation.

The Housing Act 1925 dealt with repair and maintenance of dwellings, sanitary conditions, improvement and reconstruction schemes and the provision of houses for the working classes. The Town Planning Act 1925 consolidated town planning legislation. The Public Health Act 1925 amended the Public Health Acts 1875–1907 and the Baths and Washhouses Acts 1846–99, and provided for a consolidation of powers that had been given to many local authorities through Private Bills promoted by them. The Rating and Valuation Act 1925 simplified and amended the law by transferring rating powers to county, borough and district councils. We see a good illustration here of Chamberlain's emphasis on local government and its importance; he held it to be a unifying power in government and an invaluable arm of the regulatory State.

The Poor Law Act 1927, was a monumental work containing 245 clauses and eleven schedules. It was one of the largest works of consolidation ever attempted, embracing the relative parts of more than 100 Acts of Parliament from the time of Elizabeth I. The National Health Insurance Act 1928 was a further simplification of machinery, building on Lloyd George's basically sound measure of sixteen years before.

But for the purposes of this paper it is the Local Government Act 1929, which we should note particularly. Proposals for reform had already been made in a White Paper[17]. Chamberlain himself recognized that the Bill was 'the most important Measure of the Session'[18]. He went on (at the Second Reading of the Bill on 29 November 1928): 'In mere bulk, this Bill far transcends the propositions of any ordinary Bill. When you consider the magnitude of the changes which it proposes, the variety of the interests that are affected and its possible results upon the prosperity of the country, and indeed the social welfare of the whole people, I think it must be reckoned among the greatest measures which have been presented to any Parliament for many years'. In his diary for 1 December 1928 he commented simply: 'Last Monday I moved the second reading of the Local Government Bill in a speech which lasted $2\frac{1}{2}$ hours ... when I sat down, the House cheered continuously for several minutes'[19].

It was certainly timely for a reform of local government. Urban and rural sanitary districts had been created in 1872. The county councils were created in 1888, with powers similar to those possessed by the municipal corporations. Urban and rural district councils were created in 1894. Since that time there had been no serious attempt at local government reform, but during the thirty-four years the population of England and Wales had increased from 29 to 39 million and its distribution had changed; new community services had developed and local authority annual expenditure had risen from £36m in 1891 to nearly £250m.

Chamberlain's analysis of the main defects of local government was penetrating:

(1) the continuous existence of the guardians among other local authorities with overlapping functions and boundaries;

(2) the onerous charges on county districts (particularly rural) in respect of roads;

(3) the difficulties encountered in altering boundaries to adapt to changing conditions;

(4) the inequitable system of rates which hard hit agriculture and industry;

(5) the chaotic relations existing between national and local expenditure.

In short, local government was an obsolete machine, with overlapping services, rigid boundaries, an inadequate local road system, high rates which strangled industry and agriculture, and a disharmony between local and central expenditure.

The Boards of Guardians were abolished and their duties transferred to counties and county boroughs. County councils took over rural roads together with classified roads in urban districts. A periodic review was proposed to investigate local authority boundaries, including the 500 districts with a population of less than 5000. Rating reform introduced derating with a purposive objective in employment opportunities. When the Exchequer made up to the local authorities the £24m they would lose through derating, the inequalities would be corrected, block grants being weighted with regard to loss of rates, to population, to numbers of children and to ratio of unemployment.

There were certain town planning aspects of the Act which are considered below. But central to all these measures, and certainly of significance to town planning was Chamberlain's admiration for local government. One of the features of British town planning has been the statutory system of central and local government relationships. From its inception town planning has been made a function of local government; its development in concept and practice has been cradled in local government offices to a considerable extent. The strength and nature of British local government has given a definite flavour to British town planning, which is absent in other countries. The significance of Chamberlain is that he was the responsible Minister at a very influential time for both local government and town planning.

There were some striking passages in his speech at the Second Reading of the Local Government Bill[20]. Fifty years later, the following, for example, rings very differently from any contemporary expressions:

Local government comes so much nearer to the homes, and therefore to the hearts of the people, than any national government can. To them it is something friendly, something familiar, something accessible. It is all that to them, and yet it is above them. They regard it as standing as a guardian angel between them and ill-health or injustice, and they look upon it, too, as something in the nature of a benefactor and a teacher in want. They come to it for advice. They feel confidence in its integrity. They look to it because it has ideals which they understand, and that they approve, and because it is always helping and teaching them to rise to higher things.

This reads as a remarkable testimony, but it came naturally from a man of his generation and background.

It is not everybody who had the advantage of being born and bred up in a town such as I have, a town commanding great resources, governed for many years by men who have been brought up in high and enlightened traditions, and by officials of exceptional capacity, judgment and experience. But it is just because I have seen for myself what local government can do, what I think it ought to do, because I know how many places there are in the country where it does not reach to those ideals, but where I would like to see it come up to them, and because to my mind local government reform means social reform, that I rejoice that today the opportunity has been given to me to bring forward this measure . . .

Throughout these years at the Ministry of Health, housing matters occupied much of his attention. 800,000 houses were built during the lifetime of the Baldwin Government, a peak of 273,000 in the year September 1926–27. 378,000 had been completed under the Chamberlain Act of 1923, each of which cost £4 p.a. for twenty years; 229,000 under the Wheatley Housing Act of 1924 at an annual cost of £7.10.0 for forty years. (The remainder were non-subsidy houses.) Chamberlain maintained his Birmingham concern for housing conditions. In the Second Reading of his Housing Bill, 1923, he spoke of overcrowding as constituting 'a perpetual danger to the physical and moral health of the community,. It is, I am sure, responsible for much unrest and social discontent'[21]. His keen eye on housing matters is reflected in his notebooks of visits to provincial cities between 1925 and 1927[22]. Written in his fast-flowing, but neat, meticulous hand, they tell of local conditions and personalities in frank observations as he toured to instruct local authorities, and to inspire and measure their progress. On the other hand, in spite of ample evidence of poor housing, Chamberlain had no great record in slum clearance: during his term of office just fifty-eight slum-clearance schemes were confirmed, with 31,000 people rehoused. The housing shortage was perhaps the reason for this, but in the 1929 General Election manifesto, there was a switch in emphasis to clearance, and this phase belongs to the 1930s. Lastly we might note a family connection in one aspect of housing: Ida, one of two sisters with whom Chamberlain maintained a long correspondence, was a Hampshire County Councillor and took a leading part on the Housing Committee. He consulted her during the passage of the Housing (Rural Workers) Act, 1926[23].

As Minister, Chamberlain presided over the emergent field of town planning. The Housing, Town Planning, etc. Act, 1919, had made the preparation of town planning schemes (in respect of undeveloped land) obligatory on local authorities with a population of 20,000 or more. The 1920s were devoted to patiently building up an awareness of the subject field among local authorities. The annual reports of the Ministry of Health and the Scottish Board of Health reveal the painstaking progress made in encouraging local authorities to proceed with the preparation of town planning schemes. The dates for submission of obligatory schemes were extended on a number of occasions, last by the Local Government Act of 1929 which extended the date to 1 January 1934, with power to the Minister to extend the date again, although not beyond the end of 1938. Although in acreage terms, the total area actually covered by town planning schemes was very small, by 1930, 204 out of 262 urban authorities in England and Wales had submitted proposals in the form of resolutions, preliminary statements or schemes. In Scotland, progress was much less impressive.

But in both England and Wales and in Scotland there were many useful initiatives taken in respect of regional planning through the voluntary agency of joint committees, often working with consultants. This proved to be a forcing ground in conceptual and methodological developments in planning practice, out of which grew the most significant regional exercise of all, that for Greater London. The greater spatial scale of planning was encouraged through legislation: the Local Government (Scotland) Act 1929, actually transferred the town planning powers to district committees and small burghs to county councils, while for England and Wales the Local Government Act 1929 extended to county councils the right to *share in* the preparation and administration of joint schemes.

Chamberlain himself addressed the first meeting of the Greater London Regional Planning Committee, held at the Ministry of Health in November 1927[24]. In impressing upon the various local authority representatives the complexity of the problem and the urgency of the solutions to the London situation, he offered certain principles for the committee to follow. These guidelines proved to be recurrent themes in British metropolitan planning over the next half century. For example as a spatial strategy for London he wondered 'how far there would be advantage in trying to concentrate the development in particular spots and areas by the establishment of deliberately planned new towns'. Where such new concentrations were established 'there should be representatives of all, or at any rate as many, classes as possible'; moreover they should not be dormitories (shades of Reith in 1945!). He picked up the theme of his Unhealthy Areas Committee: 'What I think we have to aim at is a decentralisation of our great city'. An important element in the spatial pattern was emphasized: garden cities should be surrounded by an agricultural belt which could accommodate parks, playing fields and hospitals. He acknowledged that the London County Council had been making a survey of the need for playing fields and the possibilities of obtaining them. All this, of course, led into the planning method of land allocation (zoning), which highlighted the problems of compensation and betterment. Chamberlain recognized that there were then no legislative powers to plan developed areas but he thought that 'such powers ought to be given and . . . as soon as I could find a suitable opportunity I should hope to introduce the necessary legislation'. Transport was not forgotten in the comprehensive study required—road, rail, canal, river and air ('I do not know what development in the design of aeroplanes may do in the direction of making it unnecessary to have large landing places but (their provision) ought not to be left out of account'); airports for London remain high on the planning agenda.

Chamberlain proposed a General Purposes and Finance Committee for the Greater London Study, and Sir Banister Fletcher of the City Corporation was duly elected. He thought that other Committees, such as a Technical Committee and a Decentralisation Committee, should follow. The LCC had contributed £3000 to this work; other proportional contributions from the bodies involved brought the total to £4400; and Chamberlain offered accommodation at the Ministry of Health. Raymond Unwin became Technical Director, and such were the origins of his subsequent Reports. There is no record of who wrote the Minister's address for that first meeting. Both Unwin and Pepler (who also attended) could have contributed, but the sentiments, particularly relating to those of decentralization were strongly in Chamberlain's own background, and to that extent his own role in the interwar planning of Greater London can be recognized.

During the 1920s, Chamberlain relied on the 1919 Act and its consolidating successor, the Town Planning Act 1925. It seemed to be the time for quiet, incremental progress. Other legislative initiatives with regard to town planning were infrequent until the local government reforms of 1929, with their implications for greater county council involvements. The Housing Act 1923 (S21) interestingly enabled the Minister to authorize the preparation of a town planning scheme for land, whether developed or not, with the object of preserving the existing character and features of a locality with special architectural, historic or artistic interest. This initiative was soon taken up in a number of historic cities, paralleling the town planning powers which were being extended by Local Acts to cover developed parts of other cities.

In all the promotional work of town planning, still a tiny section of the Ministry, the work of loyal, dedicated, enthusiastic officers was necessary. Unwin was Chief Technical Officer for Building and Town Planning, responsible until 1928 for the evaluation of all the country's housing projects. George Pepler was another, who was a critical link between the Ministry and the profession. But there is no evidence that the officers were promoting work in advance of, or under cover of ministerial head. Chamberlain himself was committed to the idea of town planning. He had been with the Institute as an Honorary Member since the earliest days: he was on the first membership list of 115 drawn up in May 1914.

How do we evaluate the place of Neville Chamberlain in British town planning? We should remember two things: first, that he was essentially a Victorian; second, that he was also a member of one of Birmingham's most influential families. These background aspects do much to explain the course of his life as a public figure and his outlooks on questions of public policy.

He was a Victorian in the obvious sense that he was born in 1869 (March 18). His formative years were those of the last quarter of nineteenth century Britain. His perceptions of British society, as well as of the problems and needs of British cities were fashioned before the Edwardian era. He was even more a Birmingham man of a very particular family and tradition. Son of Joseph Chamberlain, dynamic mayor of Birmingham for three years in the 1870s, the author of many municipal reforms and the creator of Corporation Street out of the slums of the town centre, he was born to take social duty for granted. Birmingham for many years had been governed by a succession of Unitarian mayors, and the town already had the tradition of effective and enterprising municipal government. Unitarian families, including the Chamberlains, were acknowledged leaders in many branches of local life. He was brought up therefore in an atmosphere of precept and example, which extended from public service in government to social work activated through religious conviction. Chamberlain followed his father in teaching in the Sunday School of the Church of the Messiah in Broad Street, Birmingham; a church which organized an active mission work in the adjoining slums of Ladywood.

Chamberlain belonged therefore, in outlook, ideals and assumptions, to a very distinctive coterie whose unity was a paternalist, progressive, reforming concern. Their targets were the urban evils of the turn of the century, particularly housing, where they had a strong conviction of the causal relationships between environment, health, crime and morals. They were incremental reformists; revolution and a concern for new economic and social structures were not in their book. They held that lower urban densities, better housing and improved sanitation were vital ingredients in environmental reform and social stability. They were pragmatic in their methods of arriving at a better future, although they were all 'evolutionists' in the sense that a natural, forward movement was seen to be taking place in society and this represented progress and a buoyant hope for the future. Some followed a particular propagandist line like the Garden City; Chamberlain staked much on the benefits of a local government administration of integrity and purpose. Chamberlain provides an interesting example of the sort of person first attracted to the growing town planning movement.

Within this context Chamberlain's actual contribution to town planning may be assessed. In what we have called his 'Birmingham period' his enthusiasm for town planning schemes gave a much needed fillip to the Local

Government Board as it wrestled with the virtual unknowns of the Housing, Town Planning etc. Act, 1909. Moreover, he was instrumental in pushing forward the boundaries of the concepts and practice of town planning. At national level, his early work on the Unhealthy Areas Committee laid an important seed bed for metropolitan town planning in which the planned dispersal of population and employment on a regional scale was of fundamental importance. Out of that philosophy developed the work of Unwin and Abercrombie in respect of Greater London over the next twenty years. As Minister of Health he presided over a careful but cautious development of town planning practice; a relationship with housing improvement and sound local government administration was strongly pronounced. Much of the character of British town planning has rested on its close identity with housing matters and local government as its *modus operandi;* under Chamberlain this was firmly established.

We are offered a useful glimpse of his view of planning, when, as Chancellor of the Exchequer, he spoke at a professional dinner held in Birmingham in 1934, to commemorate the 21st anniversary of the foundation of the Town Planning Institute[25]. He showed himself to be an incremental reformist within the context of good community government: he thought it 'natural that town planning which affected so closely personal interests and personal liberties, and which sought to contol those liberties, should be an example of what was called, in a familiar phrase, the inevitability of gradualness. Its progress had been gradual and cautious. As time went on new features had appeared which had brought home to the general public the fact that in the modern world it was not possible to allow complete liberty to the individual because, if that were done, the community itself might suffer'.

He was not necessarily any great visionary; he simply held to a better, more just future, attained pragmatically through orderly, rational government. He went on

> Some day, I have no doubt, the whole of the country will come under [land] control of one kind or another. I shall not live to see it, and before it comes about irreparable damage will have been done. Millions of pounds will have been wasted, and probably many thousands of lives will have been lost for want of orderly and careful planning.
>
> We must all regret this delay, but at the same time, as practical people, I think we must recognize that if the pace was made too hot there would undoubtedly be reactions which might have even more disastrous results. Therefore, I feel that if we can say that we have done something in our lifetime to make the way easier to that time when our cities will all be beautiful, when our traffic will be able to move without hindrance and without injury to itself or other travellers, when the countryside will cease to be disfigured by vulgar advertisements and hideous buildings, then we shall not have worked in vain.

We must not think that Chamberlain was the only politician in local or central Government at this time to be influential in promoting town planning objectives. From a different political perspective, for example., the work done by Herbert Morrison in London would readily be acknowledged. Moreover, Chamberlain's record in the 1930s raises questions: there is his curious failure (and indeed of most other politicians) to relate town planning to the economic problems of the disadvantaged regions, when he was in a particularly advantageous position as Chancellor of the Exchequer. However, let his professional Institute have the last word. His obituary in the *Town Planning Institute Journal* commented that 'he lost no opportunity for reaffirming his belief in planning, and whatever high office he held he remained true to this ideal and was a source of inspiration to all those who were striving to plan a better Britain and a better world'[26].

NOTES

Neville Chamberlain's private papers are held in the Library of the University of Birmingham (ref. NC below). There are three main biographies, as follows, the principal one listed first. Feiling, Keith (1946, 1970) *The Life of Neville Chamberlain.* London: Macmillan; Montgomery Hyde, H. (1976) *Neville Chamberlain.* London: Weidenfeld and Nicolson; Macleod, Iain (1961) *Neville Chamberlain.* London: Frederick Müller.

1. Cherry, Gordon E. (1974) *The Evolution of British Town Planning.* London: Leonard Hill.
2. Feiling, Keith (1946, 1970) *The Life of Neville Chamberlain.* London: Macmillan.
3. Quoted in Macleod, Iain (1961) *Neville Chamberlain.* London: Frederick Müller.
4. Cherry, Gordon E. (1975) *Factors in the Origins of Town Planning in Birmingham, 1905–14,* Working Paper 36. Centre for Urban and Regional Studies, University of Birmingham.
5. Quoted in Macleod, Iain (1961) *Neville Chamberlain.* London: Frederick Müller.
6. Quoted in Briggs, Asa (1952) *History of Birmingham,* Vol. II. Oxford: Oxford University Press.
7. General Survey Sub-Committee, City of Birmingham, 8 December 1911.
8. *Report* of the Special Housing Inquiry Committee, 1913–14, City of Birmingham, 1914.
9. List of Neville Chamberlain's speeches, 1895–1918, NC 4/1/1–2.
10. Feiling, Keith (1946, 1970) *The Life of Neville Chamberlain.* London: Macmillan.
11. *Interim Report* of the Committee appointed by the Minister of Health to consider and advise on the principles to be followed in dealing with unhealthy areas, 1920, HMSO.
12. *Garden Cities and Satellite Towns.* Report of Departmental Committee, Ministry of Health, 1935, London: HMSO.
13. *Report of the Royal Commission on the Distribution of the Industrial Population,* Cmd. 6153, 1940, London: HMSO.
14. Unhealthy Areas Committee (1921) *Second and Final Report.* London: HMSO.
15. Quoted in Macleod, Iain (1961) *Neville Chamberlain.* London: Macmillan.
16. Feiling, Keith (1946, 1970) *The Life of Neville Chamberlain.* London: Macmillan.

17. Ministry of Health (1928) *Proposals for Reform in Local Government,* Cmd. 3134.
    HMSO.
18. NC 14/1–6.
19. Quoted in Feiling, Keith (1946, 1970) *The Life of Neville Chamberlain.* London:
    Macmillan.
20. NC 14/1–6.
21. NC 14/1–6.
22. NC 2/28.
23. Macleod, Iain (1961) *Neville Chamberlain.* London: Frederick Müller.
24. Greater London Regional Planning Committee (1927) Minutes of first meeting 2
    November.
25. *Journal Town Planning Institute,* **20** (1), 1934.
26. *Journal Town Planning Institute,* **27** (1), 1940.

9

Brazilian cities old and new: growth and planning experiences

SUSAN M. CUNNINGHAM

The Latin American region inherited a strong urban planning tradition from its Spanish and Portuguese dominees during the colonial period. In Brazil, the Portuguese established this tradition on a large scale during the eighteenth century, somewhat later than their Spanish counterparts. These early planning efforts were directed towards the planting of numerous small towns. Settlements were located increasingly in the interior of the country and in frontier areas as part of a strategy designed to house European colonists, civilize the native population and also to extend Portugal's territorial claims in South America westwards. By the middle of the eighteenth century building codes had been introduced to regulate town street patterns and to standardize frontages of buildings opening on to main streets[1]. Officials appointed by the Portuguese crown were charged with the task of overseeing that basic planning rules were adhered to. After Independence in 1822 continuity with the planning philosophy was maintained, but under the terms of the 1824 Constitution and the Law of Municipal Organization (1828) responsibilities in the urban sphere (excluding public works programmes of national importance) were transferred to municipal authorities.

The remainder of the nineteenth century saw further additions to the legislation affecting urban growth and design, although in practice the capacity of municipal authorities to undertake new responsibilities was frequently limited by financial constraints[2]. Thus, by the beginning of the twentieth century, Brazil's urban planning experience was already considerable. Having said this, however, it is apparent that the pace and scale of Brazilian urban growth from roughly the last quarter of the nineteenth century to the present has far outstripped the capacity of planning structures which were developed along traditional lines to supply the demand for urban facilities. In this respect, it can be mentioned that during the late nineteenth and early twentieth centuries the coffee economy, European immigration and the growth of railways were among the principal factors stimulating urban expansion especially in the southern half of the country. Then, from about 1929 industrialization, together with changes in both the demographic base and transport became major influences upon the urbanization process and city structure[3, 4].

Against this background, the present paper concerns itself with the growth and planning experiences of four Brazilian cities: Rio de Janeiro, São Paulo, Belo Horizonte and Brasília (figure 9.1). The first two of these have had a long development history dating from the early colonial period involving both spontaneous growth and piecemeal planning efforts. The remaining two, by contrast, were planned and built as entirely new cities from 1894 and 1956 respectively, although in each case subsequent urban growth has exceeded the original plans. The paper is divided into two main parts. In the first part a

FIGURE 9.1. Brazil: basic regional division and city locations.

brief review of urban and economic trends from colonial times until 1929 provides the setting for case studies of Rio de Janeiro and São Paulo. Due weight is given to a description of their historical growth patterns including planning efforts. The second part examines more contemporary developments from about 1930 with specific emphasis upon planning experiences in all four cities. A central theme of the paper is that, despite differences in the age and development history of these cities, planning solutions have tended to be primarily concerned with macro-scale inputs while human needs at the micro-scale have assumed secondary importance. In other words, attention is drawn to the juxtaposition of economic and social criteria involved in Brazilian urban planning. At the same time it is also shown that a planning *tradition* should not necessarily be equated with planning *progress* during the twentieth century.

THE HISTORICAL BACKGROUND TO BIG CITY GROWTH

REVIEW OF TRENDS UNTIL ABOUT 1929

Two initial aspects should be mentioned with respect to the earliest urban centres established under Portuguese colonial rule. In the first place it was necessary for colonists to defend their territory from attacks by either indigenous Indians or other European colonizing forces such as the French and Dutch. For this purpose defensive hill sites close to points of navigable entry (though with access to areas of flatter land) were usually chosen for the first settlements. This was the case with the historic cities of Salvador, Recife and Rio de Janeiro. Secondly, the need for imported supplies of manufactures and labour together with the development of primary exports—first in Brazilwood and later, sugar cane—led to the growth of *entrepôt* functions in the urban centres of the coast[5].

The decline of the sugar cycle in the mid-seventeenth century was followed by a period of mineral exploitation towards the interior south of the country, particularly in the areas occupied by the present states of Minas Gerais and parts of Mato Grosso and Goiás. The onset of this new phase coincided with the later quests of the *bandeirantes* (literally flag-bearing groups) whereby earlier forays deep into the Brazilian Plateau in the search for Indian slaves gave way to increased emphasis upon the search for gold and other precious metals[6]. Discoveries of minerals were made along inland penetration routes such as the Paraíba Valley but it was with the discovery of gold at Ouro Prêto in 1695 that the country's economic centre of gravity became the landlocked region known as the General Mines *(Minas Gerais)*.

Mining activities gave rise to the first sizable interior urban settlements in Portuguese South America, notably at Ouro Prêto, São João del Rei and

Sabará, peopled by European immigrants and slave labour. Simultaneously mining also began to shift the focus of Brazilian development out of the Northeast sugar-producing areas and into the Southeast. One outcome of this change was the transfer of the capital from Salvador to Rio de Janeiro in 1763 prompted by Rio's new role as the principal port for gold exports.

Primary product export booms continued after Brazil gained its independence from Portugal. Of these coffee was the most important with large-scale production being first centred in Rio and its hinterland before spreading south to São Paulo state in the later nineteenth century. Suffice it to say here that the greatest direct impact of coffee was felt in the growing cities of Rio and São Paulo. In particular coffee revenues provided capital resources for inputs of economic infrastructure. In turn, this reinforced the position of the Southeast region and assisted the country's industrial expansion prior to the Great Crash of 1929[7, 8].

Case Study of Rio de Janeiro

The first settlement—or old town—of Rio was founded in 1565 at a defensive site provided by the gap between two hills (or *morros*)—the Pão de Açucar and Cãra do Cão–on a small coastal peninsula. This served as an initial defence point until 1567 when the town was transferred to another hilly site further north, known as Descanso do São Januário. The new site had the added advantage of more extensive adjacent flat land surrounded by several other small hills which could be used as defence posts as required (see figure 9.2).

By the early 1600s the settlement, then called São Sebastião do Rio de Janeiro, had spread down onto the flatter land. Its population numbered 4000 in 1620 and the main focus of the urban centre developed between the hills with a reticulate street pattern. Sugar cultivation took place in the environs especially under the Jesuits (until about 1760) at Engenho Velho and São Cristovão (see figure 9.3). After the discovery of gold in Minas Gerais a major new route out of the city was begun in the vicinity of São Cristovão via Barbacena to Ouro Prêto. Physical growth of the settlement continued during the eighteenth century under the impact of its new roles, first in connection with the gold boom and then with colonial administration. When, in 1808 the Portuguese court was moved to Rio from Portugal, continuous urban development occupied more than twice the area it had done a century before. Its population had grown to 60,000 with negro slaves forming a substantial proportion. Population was concentrated in the central city with smaller settlements spreading inland as far as the flatter land permitted and along the shores of Guanabara Bay.

The coming of the royal court was an event of particular significance for the city's later growth. In the first place this made Rio the effective capital of

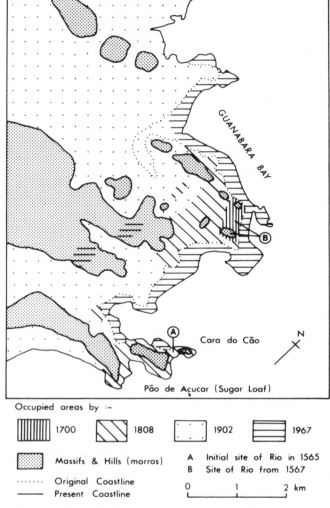

Occupied areas by :-

▥ 1700	◩ 1808	⬚ 1902	☰ 1967

▦ Massifs & Hills (morros)

A Initial site of Rio in 1565
B Site of Rio from 1567

······ Original Coastline
——— Present Coastline

0   1   2 km

FIGURE 9.2. Rio de Janeiro: relief and growth of settlement.

the Portuguese Empire (until 1822) and then of the Brazilian Empire (until 1889). Also, the initiatives of Dom João had a specific impact upon the city's urban development and these constitute some of the earliest planning efforts. The court itself was located at Quinta de Boa Vista to the north-west of the city, which had the effect of stimulating new urban growth in the vicinity of São Cristovão. In 1810 definite provisions were made for more general improvements including the widening of streets, alignment of new buildings, setting aside of small squares *(praças)*, public lighting and so on. Individual

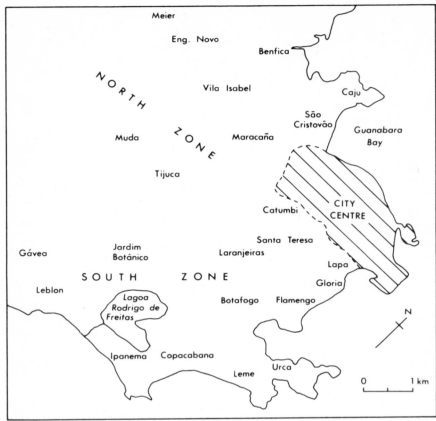

FIGURE 9.3. Rio de Janeiro: major zones and districts.

monuments and cultural landmarks were also begun during this period, notably the Botanic Garden *(Jardim Botânico),* Art Academy, Royal Library and Cathedral *(Candelária).* Above all, the presence of the court was an important force encouraging both immigration and expansion of trade (especially with England and France). In turn these had an impact upon the social mix, values and further functional roles of the city.

The development of coffee as a commodity was of additional importance. The cultivation of the crop became established in and around Rio well before Independence, spreading westwards into the Paraíba Valley during the early 1800s after which time it became more commercially viable. Coffee revenues boosted the material base for the city's aggrandizement until the 1880s when São Paulo state became the leading coffee producer. A number of particularly large projects of an infrastructural type were implemented from the mid-nineteenth century. These included a sewage system installed by the Rio de Janeiro City Improvements Company in 1864 (one of the first modern systems in the world); the new road link (144 km) to Juiz de Fora which was completed by 1862; the construction of the country's railways beginning with the short (14 km) line in Rio's port area which opened in 1854, and the Rio-Petrópolis line into the *serra* which opened in 1856 and the beginning of works for the Central do Brasil line between Rio and São Paulo during the 1850s.

In considering the territorial expansion and changing urban structure of Rio by the later nineteenth century some reference to its growing population and transport system is necessary. In the fifty years following Independence, the net increase in the city's population was about 175,000. While this was a very substantial increase by Brazilian standards over that period, much more impressive were the gains of over 247,000 between 1872 and 1890 and a further 288,000 from 1890 to 1900 indicated by Census figures. At the same time it should be made clear that increase in population density from roughly 235/km² in 1872 to 693/km² by 1900 was perhaps of greater significance than the absolute increases in numbers suggest, for it is density which provides some measure of the demand pressure exerted upon then-existing facilities. Housing was clearly a problem, since the limited flat land restricted the spread of traditional one-storey dwellings. Also, the collective dwellings (known as Pig's Heads–*Cabeças de Porco*–and Bee Hives–*Cortiços*) in which about a quarter of the population lived according to the 1890 Census could only sustain extra numbers at the expense of rapidly-deteriorating social-welfare conditions[9]. Further, real-estate speculation forced up land prices and rents in or near the city centre. These problems are set in perspective when it is realized that much of the population expansion resulted from the abolition of slavery (whereby many liberated rural-dwellers began to move cityward in search of work) and an upswing in immigration. On balance, this meant that a large proportion of Rio's new inhabitants consisted of the poorer elements then present in Brazilian society.

With respect to transport, from about 1840 horse-drawn buses and 'gondolas' made possible greater mobility within the city for those who could afford it. This led to additional residential growth in districts such as Botafogo, Engenho Velho and São Cristovão (figure 9.3). Many town-houses towards the city centre thus became available for rent on a room by room basis, eventually giving rise to squalid multi-family occupation, although as property deteriorated and land values rose there was pressure to withdraw residential land-use functions from central city locations. Plans were thus drawn up to develop new suburbs such as Copacabana in the 1850s. Also, the opening of the Central do Brasil railway in 1877 induced some shift in the pattern of residential growth to the north-west of the city, proximal to the source of the rail link. These tendencies were further reinforced after 1892 when an extensive network of electric trams was installed. By 1907 there were 290 km of tram lines with a dense network of routes leading from the city centre inland and north-westwards as far as

Meier, Muda and Tijuca. They also penetrated southwards by means of tunnels where necessary to the coastal areas between Leme and Ipanema, with up-valley routes to Jardim Botanico and Larajeiras. Journeys on most routes could be accomplished within an hour of the centre. The new transport developments facilitated urban growth beyond the old city centre and between 1890 and 1900 the proportion of suburban dwellers increased from almost 18 per cent to 23 per cent of the total population. It was only after 1920 however, when the total population had risen to over a million, that suburban residential growth took place to the virtual exclusion of central areas[10].

By the late 1920s then, Rio had expanded both its population and territory. Most of this growth was unplanned, although some initiatives concerning urban improvements were taken up from a very early date under the impetus of the Portuguese court. Perhaps more important though, from the standpoint of changing patterns of urban land use, were the controls set in train by the transport system, land and property speculation and the social mix of the population. Such factors contributed to the city having become more functionally differentiated by 1930, with the north zone showing extensive urban (and incipient industrial) growth, increased residential and commercial uses in the south zone and greater emphasis upon commercial, financial and administrative functions in the city centre.

CASE STUDY OF SÃO PAULO

From its founding by a small delegation of Jesuits in 1554 as well as its setting on the southern perimeter of the interior plateau country, São Paulo presents considerable contasts to Rio. The initial defensive hilltop site near to the confluence of two small tributaries of the River Tietê was a feature in common with other early colonial settlements, but a primary *raison d'être* of São Paulo was closely linked to religious interests and the movement of Jesuit missions up from the small coastal towns of São Vicente and Santos (founded in 1532 and 1536 respectively) to convert the native Indian plateau-dwellers. Thus, a small Indian-colonial community grew at São Paulo, receiving the status of a town (or *villa*) in 1561.

By 1600 the town had about 1500 European colonists, of whom some three-quarters were Portuguese, plus an unknown number of servile Indians. During the course of the seventeenth century the male inhabitants of the town and neighbouring small settlements of the plateau carried out numerous expeditions (or *bandeiras*) into the backlands (or *sertão*). Driven at first by the desire to investigate (and capture) Indian supplies, such ventures later provided the means by which Portugal extended her territorial claims in South America, especially after the discovery of gold by *bandeirante* groups in 1695[11].

Having become the capital of the Captaincy of São Paulo in 1683, the town was given the status of a city in 1711. Even so, its population was only 14,760 free men and 6000 slaves in 1765[12]. This relatively small population was largely the result of the Jesuit strategy of establishing numerous settlements for 'domestication' of indigenous *planalto* Indians as well as natural wastage during expeditions. São Paulo thus became the centre of a polynuclear settlement region rather than a city which expanded outwards from a central core (see figure 9.4). This trend persisted under the later colonial policy of new town creation which aimed at stimulating further the peopling of the *planalto*.

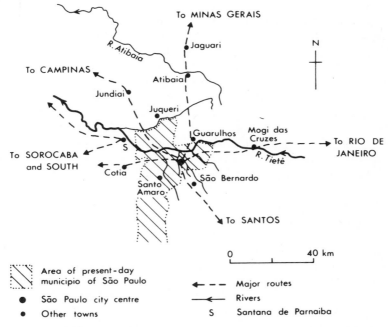

FIGURE 9.4. São Paulo: location, early route pattern and neighbouring towns.

Economic activity in the São Paulo region centred mainly upon subsistence agriculture, although during the course of the eighteenth century trading activities with the interior and southern regions of the country became increasingly important. In particular, mules from Rio Grande do Sul in the far south, were taken to be sold in the mining areas via São Paulo, in return for cotton goods and sugar. Further trade was built up with Rio via both the Paraíba Valley and the port of Santos. In connection with these *entrepôt* functions, São Paulo saw further development of its centrifugal pattern of routes (shown also in figure 9.4) which had begun to be important soon after the initial phase of colonization. Such routes extended outwards from the city centre to local regional centres (Jundiaí, Campinas, Sorocaba), the interior (towns of southern Minas, Mato Grosso) and the coast (Santos via descent of the *serra* to the south, Rio via the Paraíba route to the east).

By the beginning of the nineteenth century, the route pattern had shaped the basic plan of São Paulo, with the north-south (Minas-Santos) axis being predominant. The population of the still small 'city region' had not grown dramatically, there being 21,300 in 1798 and 25,000 in 1816. According to Morse[13] the central zone of the city could boast some development of occupations other than agriculture by 1818. These included 566 in military service, 220 merchants, 271 skilled workmen and 98 labourers. However, at this time at least a quarter of the population were slaves. The layout of the city was roughly rectilinear in parts, although the centre had only about a dozen streets with un-numbered dwellings not always well ordered. Churches were the main public buildings. Further residences and agricultural homesteads (*chácaras*) grew out along principal routes. By Independence therefore, São Paulo retained the basic characteristics of a semi-rural town set in an agricultural hinterland of about 200,000 people.

After Independence the city gained a new role as a provincial political and administrative centre, by virtue of which it was to have a Law Academy (one of only two then designated in Brazil) and a public press. As with other municipalities, official impetus for planning was given by the provisions of the 1824 Constitution and the Law of Municipal Organization (1828). Yet the subordination of local autonomy to the court in Rio and Acts which restricted the financial resources of municipal authorities frequently limited the planned expansion of urban development. By 1840, São Paulo had almost two dozen named streets and it had acquired one major new amenity in the form of a botanical garden, although few other improvements had been made. Routes out of the city were poorly maintained, street drainage was lacking, rivers which traversed the city continued their uncontrolled flooding, bridges were in bad repair and there was some new pressure for extra accommodation brought about by the small inflow of immigrant workers which began shortly after Independence. While the severity of these problems should not be over-stated given the city's relatively small size and low population density, it is of some significance that such a backlog of needs already existed even before new social and economic changes began under the impact of coffee.

Coffee-growing had spread down into the state of São Paulo along the Paraíba Valley and output began to be substantial by mid-nineteenth century. In addition, planting of coffee trees was under way throughout the state except the far west and south. An immediate effect of coffee expansion was to reduce the production of foodstuffs which had been a major output of farms in the vicinity of São Paulo. At the same time, coffee rapidly reduced the carrying capacity of the land which meant that the coffee frontier had to expand continually. The crop thus ushered in two major changes which were to transform the course of São Paulo City's development. First, the need for large numbers of farm labourers was initially responsible for stimulating migration of ex-slaves from other regions of the country, backed by an upswing in foreign immigration. These trends were even more pronounced as the movement for abolition of slavery reached its climax in the 1870s and 1880s and government policies were introduced to encourage large-scale immigration. Some 263,000 immigrants (mostly Italians) disembarked at Santos from 1882–91. Secondly, the commercialization of the coffee crop and its extensive land use required improved transport links. The 1860s thus saw the onset of rail construction, linking the interior state coffee regions via São Paulo to the port of Santos from which exports proceeded. The Santos-Jundiaí line was opened in 1867 and proved to be a further stimulus to coffee plantings. By 1875 four other railroads connected São Paulo with its wider hinterland and provided the main arteries of an extensive rail system installed between 1880 and 1940.

As was indicated above, the primary purpose of the railways was the transport of coffee from the production regions to Santos for export. But of additional importance was their role in transporting incoming workers and pioneer settlers[14, 15]. At first, new colonists from abroad, whose expenses were subsidized by the state government of São Paulo, were obliged to work on the coffee *fazandas,* being given a rail passage to interior destinations. Later, however, these colonists were free to move elsewhere. The dramatic growth of São Paulo city between 1890 and 1900 from 65,000 to just under 250,000 tends to suggest that many immigrants eventually gravitated back towards the city. As in Rio, this was often reflected in new patterns of residential growth near the source of the rail links.

The new demographic dimension of São Paulo as a city of a quarter of a million people by 1900 brought about strongly competing demands upon land use from industrial, commercial and residential interests. Such demands intensified the scramble for living and working space and proved the inadequacy of existing facilities as the city changed its status from pre-industrial to industrial. It should be pointed out that some efforts had been made to put in new infrastructure (water supplies, roads, lighting etc.) during the last quarter of the nineteenth century, but these fell far short of requirements. Spontaneous solutions thus prevailed over planned ones in the wake of a real-estate boom. New constructions were erected in haphazard fashion without recourse to even the most basic overall plan to integrate building with public utilities such as water supplies, sewage and transport. Frequently, in the city's central zone, the rapidity of growth coupled with the operations of land speculators, who sold off plots irrespective of the buyer's land-use intentions, produced congested multi-purpose developments. Simultaneously, the subdivision of suburban land began to take place on a larger scale, although this was often done along the more planned lines of rectilinear street patterns.

In sum these changes combined to produce a city which was highly disarticulated. Housing shortage was also a specific problem to be faced by the city's poorer elements whose main choice of accommodation consisted of the communal *cortiço* type of dwelling, towards the city centre (some of these having been constructed by 'benevolent' early industrialists) or in improvised shacks often on the outskirts, distant from work opportunities. These problems persisted as the city's population expanded further under the impact of continued immigration (a net inflow of some 500,000 people to Brazil was recorded between 1908 and 1933) and industrialization. By 1920, São Paulo city had almost 600,000 people, while there was a total of 4.6 million in the state as a whole.

BIG CITY GROWTH AND PLANNING EXPERIENCES SINCE 1930

TRENDS SINCE 1930

Since 1930, immigration has ceased to be of major importance as a source of population growth in Brazil. Instead, falls in the death rate and continued high rates of natural increase have been principal factors in expanding the population at rates currently averaging 2.9 per cent per annum. Population tripled between 1920 and 1970 rising from 30 million to 93 million and it is estimated at about 123 million in 1980[16]. Turning to the economy, the collapse of the world coffee market after the Great Crash of 1929 gave new impetus to industrialization through import substitution policies[17, 18]. These factors contributed to intensified levels of urbanization during the post-1930 period. Put simply, increasing numbers of the rural population have migrated to urban areas which in general have gained most of the new non-agricultural activities[19]. In 1970, therefore, more than half the population (52 million out of 93 million) was classified as urban by the census.

As might be expected, these trends have been even more pronounced in the country's largest cities. São Paulo is outstanding in this respect. The capital itself increased its share of state population from 18 per cent in 1940 to 33 per cent in 1970, while its total population rose from 1.3 million to 5.9 million. Rio de Janeiro's net growth rate has been slightly below that of São Paulo since about 1950, although increases in density were much greater. The newer, planned cities of Belo Horizonte and the Federal District of Brasília had populations of 1.2 million and over half a million respectively in 1970. In the case of Brasília such growth is remarkable given the fact that the city was only officially opened in 1960. Extensive metropolitan growth has also been a feature of the urbanization process. Nine metropolitan areas are now recognized by the government for planning purposes, although only São Paulo and Rio constitute large-scale metropolises by world standards with joint populations of nearly 15 million in 1970 and over 18 million in 1975. As in the past, the growth of big city populations has meant that the demand for mass housing has far exceeded supply. However, the greater absolute size of demand and the failure of planning—or other measures—to cope with this has resulted in the widespread adoption of self-help solutions to housing shortage. In this context the *favelas* of Rio, São Paulo and other urban centres have become the well-known ambassadors of the informal housing developments which sprang up throughout Brazil and indeed, Latin America[20–24].

Finally, as a general point it should be mentioned that the development of road transport has given an additional dimension to big city growth since 1930. In particular the expansion and improvement of inter-city road networks (especially between São Paulo, Rio, Belo Horizonte, Salvador and Brasília etc.) has increased the availability of transport by bus, so facilitating internal migration. Frequently, road routes have become new arteries of residential and industrial growth towards the city outskirts. At the same time, larger numbers of private passenger cars, taxis and goods vehicles have generated further problems of congestion and pollution. In turn, the building of fast intra-urban freeways has sometimes taken up large tracts of land which might have been used for residential purposes.

PLANNING EXPERIENCES OF BIG CITIES SINCE 1930

The trends sketched above give some indication of the scale and variety of problems confronting planners. In examining the planning experiences of the four selected cities, attention is drawn to two categories: first, the long-established colonial cities of Rio and São Paulo; and second, the planned cities of Belo Horizonte and Brasília. Yet, in spite of these contrasts in history, it is also shown below that in both categories planning solutions have generally been insensitive to the basic needs of the bulk of city populations, particularly concerning housing provision and public amenities.

RIO DE JANEIRO

Between 1927 and 1930 the city was subject to scrutiny by a planning team under the direction of Alfred Agache, a French engineer-urbanist and exponent of the City Beautiful movement. A plan, referred to as the Agache Plan, was produced. Under this plan, Rio was to be transformed into a monumental city based upon its transport network in the configuration of a hand whose palm was the city centre whilst routes via valleys and beaches were the fingers. The construction of new tunnels through the *morros* and a metro system were to interlink the parts; buildings and residential complexes were to be arranged in functional relationship with the transport pattern. A strategy for the setting up of worker accommodation districts, satellite towns and other residential projects was also included, together with further inputs of water supplies, sanitation and transport. Although somewhat utopian in its basic concept the foresight of the plan was remarkable, since it took into account the likely growth trends of the city over the following thirty years. In the event the plan was not implemented.

By 1960 the severe imbalance between supply of and demand for facilities and services was readily apparent. Very limited provision had been made to serve the needs of the city, which had more than doubled its population from 1.4 million in 1930 to 3.3 million by 1960, or its suburban zones. *Favelas* occupied spare ground wherever possible, including locations on the steep-sided hills and on low-lying ground along the northern shores of Guanabara Bay. Some 16 per cent of Rio's total population in 1960 were living in these settlements[25]. In the higher-income residential areas of the city's south zone (Flamengo, Leme, Copacabana, Ipanema) multi-storey apartment blocks superseded low-rise buildings in all but a few districts (Urca, Santa Tereza and parts of Botafogo). Public utilities such as electricity, water and telephones were stretched. This situation reflected not only a lack of provision to meet increased demands, but the fact that Rio had experienced some relative decline in its economic fortunes especially after the building of Brasília was designated in 1956. Also, São Paulo had expanded its base with respect to both industrial development and population growth which detracted from Rio's position.

The urban planner Doxiadis (of *Ekistics* fame) was called in to advise on solutions to Rio's problems in 1960, although the extent to which his advice formed the basis of the eventual Action Plan (1961-65) issued in December that year is not clear. The plan gave priority to social and economic infras-tructure provision—in theory—and was at pains to consider the spatial aspects involved. Nevertheless, one of the main targets of the plan was the eradication of *favelas* using funds from the newly-set up USAID scheme to support housing construction programmes. In this respect, the plan bore the indelible stamp of Carlos Lacerda, the then governor of Rio. New housing developments such as Vila Kennedy were located in inconvenient and distant areas, and the extent to which these have eased the demand for housing appears to have been limited. A further project in the plan was the building out of the shoreline (see figure 9.2) between the city centre and Botafogo, to provide space for an urban coastal freeway (the Beira Mar highway) complete with gardens (designed by Roberto Burle Marx) and the Santos Dumont domestic airport complex. Essentially, this was a prestige development.

Subsequently, other projects have been under way, including the con-struction of the Rio-Niterói bridge, building of new tunnels, a metro, viaducts and roads to help ease traffic congestion and a new supersonic airport complex at Galeão. Further attempts have also been made to expand low-income housing especially after the setting up of a national housing bank (the BNH) in 1965. It remains difficult however to assess how far recent projects have gone towards solving city problems. Census data for 1970 show that in the local authority area of Rio itself urban infrastructural inputs to existing dwellings had achieved high rates. Over 80 per cent of dwellings were supplied with water and electricity while sewage links were less well developed. Some negative indicators include marked contrasts in provision between different zones of the city (particularly north–south differences) and a doubling of the proportion of *cariocas* living in *favelas* (from 16 per cent of the total in 1960 to 32 per cent in 1970).

SÃO PAULO

The development of São Paulo after 1930 proceeded in much the same random fashion as it had done from the late nineteenth century although there is little doubt that it benefited from national policies designed to stimulate industry and trade. The city was also fortunate in being able to draw upon the capital, infrastructure, labour force and entrepreneurial skills built up during the coffee period[26]. Such advantages as these seemed not to warrant the strictures planning might impose. Indeed, São Paulo avoided contracting the services of an Agache or a Doxiadis. The city's spatial structure continued to be shaped instead by its historical legacy, infrastructural inputs and real-estate values. It is true that some local municipal codes and practices were laid down but these were restricted in scope and not always observed. The only common guiding principle throughout the metropolitan area was the Sanitary Code of 1951 which established certain minimum criteria to be fulfilled in the process of selling off land parcels for single-family dwellings. One major outcome of this was the perpetuation of low-density suburban development with considerble 'gaps' being left vacant in the urban fabric to accrue in value. In turn, this produced a demand for services (water, sewage, roads etc.) over a very extensive area which meant that the cost of providing these was exceptionally high[27]. As before, high and above-average income residential growth took place in the 'better' inner areas, or, with the use of private transport, selected suburbs, while lower income groups were relegated to less-salubrious districts with more limited services, or *favelas* on plots of vacant land.

In the *município* of São Paulo itself soaring land values drove constructions heavenwards to produce the well-known tower-block skyline with commercial enterprises occupying the most central locations. Industrial and lower income residential land use tended to spread along the major transport routes. This process of spontaneous urbanization did not include any setting aside of land in the most intensively used zones for recreational use or as 'green belt'. Similarly, little attempt was made to plan links between the radial transport routes.

The outcomes summarized above only began to be substantiated by statistical evidence during the course of the later 1960s when attention at last came to focus upon the structure of the city and its metropolitan region as part of a broader trend directed towards the wider uses of planning in São Paulo state. Particular interest centred upon the creation of a metropolitan area planning authority (GEGRAN) and studies were carried out to identify principal problems. Among other results it was found the in 1967/68 water supply problems affected some 60 per cent of the population; poor integration of public transport systems and central city congestion required long daily journeys to work averaging three hours per day; with respect to housing, there was an estimated lack of 375,000 units affecting 1.7 million people, while 40 per cent of dwellings were without sewage links and refuse collection was absent over 50 per cent of the metropolitan area.

These findings were used as the basis for an urban plan[28] and then a development plan for the metropolitan area[29]. The latter was in fact a perspective plan reviewing alternatives for spatial organization of the region until 1980, rather than a set of concrete proposals. While no attempt is made here to evaluate the results, a study published in 1976 suggested that limited progress had been made by the mid-1970s[30]. Moreover, the acquisition of land by those relatively few in a position to afford it continues to be the best inflation-proof investment, thus perpetuating the tendency for property and land speculation.

BELO HORIZONTE

Belo Horizonte was Brazil's first major planned city in the post-Independence period, being created as the new capital of Minas Gerais state to replace the historic capital of Ouro Prêto. The site was chosen in 1893 and construction began in 1894 with the official opening taking place in 1897.

Irrespective of the undulating topography, the city was laid out without considerable deviation from the standard grid-iron pattern. In this case, however, the basic plan was set by wide avenues with each sector of the grid being traversed by a system of streets at right angles. A large municipal garden was incorporated in the plan being located just off-centre, as well as several smaller parks and squares at avenue junctions. The city was also circumscribed by a continuous perimetral road, the *Avenida do Contorno,* leading off from which were roads to the state interior, São Paulo and Rio.

The city remained fairly small in terms of population during the early twentieth century, having only about 55,000 people by 1920. Much of its area was given over to residential, commercial and administrative uses. After this, it began to experience considerable growth, having over a fifth of a million people in 1940. The relative decline in agriculture and the new emphasis upon government-sponsored economic (and industrial) expansion were both important stimuli to this growth. By 1970 Belo Horizonte ranked as Brazil's third largest city with over 1.2 million people, and almost half a million more in its suburban zones. The current urban area is over twelve times the size of the original city. Clearly, much of the recent expansion could not have been foreseen by the original plan. Some revisions to the master plan were in fact made during the 1940s. One specific result of the revision was the setting up of an industrial district at Contagem to the west where appropriate economic inputs such as power, transport and lighting would be provided to attract and serve incoming industry. While this—and other—estates have successfully served the purpose of separating out industrial land use[31], the absence of land-use controls elsewhere has often led to the spontaneous mushrooming of industrial, residential and other uses, these being subject to similar real-estate dictates as in other cities. In particular, rising land values towards the centre have contributed to the development of a multi-storey skyline and decentralization of residential uses.

Inevitably, the bulk of new growth has had to take place outside the planned area of the city, tending to spread along principal road and rail routes, although the *serras* to the south and east have acted as controlling factors. In line with other cities, provision of public services and dwellings has lagged behind the newer demands of an enlarged urban area. As yet, however, the demands have been small in comparison with those in São Paulo or Rio de Janeiro.

Some attempts were made to plan ongoing growth during the 1970s both in the context of the two state development plans[32, 33], and through the metropolitan agency PLAMBEL created in 1971. One particular scheme, announced during 1973, was that two new towns were to be constructed within the metropolitan area. One was to be located in Betím-Contgem to the west with access to the industrial districts, and the other in the little-urbanized area of Vespasiano to the north. The need for an integrated approach to public transport, other services and for the breaking of the cycle of land and property speculation has also been recognized. These may be seen as steps in the right direction if the needs of lower-income families who form the bulk of the population are to be served[34], although implementation of such measures as are implied are strongly dependent upon financial, administrative, technical and other abilities of state planning agencies. In turn, these also depend upon the decisions and financial allocations of federal agencies.

BRASÍLIA

The designation of Brasília as the new federal capital of Brazil in 1956 by President Kubitschek was the outcome of a long sequence of deliberations which had begun in earnest in the early nineteenth century. The city cannot, therefore, be viewed simply as a specially-conceived scheme designed to alleviate pressure on the country's already overburdened urban areas.

Certainly, such an objective may have seemed logical by the late 1950s, but more important factors were the development-oriented approaches in certain quarters of the Brazilian polity, together with the personal wishes of the president himself[35, 36]. Nevertheless, the instant appeal of the proposed city was registered by the rapid growth of population during the construction phase, although this was stimulated by the prospect of high wages offered to construction workers.

By 1959 there were over 64,000 people in the Federal District. Many of these were involved in some way with the construction effort and related services. The inauguration of the city in 1960 saw the transfer of some 50,000 civil servants from Rio, and the attraction of about 30,000 migrants to Brasília. Continued in-migration and transfers of government personnel since then have expanded the population still further, although in 1970 no more than 50 per cent of the Federal District population (roughly 270,000 out of 537,000) could be classed as civil servants, their dependents or other professionals involved with national or international agencies. These population trends indicate that Brasília in reality cannot be regarded as the pure product suggested in Lúcio Costa's Pilot Plan for Brazil's 'city of the future'. This plan was drawn up with the idea that the future city would be a single functional unit, housing the whole population. Yet, it became apparent at a very early stage that the Brasília of the Pilot Plan would have to be modified if the migrant population drawn in during the construction period was to remain.

Thus, while the principal monumental design of the city centre has been immortalized in concrete, steel and glass, other features not anticipated by the plan are in evidence. These consist of a number of satellite towns at varying distances from the city centre, as well as some quasi-legal squatments in parts of the inner area. Epstein's study[37] has demonstrated that these urban nuclei are the outcomes of decisions taken by NOVACAP (the agency responsible for building Brasília) whereby the spontaneous squatter settlements which had sprung up within and along routes into the city were 'legalized' in alternative out-of-centre locations. At first, early squatter settlements had been tolerated by the authorities since it had proved impossible to house all comers in the main construction camps or the Free Town. But as soon as the situation appeared to threaten public order or the execution of the plan, NOVACAP's director proposed that a satellite town—Taguatinga—should be set up outside the boundary of Brasília's central zone.

Taguatinga was improvised at first, but later became consolidated as basic utilities were installed. From an initial population of 3677 in 1959 it had grown to over 26,000 by late 1960, 69,000 by 1964 and 107,000 in 1970. The town now ranks as the second largest urban nucleus after Brasíla itself. Other satellite towns—such as Gama and Sobradinho—were also set up and the pre-existing rural settlements of Braslândia and Planaltina have received some official support. The extent of assistance to these towns has been the input of utilities and subdivision of lots to be sold or distributed for residential use. If housing was built, it generally consisted of poorly constructed individual shacks. Since 1964, the population of these satellite towns has made up over 50 per cent of the total living in the Federal District. In effect, they serve the function of segregating low-income families from the better-off residents of the city centre. This is not so very different from the net effect of spontaneous *favela* development in Rio and São Paulo, although in the case of Brasília the removal of low-income groups at the planning stage has ensured that the greater part of poor housing is kept from the view of international visitors and top civil servants. It can be argued of course that such a strategy at least represents some solution to the problems of the lower strata, in that facilities were provided (however limited) and the worst features of exploitation or exclusion may have been avoided. Yet, given that the principal sources of paid employment are in central Brasília, and that the satellite towns are some distance away (10–45 km) often being badly-served by public transport, it is difficult to agree that such a strategy has been fully acceptable.

Without labouring the point, the observations above illustrate some of the problems of a city which was planned towards the future and give an insight into the aphorism 'it is difficult living in Brasília' (*é duro morar em Brasília*). Such difficulties have not been completely disregarded by government planning agencies. In the later 1960s efforts were made to increase the supply of housing—popular as well as medium and higher income types—although new dwellings have rarely fulfilled existing demands. Two special programmes were also devised for Brasília operating on two different levels. The first was a programme for the 'Geo-economic' region approved in February 1975; the second was an urban development package for the Federal District announced in March 1976, which made technical and financial resources available. It is too early to assess the impact of these programmes, but what is clear from the foregoing review is that Brasília was not intended to be, and has not been allowed to become, a city which presented a new blueprint for urban development.

CONCLUSIONS

This paper has demonstrated, albeit selectively, the limited success of planning attempts as applied in four Brazilian cities. The main emphasis of planning projects has been upon the provision of urban and economic 'hardware'. Thus, the poorer social strata have often been excluded from the benefits of public utility investments and have also been adversely affected by housing shortages. This was shown to apply in the case of the planned as well as the unplanned cities. In part, such outcomes reflect the general constraints on planning in Brazil—and indeed, much of Latin America. These include rudimentary planning facilites, few planners, administrative and financial constraints[38–39]. A further—and possibly more serious—factor, relates to the overall *concept* of planning, and specifically, the objectives pursued by urban planning. In this context, it should be made clear that since at least the later nineteenth century city growth experiences have been an expression of trends in the broader political economy of the country. During the last fifty years, economic development policies have been especially influential. Such policies have not been able to achieve the multiple (and often, conflicting) objectives of increasing national economic growth while simultaneously reducing social and spatial inequalities and creating substantial numbers of well-paid employment opportunities. As has been shown, many of the fundamental problems still to be faced in the cities studied depend upon planning approaches which include a greater sensitivity to basic human needs for more housing, jobs and better incomes. This latter observation provides both a criticism of past planning efforts and a suggestion about the redirection of planning priorities in future.

NOTES

1. Delson, R. M. (1976) Planners and reformers: urban architects of late eighteenth-century Brazil. *Eighteenth Century Studies,* 10 (1), pp. 40–51.
2. Delson, R. M. (1979) Land and urban planning: aspects of modernisation in early nineteenth century Brazil. (Mimeographed)
3. Reis Filho, N. (1969) *Evolução Urbana do Brasil.* Rio de Janeiro: Pioneira Editora..
4. Singer, P. (1969) *Desenvolvimento Econômico e Evolução Urbana.* São Paulo: Compania Editora Nacional.
5. Furtado, C. (1959) *Formação Econômica do Brasil.* Rio de Janeiro: Fundo de Cultura.
6. Morse, R. (1958) *From Community to Metropolis: A Biography of São Paulo, Brazil.* Gainsville, Florida: University of Florida Press.
7. Baer, W. (1965) *Industrialization and Economic Development in Brazil.* Homewood, Illinois: Irwin.
8. Dean, W. (1969) *The Industrialization of São Paulo, 1880–1945.* Austin, Texas: University of Texas Press.
9. Pearse, A. (1961) Some characteristics of urbanization in the city of Rio De Janeiro, in Hauser, P. (ed.) *Urbanization in Latin America.* New York: UNESCO, pp. 191-205.
10. *Ibid.*
11. Morse, R. (1958) *From Community to Metropolis: A Biography of São Paulo, Brazil.* Gainsville, Florida: University of Florida Press.
12. Marcilio, M. L. (1974) *A Cidade de São Paulo.* São Paulo: Pioneira Editora.
13. *Ibid.*
14. Milliet, S. (1938) *O Roteiro do Café.* São Paulo: Departamento de Cultura.
15. Monbeig, P. (1952) *Pionniers et Planteurs de São Paulo.* Paris: Armand Colin.
16. Instituto Brasileira de Geografia e Estatistica (1975) *Anuário Estatístico.* Rio de Janeiro: Serviço Gráfico IBGE.

17. Baer, W. (1971) Industrialization and policy-making in Brazil. *Economic Development and Cultural Change,* **19** (2), pp. 181–93.
18. Bergsmann, J. (1970) *Brazil: Industrialization and Trade Policies.* Paris: OECD.
19. Graham, D. and Hollanda, S. B. (1971) *Migration, Regional and Urban Growth and Development in Brazil: A Selective Analysis of the Historical Record 1872–1970.* São Paulo: University of São Paulo.
20. Hauser, P. (ed.) (1961) *Urbanization in Latin America.* New York: UNESCO.
21. Mangin, W. (1967) Latin American squatter settlements: a problem and a solution. *Latin American Research Review,* **2** (3), pp. 65–98.
22. Morse, R. (1961) Latin American cities: aspects of function and structure. *Comparative Studies in Society and History,* pp. 473–93. Morse, R. (1965) Recent studies on Latin American urbanisation: a selective survey and commentary. *Latin American Research Review,* **1** (1), pp. 35–74. Morse, R. (1971) Trends and issues in Latin American urban research, 1965–70. *Latin American Research Review,* **6** (1), pp. 3–52; **6** (2), pp. 19–75.
23. Hardoy, J. (ed.) (1975) *Urbanization in Latin America—Approaches and Issues.* New York: Anchor.
24. Perlman, J. (1976) *The Myth of Marginality.* Berkeley: University of California Press.
25. *Ibid.*
26. Dean, W. (1969) *The Industrialization of São Paulo, 1880–1945.* Austin, Texas: University of Texas Press.
27. Bolaffi, G. (1975) Habitação e urbanismo: o problema e o falso problema. *Ensaios de Opinião,* Julho, pp 73-85.
28. Grupo executivo para Grande São Paulo—GEGRAN (1968) *Plano Urbanístico Básico.* São Paulo.
29. Grupo Executivo para Grande São Paulo—GEGRAN (1969) *Plano Metropolitano de Desenvolvimento Integrado.* São Paulo.
30. CEBRAP (1976) *São Paulo: Crescimento e Pobreza.* São Paulo: CEBRAP.
31. Dickenson, J. P. (1970) Industrial estates in Brazil. *Geography,* **55** (3), pp. 326–9.
32. Estado do Minas Gerais (1971) *I Plano de Desenvolvimento Mineiro.* Belo Horizonte.
33. Estado do Minas Gerais (1975) *II Plano de Desenvolvimento Econômico e Social.* Belo Horizonte.
34. Merrick, T. (1976) Employment and earnings in the informal sector of Brazil: the case of Belo Horizonte. *Journal of Developing Areas,* **10** (3), pp. 337–54.
35. Meira Penna, J. (1958) *Quando Mudan os Capitais.* Rio de Janeiro: IBGE.
36. Epstein, D. G. (1973) *Brasília—Plan and Reality.* Berkeley: University of California Press.
37. *Ibid.*
38. Wilheim, J. (1969) *Urbanismo no Subdesenvolvimento.* São Paulo: Editora Saga.
39. Da Costa, J. G. (1971) *Planejamento Governamental.* Rio de Janeiro: Fundação Getúlio Vargas.

10

Exporting planning: the colonial and neo-colonial experience[1]

A. D. KING

We want not only England but all parts of the Empire to be covered with Garden Cities.[2]

I hope that in the new Delhi we shall be able to show how those ideas which Mr. Howard put forward . . . can be brought in to assist this first Capital created in our time. The fact is that no new city or town should be permissable in these days to which the word 'Garden' cannot be rightly applied. The old congestion has, I hope, been doomed forever.[3]

In 1945, the sphere of influence of the English [Town and Country Planning] 1932 Act as developed in the West Indies extended to the continent of Africa . . . Uganda, in . . . 1948, adopted the original Trinidad scheme . . . The influence spread further afield. Fiji legislation shows distinct traces of its West Indian origin . . . Aden has town planning laws . . . closely related to the Uganda ordinances; Sarawak has legislation which finds its roots in Sierra Leone and Nyasaland. In the Indian Ocean, the Seychelles passed legislation derivative from the English Act. Mauritius . . . adopted legislation based on Uganda.

Thus, the 1932 Act has left its mark in all corners of the world . . . Modern developments in British planning procedure are followed closely by colonial planning officers who are always ready to profit by the experience of the mother country.[4]

. . . we have exported, through the media of planning education, some of the worst artifacts of the planning and development process of this country.[5]

SOME DELIMITATIONS

This paper arose from a concern that, in focusing largely on European and North American developments, the history of urban and regional planning might overlook modern planning experience in other areas of the world occupied by two-thirds of its population. Moreover, if 'modern' (i.e. post-1850, 'urban industrial') planning in Europe is to be perceived within a context which ignores the central part played by colonial economies in the industrialization of Europe (especially Britain) and hence—indirectly as well as directly—in the development of modern planning, a major omission is being made[6]. Whilst the unlikely task of discussing a myriad cases of 'planning' in Asia, Africa, the Middle East and Central America has been eased by subsequent contributors, it is nonetheless the original unrealistic proposal which determines both the content and structure of this paper.

Conceivably, the scope of such a theme would cover the activities of those metropolitan societies—France, Britain, Belgium, Portugal, Spain, Holland, Italy, Germany, the United States and also South Africa, with colonial possessions in south and south-east Asia, middle America and Africa over the last hundred or more years[7]. To be technically correct, it would be necessary to include other continents—such as Australasia—politically defined as 'colonies' during part of the period. It should purportedly deal, not only with the 'grand designs' for Delhi, Lusaka, Canberra, Salisbury, Nairobi, Kaduna or Kuala Lumpur, but with a myriad cases from Fez to Djibouti, Casablanca to Luanda where some forms of conscious planning took place, if not in the particular British manner of town planning ordinances, improvement trusts or master plans. It would deal with the activities of Lutyens, Baker, Geddes, Lanchester in India (Dehli, Calcutta, Madras), with Baker or White in South and East Africa (Pretoria, Nairobi), with Reade in Malaya, Adshead in Northern Rhodesia (now Zambia), Ashbee in Palestine, Gardner-Medwin in the West Indies, or their French counterparts in Morocco, Algeria, other parts of colonial Africa, in Saigon, Cholon or the Treaty Ports of China[8].

If this is the possible scope for the field, this paper is limited to the British colonial experience as it relates to those areas where subject populations were incorporated, on a large scale, into the political, economic and cultural system of the metropolitan society. Hopefully, it may spur others to look into this grossly under-researched area, including the experience of France, Belgium, Portugal, Spain, the United States, as well as of the Soviet Union in inner Asia. It is an area not only of immense importance for present-day planning practice in the 'Third World' but one that offers insights into fundamental theoretical and methodological issues in planning[9].

Two conceptual clarifications are needed. Following Emerson, colonialism is understood as 'the establishment and maintenance, for an extended time, of rule over an alien people that is separate from and subordinate to the ruling power ... It is no longer closely associated with the term "colonisation" which involves the settlement abroad of people from the mother country'[10]. For a proper understanding of the processes of 'colonial planning', however, some basic conceptual distinctions would need to be made between different colonial situations: for example, regarding the numbers of an indigenous people existing in the colonized country, their culture and state of economic development including the presence, if any, of urban settlement; the number, activities and degree of permanence of colonial settlements; and the degree of social, economic and political incorporation into the colonized society of the indigenous inhabitants[11].

Second, what is to be understood by 'urban and regional planning'? In an earlier paper, a plea was made for a *wider* definition of planning, to be understood as 'environmental decision-making'[12]. The history of urban planning in any society demonstrates a long continuity—in terms of emerging ideas of social policy, social and cultural values, the distribution of economic and social power and the development of political institutions—between an age when there was no governmental responsibility for 'town planning' described as such and a period (in Britain, from 1909) when there was. This continuity is especially evident in colonial territories[13]. In this context, therefore, the modern history of 'exporting planning' can be usefully divided into three phases.

(a) A period up to the early twentieth century when settlements, camps, towns and cities were consciously laid out according to various military, technical, political and cultural principles, the most important of which was military-political dominance[14]. In certain cases (as with Coleman's plan for Singapore in 1819 or the lay-out of towns in Natal or Cape Colony[15] a greater degree of strictly 'professional' skill may have been utilized.

(b) A second period, beginning in the early twentieth century, which coincides with the development of formally-stated 'town planning' theory, ideology, legislation and professional skills in Britain, when the network of colonial relationships was used to convey such phenomena—on a selective and uneven basis—to the dependent territories.

(c) A third period of post- or neo-colonial developments—depending on the standpoint taken—after 1947 in Asia and 1956 in Africa[16], when cultural, political and economic links have, within a larger network of global communications and a situation of economic dependence, provided the means to continue the process of 'cultural colonialism' with the continued export of values, ideologies and planning models. It is taken for granted that in all three periods the traffic of ideas has been largely unilateral.

Moreover, in discussing urban planning in relation to colonial territories, it is impossible to disassociate a more limited notion of 'planning' from, at one level, a range of related topics such as social housing, architectural style, health, house form, legislation, building science and technology and these, at another level, from the total cultural, economic and social system of which they are a part. The introduction of modern 'planned' environments based on Western notions of civilization, when compared to the traditional indigenous city of Kano (northern Nigeria) or the Malayan village, has obviously modified far more than just the physical environment[17].

The aim of this paper, therefore, is to suggest five interrelated themes which seem to the author to be central to any discussion regarding the 'exporting of planning' in a colonial situation. By the multiplicity of the historical-geographical circumstances covered and the change, during the period, governing the metropolitan-colonial relationships, it is fully recognized that sweeping generalizations will be made. Moreover, the issues raised and the way they are discussed are significantly more dependent on an initial moral stance, not only towards the historical experience of colonialism but more expressly, towards present-day inequalities in the world than would possibly be the case when discussing planning in our own society.

The Political-Economic Framework

Colonialism, as a political, economic and cultural process, was the vehicle by which urban planning was exported to many non-Western societies. How were the aims and activities of planning affected by this? How did urban planning contribute to or detract from the larger colonial situation? What is the present-day structure of political and economic relationships which enables the assumptions and aims of planning to be transferred to ex-colonial societies?

As suggested above, a consideration of these questions presupposes an intellectual and moral stance. Stated as a simplistic dichotomy, this may be an analysis which treats imperialism as 'the highest state of capitalism' (Lenin) where subject populations (and environments) were incorporated into the metropolitan capitalist economy with the attendant consequences for good or ill inherent in that system; at the other end of the spectrum, colonialism can be seen as the primary channel by which the benefits of Western civilization, 'the ideas and techniques, the spiritual and material forces of the West' have been brought to a large portion of mankind[18].

In the simplest analysis, colonialism was a means by which the metropolitan power extended its markets for manufactured goods and by which the colonies, in turn, supplied raw materials to the metropolis. Though such an over-simplification represents a caricature of the complex historical situation, the notion of economic dependency, characteristic of both colonial and post-colonial situations, has obvious utility. An aspect of the notion is what Castells[19] has termed 'dependent urbanization', i.e. industrialization, which historically was closely related to urbanization in the development of modern Western societies, in the colonial case took place in the metropolitan society whilst the urbanization (without industrialization) took place in the dependent colonial society. Urban planning in the colonies, along with its associated activities such as housing and transport developments, in any of the three periods indicated, may be viewed as part of this phenomenon of 'dependent urbanization'. The evolution of urban systems (regional planning?) and the organization of urban space (urban planning) in the colonial society can be accounted for by 'the internal and (especially) the external distribution of power'[20].

The developing ideas of dependency theory have been summarized by Friedmann and Wulff[21].

> Basically, it involves the notion that powerful corporate and national interests, representing capitalist society at its most advanced, established outposts in the principal cities of Third World countries, for three interrelated purposes: to extract a sizable surplus from the dependent economy, in the form of primary products, through principally a process of 'unequal exchange'; to expand the market for goods and services produced in the home countries of advanced monopoly capitalism; and to ensure stability of an indigenous political system that will resist encroachment by ideologies and social movements that threaten to undermine the basic institutions of the capitalistic system. All three forms of penetration are ultimately intended to serve the single purpose of helping to maintain expanding levels of production and consumption in the home countries of advanced capitalism.
>
> . . . (Later versions of this theory see the domination of peripheral economies primarily of help in the expansion of multi-national corporations that exhibit a growing independence of action from national commitments and control.)
>
> In the course of this process, local elites are co-opted. Their life-style becomes imitatively cosmopolitan . . . As part of this process massive transfers of rural people are made to the urban enclave economy.

According to Friedmann and Wulff, this theory of dependency, or more accurately, *dependent capitalism,* seems to account for certain forms of spatial development in newly-industrializing societies[22].

Whether this analysis is accepted *in toto* or only in part, there are nonetheless certain aspects which, when applied to the urban planning experience of the colonial (irrespective of the post-colonial) period, explain a great deal. Translated into tangible schemes for the location, lay-out and institutional provision of specific planned environments, it is apparent that many specifically colonial phenomena in the built environment can be explained by dependency theory.

Thus, in India, the most widespread example of conscious urban planning prior to the twentieth century is the location and lay-out of military cantonments, the primary purpose of which was to provide for the ultimate sanction of force over the colonized population. The informally planned 'civil station', located alongside, accommodated the political-administrative 'managers' of the colonized society. The major cities resulting from the colonial connection (Madras, Bombay, Calcutta), all subject to various planning exercises in the early twentieth century, were not primarily industrial centres but commercial, *entrepôt* ports oriented to the metropolitan economy[23]. The major city-building exercise during two hundred years of informal and formal colonial rule—the planning and construction of New Delhi (1911-40)—involved the creation of a capital city almost entirely devoted to administrative, political and social functions with virtually no attempt made to plan for industrial development. The so-called 'hill stations'—a major example of specifically colonial urban development—had primarily political and socio-cultural functions, the most famous of them, Simla, described by Learmonth and Spate as 'parasitic' in relation to India's economy[24].

In Africa, for much of the colonial period, the functions of newly-established centres were political, administrative and commercial, not industrial. The built environment of the 'ideal type' political administrative capital was characterized by those buildings housing the key institutions of colonialism: government or state house, the council or assembly buildings (if any), army barracks or cantonment, the police lines, hospital, jail, government offices and the road system, housing and recreational space for the expatriate European bureaucracy and occasionally, housing for local government employees. At its most extreme, as at Lagos, the place of the central business district was occupied by the race course.

The economic institutions of colonialism were expressed in physical and spatial form: the penetration of finance capital in the construction of banks, insurance buildings and the headquarters of the multi-national corporation; the incorporation of labour power in the 'native townships', mining compounds and the 'housing for labour'. The whole relationship between the economic system, the supply of 'native labour' by induced migration from rural areas and the provision or, more accurately, lack of provision for their accommodation is too large an issue to be discussed here, having, to quote Collins, 'a literature of its own'[25]. The underlying assumption of the system of circulatory labour migration in the Copperbelt was that 'the towns were for Europeans and the rural areas were for Africans. It followed that no African should be in town except to provide labour as and when required by a European employer. Only men were required . . . Urban housing was therefore rudimentary'[26].

In the more 'liberal', pre-independence phase in Africa, considerable effort was placed in planning and construction of 'African housing'. Such efforts can be viewed, on one hand, as evidence of changing values and priorities in the postwar period, a humanitarian concern for what were seen as the unsatisfactory conditions of indigenous rural migrants living in shanty towns on the edge of the city: 'low-cost' and 'planned' housing, with sanitation, electricity and water supply constructed as part of a new social welfare programme of the Colonial Office. It can also, however, be seen as a means of incorporating labour into the colonial economy[27]. Built and let by the metropolitan government, housing in this sense represented a subsidy to wages—either to government employees or metropolitan enterprises—as well as a potential instrument of social control. The planning, design and building of such housing estates—as also of 'Asian' and 'European' housing (of somewhat different order)—in separate parts of the town is patently 'town planning' and the nature of the activities are part of the larger colonial enterprise[28].

The metropolitan government, in developing these low-cost housing programmes, generates and exchanges information on standards, costs and design with other European powers with interests in Africa: the Belgian Office des Cités Africaines in the Congo (later, Zaire); the French Bureau Central d'Etudes pour les Equipments d'Outre-Mer (on 'tropical housing') of the Secretariat des Missions d'Urbanisme et d'Habitat, and the South African National Housing and Planning Commission (on minimum standards for housing non-Europeans). Information is also exchanged with major metropolitan private concerns with their own housing programmes for African workers: Imperial Tobacco, Fyffes or the Union Minère (later, Gecamines) in the Congo[29]. In brief, 'official' housing and planning policy is primarily directed to ensuring basic minimum standards for the local labour force and government employees as well as government buildings, administrative and welfare buildings (schools, hospitals, colleges). Industrial development, such as it is, is the responsibility of local, or more usually, metropolitan private enterprise.

THE CULTURAL, SOCIAL AND IDEOLOGICAL CONTEXT OF COLONIAL PLANNING

The history of 'town and country planning' in Britain in the industrial and post-industrial era is a unique and culture-specific historical experience. True, common factors resulting from the influence of industrialization or modern automotive transport may induce a structural similarity in urban environments of different industrial societies: in some respects, Birmingham is like Berlin in the same way as pre-industrial Fez is like pre-industrial Baghdad or Katmandu. Yet given such economic or technological determinants, the extent to which urban forms and planned environments differ clearly depends on other factors: cultural values, unique historical experience, geography and, above all, the values and ideological beliefs of those power-holding groups responsible for structuring and implementing decisions about urban planning and the overall shape of towns.

The particular ideological and cultural context of British planning in the first half of the twentieth century, as dominated by the Garden City movement, is well known. The primacy of 'health, light and air', combined with a set of social and aesthetic beliefs, as a reaction to the nineteenth-century industrial city[30] was expressive of an implicit environmental determinism which pursued physicalist solutions to social, economic and political problems ('the peaceful path to reform'). It was an ideology, however, which also rested on assumptions of social and political stability.

From this nineteenth- and early twentieth-century experience grew the theory of physical planning, as well as planning legislation and the mechanisms to implement it, which—until relatively recently—was accepted as a form of 'technical expertise' by which environments were modelled or controlled in accordance with an assumed 'public good'.

It was this 'expertise' which, with its assumptions, values and mechanisms and partly modified by local conditions, was exported to colonial societies. There are many aspects of this process only some of which can be touched on here.

As discussed in the preceding section, physical planning notions and legislation were introduced as part of the overall economic and political context of colonialism. The basic divisions of the society, inherent in the colonial process, between ruler and ruled, black (brown) and white, rich and poor, 'European' and 'native', were taken as givens. In this situation, the 'techniques' and goals of planning—'orderly' development, easing traffic flows, *physically* 'healthy' environments, planned residential areas, reduced densities, zoning of industrial and residential zones, and the rest, were introduced, each according to the standards deemed appropriate to the various segregated populations in the city—and all without disturbing the overall power structure.

Secondly, the over-riding, even obsessive concern with 'health' (referred to by Swanson[31] as the 'sanitation syndrome') was, after the implicit political and economic function of planning, taken as the driving force behind planning in all colonial territories. The creation of physically 'healthy' environments, defined according to the cultural criteria of the metropolitan power, became a major objective. It is 'health' (in quotes) rather than health because the basically relative nature of health states and their overall cultural and behavioural context (discussed below), if appreciated at some times, were ignored at others. Indigenous definitions of health states, the means for achieving them and the environments in which they existed were replaced by those of the incoming power in a total ecological transformation. Thus, vital statistics from the metropolitan society are used as the reference point to 'measure' health states in the colonial population; historically- and socially-derived concepts of 'over-crowding' developed in the metropolitan society are applied to the indigenous environment, irrespective of the cultural context or the larger economic and political situation[32]. In the interests of 'health', new environments are created—rows of minimal 'detached' housing units, surrounded by 'light and air', 'open space', gardens, and recreational areas in total disregard of the religious, social, symbolic or political meaning of built environments as expressed in the indigenous villages and towns[33].

Health care defined according to metropolitan cultural norms, with its system of inspections, regulated environments and controls over behaviour becomes, like the police, housing or employment, another means of social control. Because of the racially segregated nature of the society, as Swanson points out, 'problems of public health and sanitation, overcrowding, slums, public order and security are perceived in terms of racial differences'. Though many of the objectives of municipal government (abatement of health dangers, slum clearance and housing) were legitimate and necessary, in a colonial society the pursuit of class interest and the exercise of prejudice regarding race, culture and colour, mixed up these objectives with racial and social issues[34]. The culture and class-specific *perception* of health hazards more than actual health hazards themselves was instrumental in determining much colonial urban planning policy[35].

From a purely physical and spatial viewpoint, environmental standards, norms of building and design (as well as the urban institutions themselves), derived from the historical experience of the capitalist industrial State and overlaid with its particular cultural preferences, were transferred to societies with totally different economic and cultural experience[36]. Though a revision of these norms and standards has been slowly taking place to a greater or lesser extent in the last decade, in 1971 'European planners' were still planning 'Garden Cities in countries which have never known an industrial revolution [forcing] workers to make even longer journeys to work. Few of their plans show any depth of political and social analysis or recognise the necessity for an Afro-centric outlook'[37].

Where substantial numbers of 'ex-patriates' or 'settlers' were exported, as in Lusaka, Nairobi or Delhi, very low density residential developments were built to suit their convenience. In the Master Plan for Nairobi of 1948, revisions to the original lay-out of the town, founded in 1896, suggested that densities in the European area be raised from 1 to 15 per acre[38]. Low densities, extensive intra-urban distances, large housing plots, and lavish recreational space were all based on the assumption of the availability of motorized transport and the telephone, as well as cheap 'native labour'; i.e. on a technology for which the colonized country was dependent on the metropolitan. The assumption in such plans was presumably that the 'industrial', fully-motorized society 'must come', an assumption which, in the post-colonial era of independent development has meant not only vast journeys to work, but excessive expenditure on basic services (water, sewers, road, electricity), inefficient land use and a need for fundamental 're-desification'[39].

Given the fact that metropolitan environments were introduced, or rather, colonial versions of such environments[40], it could be argued that the legislation was necessary to maintain them, hence, the widespread introduction of the 1932 Act and other legislative orders (see opening quotations). Some—if not all—of this legislation, where it was implemented, may have benefited the total population. Yet two points can be mentioned. The first concerns the transfer of particular environmental categories from the metropolitan to the colonial society, of which the basic dichotomy between 'town' and 'country' was one of the more important[41].

Another is the diffusion of what, at a 1977 seminar[42] were referred to as peculiarly British 'hang-ups': of these, the most easily identified are those values of historicism and sentiment expressed in the 'preservation' syndrome. In the colonial context, this has a double irony. Not only does planning effort go into inculcating the colonized culture with similar values but, more important, the values and criteria of the colonial power are used to define and 'preserve' 'buildings of architectural and historic importance' while remnants of the indigenous culture are allowed to disappear[43].

A further assumption is that which relates to the supposed influence of designed environments on forms of social organization. It has been suggested that, for many years, planning was seen as a professional 'technical' process. In recent years, the range of social assumptions on which design decisions have been made has been increasingly questioned. Thus, concepts of 'community' and 'neighbourhood' have come under scrutiny[44], particularly when applied to the planning of housing or residential areas. These and similar concepts have—even within the totally different cultural context— been part of the planning concepts used in the design of colonial environments.

COLONIAL PLANNING: THE SOCIAL DIMENSION

The central social fact of colonial planning was segregation, principally, though not only, on racial lines. The segregated city not only resulted from but in many cases, created the segregated society. In southern Africa, the indigenous population was kept out of cities; here and elsewhere, it was confined to 'native locations' or 'townships'[45] or it 'squatted' on the perimeter. In India, an implicit apartheid based on economic and cultural criteria governing occupation of residential areas was practised. In other south-east Asian cities zoning of Asian and European areas was the norm[46].

In South Africa, as labour migration increased, 'native housing' was provided in locations on the edge of the city. As urbanization proceeded, Africans were 'brought into' the urban system in the form of segregated cities, thus, as Swanson[47] describes, learning to see themselves in the new social categories imposed by the ruling white minority. 'The urban nexus explains why the policies of segregation and separate development emerged as the dominant concerns of local and national government', the Native (Urban) Areas Act of 1923 embodying, for the first time, national recognition of the impact of urbanization. The segregated city has been fundamental in the development of 'categorical' relationships, the stereotyping of one race and its behaviour by another[48].

Even within the larger racial divisions, however, transformations have also occurred as a result, in later times, of particular planning and housing policies which have allocated different social groups to housing types and residential areas built and allocated according to economic (i.e. income bracket) criteria. Because of the lack of finance or capacity in the private sector, in many colonial and ex-colonial societies, a large proportion of housing has been undertaken by government, particularly in newly-created urban centres such as Tema (Ghana). The design and allocation of housing and area according to occupation and income group has been significant in structuring perceptions of social stratification[49]. Similar practices—a continuation of the colonial Public Works Department tradition—can be found in Chandigarh or Islamabad.

Nothing could be more different than the traditional Ashanti village and the low-cost, grid-iron planned suburban housing unit estate of Accra[50]. The symbolic meaning of space in the traditional village, whether expressed in terms of house or compound size, dwelling form, or distance between dwellings, in all cultures relates to social, cultural or religious meanings. New urban environments based on income and occupational differentials clearly affect the perception of social differences. Yet in Ghana, it was assumed that such planned housing could be used *as a means* to break down traditional tribal and kinship bonds and help to establish a 'law-abiding' and, with the introduction of privately-owned, single-family dwellings, an implicitly consumer society[51].

The effect of changes in land ownership and tenure on social structure and relationships is also an important area for investigation.

THE INTERACTION OF ENVIRONMENT AND BEHAVIOUR

Urban planning relates, on one hand, to the actual creation of planned areas and, on the other, to the regulation and modification of other parts of the environment by means of statutory legislation and municipal controls. In democratic societies, it is assumed that statutory control—the law— represents the 'collective will' of members of the society. In theory, therefore, members of the society are, by and large, in agreement with the law and, in a stable polity, accept it as legitimate.

A more important factor controlling the use and modification of the environment—determining how houses are built, how public space is used, how people behave in specific areas—is the whole realm of 'unwritten law', the taken-for-granted rules and codes, based on shared values, which are part of everyday cultural behaviour[52].

In the case of planned environments as well as planning legislation exported to culturally alien colonial societies, neither of these two assumptions apply. By definition, such societies are not democratically governed. Legislation is imposed after being conceived primarily for the interests of the ruling elite acting 'in trusteeship' for the people over whom it rules. In ensuring that such legislation is enforced, resort must be had more frequently to the instruments of social control—police, army, judiciary or the informal, but effective, para-judicial powers of members of the ex-patriate community.

Equally important, in a totally different culture, the taken-for-granted cultural rules governing people's relation to their environment simply do not apply to culturally-different 'imposed' environments; indeed, most of the indigenous cultural code is likely to conflict with that of the incoming colonial society, most obviously, for example, in relation to building practice, sanitation behaviour, and the holding and transfer of land. Hence, over time, two interrelated processes take place. New laws and regulations are enforced by municipal or national governmental authorities by a mixture of penalties and example; secondly, the life-style and cultural behaviour of local inhabitants may be modified as they emulate the ruling colonial elite—in effect, 'Westernization'[53].

If illustration of this interdependence is needed, it can be found by noting the very rapid change which has overtaken colonial environments when abandoned by the colonial power and where they have not been subsequently maintained by a Westernized indigenous elite[54]. The same phenomenon is, of course, observable in any environment where the social composition of its inhabitants changes over time.

EXPORTING PLANNING: THE MECHANISMS

If the central fact about colonial planning is the export of values and ideologies—and not least, the economic ideology of industrial capitalism—from metropolitan to colonial society, a key task is to identify the mechanisms—the agencies or brokers—which enabled this transfer to take place.

In early nineteenth-century India and elsewhere, planning activity, as part of urban development in general, was largely the responsibility of military engineers: specialized knowledge dealing with the lay-out of cantonments as well as building and architecture (the responsibility of the 'Military Board') was taught at army academies at Chatham and Woolwich and in India, from the mid-century, at Thomason Engineering College (later Roorkee University) and Madras Engineering College. Later in the century, these activities were supplemented by surveyors and civil engineers attached to municipalities. As sanitation was a major consideration, both legislation and institutions to enforce it were based on adaptations of metropolitan models.

The rise of professional organizations and the growth of a specialized press dealing with engineering, surveying, architecture and building matters developed especially from the mid-nineteenth century. Not only were civilian professionals (engineers, surveyors and occasionally architects) recruited into colonial administrative and technical services (in India, into the Public Works Department founded in the 1850s) but in the 1860s, an increasing interest is expressed in the professional 'environmental' press regarding developments in the colonies. An institute for the specialized training of civil engineers for India was established at Coopers Hill, Surrey, in the late nineteenth century. It also seems likely that many of the principles of 'tropical' environmental design and planning were transferred from India to Africa[55].

The Garden City and Town Planning movement, the passing of legislation (1909), the establishment of the Town Planners Institute and the institution of town planning as a subject to be taught at university, in the early years of the twentieth century, all had their effect on the transmission of techniques and ideologies abroad—as also did the founding of professional and lay journals at the same time. These carried ideas abroad as well as reports from the colonies of the work being done by engineers, architects and administrators. The involvement of leading practitioners such as Baker (with close relations to Rhodes) or Lutyens in planning and architectural work in South Africa and India stimulated general interest, as also did the building of Canberra. The well-known activities of Geddes and his plans for remodelling Indian cities increasingly made colonial governments and administrators aware of town planning activities. Alongside—and long prior to—these developments was the long-standing interest in public health questions, tropical medicine and the work of the Public Works Department, in many ways more important than the 'grand designs' in shaping settlement forms around the world.

Just how much metropolitan influence in the town planning sphere there was in the Empire between the wars is difficult to establish without much-needed further research. A government town planner was appointed to the Federated Malay States in 1921 (C. C. Reade) and another in Nigeria shortly after. S. D. Adshead prepared the plan for the new capital of Lusaka in Northern Rhodesia in 1931[56]. It would be naive to assume, however, that because no officially-designated 'town planner' was appointed or 'planning' legislation passed, no 'planning' existed as part of ongoing urban development. Such activity continued according to what may best be described as colonial 'ethnic planning' practices—the understood professional and cultural principles of the Public Works Department.

The postwar period saw such links made more tangible. Funded through development and welfare funds of the Colonial Office from 1940, town planning, housing and building expertise was increasingly made available to the colonial territories, especially Africa, the West Indies and elsewhere. By 1947, some forty-seven British architects and planners were working in colonial administrations. In 1948, as a result of collaboration between the Colonial Office and the Building Research Station, a Colonial Liaison Unit was set up at the BRS to deal with requests from overseas administrations concerning housing, building and planning matters and to disseminate information on these activities[57]. From this arrangement emerged the *Colonial*

Building Notes (1950-58), continued, when the Unit became the Tropical Section and subsequently, the Overseas Division, as the *Overseas Building Notes* (1959–present). The notes, containing 'technical information' generated by the BRS and collected from colonial and other tropical areas also contain considerable data on metropolitan and overseas planning, housing and architectural practice and were circulated to colonial and ex-colonial societies[58].

By 1950, the growth of international networks of communication was so extensive as to make these more localized channels less important. In particular, the existence of numerous international organizations, especially those sponsored by the United Nations, became important means by which planning knowledge was diffused to the colonial and, from 1960, to the ex-colonial societies[59]. Compared to the small numbers of colonial students who studied in the metropolitan society prior to 1939, an increasing number arrived after 1950. The recognition that planning and architecture in these societies required skills which British planning schools were not equipped to offer resulted, in 1955, in the setting up—at the suggestion of the Colonial Office and others—of courses in Tropical Architecture at the Architectural Association (subsequently to form the basis for the Development Planning Unit, University College, London).

This increasing flow of students from 'developing' countries led to the further establishment, from 1967 onwards, of special courses in planning 'designed to meet the needs and problems of developing countries'. The first of these, established at Edinburgh University, was followed by the setting up of other centres at Nottingham, UWIST, Sheffield and Newcastle Universities. Other courses relating to aspects of regional and 'development' planning were to be established at Swansea, Birmingham, East Anglia and Sussex Universities. In addition, countless other students from 'developing' countries attend courses in polytechnics and further education institutes in subjects related to environmental management, such as housing administration and quantity surveying. The financing of many of these centres, including the funding of some students and staff positions (filled in certain cases by architect-planners with earlier professional experience in colonial administrations), is supported by the Foreign Office through its subsidiaries, the Ministry of Overseas Development and the British Council. Apart from students sponsored on these courses, it was recently reported that practically one in four of all students on post-graduate planning courses at U.K. universities are from 'developing countries'[60].

To complete this outline of 'mechanisms' it would be necessary to mention various advisory and consulting roles taken up by firms of British planners (financed by the Ministry of Overseas Development) which have resulted in comprehensive redevelopment plans for down-town Kingston, Jamaica, Cyprus, for Kaduna in Nigeria, Francistown in Botswana and many more. In addition, teaching and planning staff from 'developing countries' are sponsored to undertake courses in Britain; study tours to see recent examples of British planning and housing problems are arranged. Planning advice in the preparation of planning legislation is offered, in recent years, to Cyprus, Malta, Nigeria, Trinidad and Tobago. A further source of diffusion is through professional institutes and associations, including the Commonwealth Association of Planners and the Royal Town Planning Institute of whose over four thousand corporate members in 1970, some 760 were overseas[61]. Since 1957, the Institute has had an Overseas Section at its annual Summer School devoted to planning in 'Third World' countries.

The issue here, therefore—if it need be explicitly stated—is not whether the ideas, values or models of urban planning exported abroad are 'good' or 'bad', functional or disfunctional in relation to ex-colonial or 'developing' societies. Some reference will be made to this in the conclusion below. The issue is rather to show that the mechanisms and institutions for the export of planning—with its ensuing cultural dependence—not only persist but grow[62].

This is particularly so in the field of education. On one hand, it is intended to reduce the number of overseas students in Britain. On the other, 'aid' policies bring in practitioners and students from 'developing' (often ex-colonial) countries. In these policies, the British government makes no secret of the fact that 'aid' is as much in Britain's own economic and political interest as it is in that of the recipient countries. Whatever its intentions in theory, aid is an instrument of cultural imperialism. In education, it is especially effective. In a subtle process of cognitive colonialism, values, language, methods and professional ideologies are largely transplanted. Students, often more interested in the professional qualification than the education it represents, become bearers of the new expertise. The metropolitan degree is a badge which reinforces the cultural dependence of the ex-colonial country[63]. The export of educational software—ideas, values, beliefs—is of far more import than that of hardware. The ideas go first (the mass transit system, public housing, the 'modern movement')—the consumer goods flow later. In the old days, trade followed the flag; now, it is assumed, it follows the diploma.

The implications of aid and technical assistance are many, for research, teaching and practice: it means that 'aid' money is available for research on urban policies in Tanzania but not in Cuba; that metropolitan academics or practitioners attracted abroad under 'technical assistance' programmes often find themselves trapped in the 'development industry' on return; jobs, even departments (let alone consultancy trips abroad) depend on ODM funds; students from ex-colonial countries arrive in the 'mother country' to find a cultural environment in which they feel thoroughly at home. Why, therefore, should they question their own assumptions and standards?

In many, if not all cases specialized 'aid'-funded courses for overseas students inhibit rather than encourage the development of a genuine

comparative, cross-cultural approach to the teaching of planning and
architecture to native (British) students. 'Culture' is seen as necessary to
understand the Cameroon but not Croydon; bureaucracy and the power
structure as a factor to be coped with in Mali but not Merseyside.

Whilst these issues are more than familiar to the participants involved
(and are far more subtle than can be set out here), only rarely are they made
public or explicit[64]. Even more rarely do they figure in the syllabus of
planning courses. Despite modifications in recent years, planning is still too
frequently seen as a technical process. If the curriculum has been revised to
incorporate the discussion of planning as part of a local, regional or national
system of economic and political power, we are still a long way from making
students aware that it is also part of an *international* power system[65].
Whatever one's political views, the history of architecture and planning
'overseas' (and not only there) has frequently been one of providing a
'back-up service' for the capitalist (or occasionally socialist) transformation
of dependent economies.

Yet despite the comparatively large number of non-British students on
courses in Britain, in the history of planning, minimal attention is apparently
given to the subject of 'overseas planning'; hardly any of the twenty-eight
most frequently cited texts used on such courses refer to planning practice
either in Latin America, Africa or Asia—whether colonial or indigenous[66].
When the topic is eventually introduced, a useful examination question might
be 'Discuss the underlying assumptions behind concepts of "colonial
architecture and planning" (1920s), "planning and architecture in the
tropics" (1950s) and "development planning" (1970s).

EXPORTING PLANNING: THE CONTENT

Attitudes concerning the value of exporting planning and its ideas to other
parts of the world—as expressed in the different viewpoints between 1907
and 1976 (opening page)—have radically changed, especially in the past
decade. Failing confidence in planning as a solution to social ills is only part
perhaps of a more general late-twentieth-century malaise and the failing
confidence in aspects of Western values and civilization. The missionary zeal
of the nineteenth century which saw imperialism as a means of bringing the
benefits of Western civilization and material wealth (through free trade) to
'the darkest corners of the earth' was reflected in the confidence with which
metropolitan institutions, including 'town and country planning', were
introduced abroad. Similar zeal and self-confidence in the Garden City and
Town Planning movement in the twentieth century, successfully pursued 'at
home' till comparatively recently, was, in the colonial territories, to come up
against social and political movements of far more urgent import.

Within the planning profession itself, beliefs and values have radically
changed. In the immediate post-1945 decade, there was still confidence that

physical planning was an unquestionable exportable good, though requiring adaptation at the country of reception and the need to revise earlier measures and legislation. British experience of new towns, social housing, school design, town planning legislation, however, was still looked at with admiration. But from the late 1960s hesitation had begun. In the ex-colonial 'developing' countries, the looked-for 'take-off' had not occurred; in metropolitan planning itself, stimulated by greater public awareness, self-doubts had begun to set in. By the 1970s, many things had changed. Planning was no longer a 'technical expertise' but a highly politicized and value-laden activity, increasingly coming under public scrutiny. Events abroad—in Latin America, Vietnam, Africa—and the continuing poverty of ex-colonial societies found Rostow's 'Stages of Economic Growth', and other analyses of the 1960s, replaced by far more radical views of the world power structure[67]. Despite the shift to a notion of 'development planning', increasing awareness of world inequality and poverty, through the media or at first hand, have undermined earlier assumptions.

The 'environmental crisis', with its consciousness of wasted human and material resources, has likewise sapped confidence in the 'benefits' of Western industrial civilization: the energy crisis was, in many ways, the last straw, exposing the vulnerability of urban environments in the West as they have developed in the twentieth century as well as the amazingly unquestioned assumption about the energy and technological foundations on which they are based.

Energy consciousness has stimulated interest in low-energy environments, intermediate technology and, in relation to one-time colonial societies, 'ethnic' architecture and planning[68]. Unquestioned belief in the superiority of European ideas and values has been tempered by greater interest in indigenous design, the variability of standards[69] and indigenous solutions to housing and planning which, in some cases, were being advocated twenty-five years ago and earlier[70]. If current discussions among teachers of planning for planning students from 'developing countries' are representative, there would seem to be very serious doubts about what, if anything, of 'Western planning' is relevant to non-Western societies in the 'developing world'; even, indeed, if it is still relevant to societies in the West[71].

Yet irrespective of the *content* of this debate about 'relevance', and increasing consciousness that such planning education should take place in the indigenous environment, it nevertheless still continues in the metropolis, the 'Third World' planners exposed to Western environments and ideas. Meanwhile, the entire controversy has been restarted, *ab initio* with the export of architecture and planning to the Middle East[72].

NOTES

1. This chapter is a revised version of the 1977 conference paper which subsequently appeared in *Urbanism Past and Present,* 5, Winter 1977-8. Some of

the issues are discussed further in the author's *The Bungalow. A Cultural History and Sociology* (Routledge and Kegan Paul, forthcoming, 1981). I should like to acknowledge valuable comments from Messrs. G. A. Atkinson, Hubert Morsink, Michael Safier and Professors Peter Hall and Gordon Cherry in the preparation and revision of this paper. The views expressed, however, are entirely my own.

2. (1907) *Garden City,* 2 (15).
3. Swinton, G. (1912) Planning an Imperial Capital. *Garden Cities and Town Planning,* 2 (4), (NS). Capt. Swinton was Chairman of the LCC and a member of the Planning Committee for New Delhi.
4. Stevens, P. H. M. (1955) Planning legislation in the colonies. *Town and Country Planning,* March.
5. Atkinson, S. (1976) Possible directions for Third World planning education in Britain. EPA Workshop 1, Planning Education for Developing Countries.
6. That is, how far did overseas trade and imperialism finance British urbanization and the planning which emerged from it? More specifically, where did Bournville's cocoa come from or (in relation to Port Sunlight) the cocoanut oil for Lever's soaps?
7. In Africa in 1919, Algeria, Tunisia, Morocco, French West Africa, French Equatorial Africa, Somaliland, Togoland, Cameroon, Madagascar, Congo, Guinea, Angola, Mozambique, Cabinda, Rio de Oro, Rio Muni, Spanish Guinea, Eritrea, Italian Somaliland, Gambia, Sierra Leone, Gold Coast, Nigeria, South West Africa, Bechuanaland, Swaziland, Basutoland, Southern Rhodesia, Northern Rhodesia, Nyasaland, Tanganyika, Zanzibar, Uganda, Kenya, Sudan, Egypt.
8. See *(passim) Garden City,* 1904-1910; *Garden Cities and Town Planning,* 1911-32, *Town and Country Planning,* 1932-; Gardner-Medwin, R. *et al.* (1948) Recent planning developments in the colonies. *RIBA Journal,* 55 (February); Ginsburg, N. (1965) Urban geography in non-Western areas, in Hauser, P. M. and Schnore, L. F. (eds.), *The Study of Urbanization.* New York: Wiley, pp. 311–46.
9. See King, A. D. (1976) *Colonial Urban Development.* London: Routlege and Kegan Paul, pp. 13-15; on Belgium, see Fetter, B. (1976) *The Creation of Elizabethville, 1910-40.* Stanford: Hoover Institute Press. Bibliographies (including references to colonial planning) exist in King, A. D. (1976) *ibid.,* Friedmann, J. and Wulff, R. (1976) *The Urban Transition: Comparative Studies of Newly Industrializing Societies.* London: Edward Arnold; and Abu-Lughod J. and Hay, R. (eds.) (1977) *Third World Urbanization.* Chicago: Maroufa Press.
10. Emerson, R. (1968) Colonialism, in *International Encyclopaedia of Social Sciences.* New York: Macmillan.
11. Horvath, R. V. (1969) In search of a theory of urbanization: notes on the colonial city. *East Lakes Geographer,* 5, pp. 68-82; Horvath, R. V. (1972) A definition of colonialism. *Current Anthropology,* 13 (1), pp. 45-57; King, A. D. (1976) *Colonial Urban Development.* London: Routledge and Kegan Paul, pp. 17-18.
12. King, A. D. (1974) History of planning. Opportunities for new theory and method. Paper presented to the British History of Planning Group, April (unpublished).
13. King, A. D. (1976) *Colonial Urban Development.* London: Routledge and Kegan Paul.

14. For example, 'I moved the HQ from that close, unhealthy and altogether hateful spot Kampala to a lovely place on the Lake; two great grassy hills, like the Kingsclere Downs, rising almost straight out of the water; and a view over the Lake like over the sea dotted with a dozen islands. I put the European quarters on the highest hill, and the Soudanese troops on the lower one, and we marked out all the streets and divisions giving each man a small compound, and established a market place, and cut great wide roads in every direction. Before I left there was already quite a neat town of about 1000 inhabitants, ten times more healthy than at Kampala ... The name of the settlement is Port Alice'. Portal, Sir G. (1894) *The British Mission to Uganda.* London: Arnold (subsequently to be Entebbe, Uganda). Quoted from *Colonial Building Notes,* No. 42, January 1957, p. 13. Nairobi was established in 1896 as a railway capital, laid out by a sergeant of the Royal Engineers (*Overseas Building Notes,* No. 141, December 1971). The site was 'badly chosen ... the same mistakes of overcrowding and insanitary conditions as existed in England in the early nineteenth century have a tendency to repeat themselves in new countries'. *Report on Sanitary Matters in the East Africa Protectorate, Uganda & Zanzibar,* 1913 quoted in White, L. W. T. *et al.* (1948) *Nairobi: Master Plan for a Colonial Capital.* London: HMSO.

15. Lewcock, R. (1963) *Early Nineteenth Century Architecture in South Africa.* Cape Town: Hobbema.

16. National Independence dates in Africa: South Africa 1909, Egypt 1922, Libya 1951, Tunisia, Morocco, Sudan 1956, Ghana 1957, Guinea 1958, Mauritania, Mali, Senegal, Togo, Dahomey, Ivory Coast, Upper Volta, Niger, Nigeria, Chad, Somali, Cameroun, Central African Republic, Gabon, Congo-Brazzaville, Congo Republic, Malagasey 1960, Sierra Leone, Tanzania 1961, Ruanda, Uganda, Burundi, Algeria 1962, Kenya 1963, Zambia, Malawi 1964, Gambia, Rhodesia (UDI) 1965, Lesotho, Botswana, Swaziland 1967, Ifni 1969, Guinea-Bissau 1974, Mozambique, Cape Verde, The Comoros, Sao Tomé and Principe, Angola 1975.

17. King, A. D. (1977) The westernization of domestic architecture in India. *Art and Archaeology Research papers,* 11 (June), pp. 32-41.

18. Emerson, R. (1968) Colonialism, in *International Encyclopaedia of Social Sciences.* New York: Macmillan.

19. Castells, M. (1972) *La Question Urbaine.* Paris: Francois Maspéro, p. 64. See also Harvey, D. (1973) *Social Justice and the City.* London: Edward Arnold, pp. 228-32.

20. Friedmann, J. and Wulff, R. (1976) *The Urban Transition: Comparative Studies of Newly Industrialising Societies.* London: Edward Arnold, pp. 13-14.

21. *Ibid.*

22. *Ibid.*

23. Brush, J. E. (1970) The growth of the Presidency Towns, in Fox, R. G. (ed.) *Urban India: Society, Space and Image.* Durham, N.C.: Duke University Press, pp. 91-114.

24. Learmonth, A. T. L. and Spate, O. U. K. (1965) *India: A Regional Geography.* London: Methuen; King, A. D. (1976) *Colonial Urban Development.* London: Routledge and Kegan Paul, pp. 156-79.

25. Collins, J. (1980) Lusaka: Urban planning in a British colony, 1931-64, pp.

227–41 in this volume, but especially Gugler, J. (ed.) (1970) *Urbanisation in Sub-Saharan Africa.* Kampala; Rex, J. (1973) *Race, Colonialism and the City.* London: Routledge and Kegan Paul; Amin, S. (ed.) (1974) *Modern Migrations in Western Africa.* London: Oxford University Press.

26. Collins, J. (1980) Lusaka: Urban planning in a British colony, pp. 227–41 in this volume.

27. Thus, 'social housing' built in the Gold Coast in the 1950s is 'to house labour required at the harbour'; housing in Jinja, Uganda, are 'units for Labourers, Waluka Labour Estate'. Housing in Nairobi in the late 1920s, and elsewhere, was constructed on the 'bed space' principle to accommodate single male labourers. (*Colonial Building Notes*) *passim.*

28. Between 1945 and 1957, the number of Africans employed in urban factories in Southern Rhodesia rose from 95,000 to 300,000. 'This increasing demand for labour was most fortunate for whilst it was developing, the population of the rural areas was rising rapidly, largely because of the steep reduction in infant mortality which followed the introduction of medical services into the countryside.' In 1953, the shortfall of 'single quarters' in Salisbury was 13,500. As 'a certain amount of disquiet had been felt about the earlier system of housing large numbers of single men in hostels' it was thought that such in-migrants would be more comfortable and 'socially more stable' if married householders could be encouraged to accept lodgers of their own choosing (each working African receiving £1 housing allowance per month). In the housing scheme devised, costs were cut to a minimum to result in over 2000 units of housing being built for approximately £140 each outside Salisbury. The Treasury Accounts report, 'The cost per square foot obtained is probably the lowest on record in Africa and it is possible that a world low record has been achieved for the construction of this type of building today'. Report on Rhodesia African Home Ownership Scheme. *Colonial Building Notes,* No. 60, June, 1959.

29. *Colonial Building Notes, passim.*

30. Tarn, J. N. (1974) *Five Per Cent Philanthropy.* London: Cambridge University Press.

31. Swanson, M. W. (1970) Reflections on the urban history of South Africa, in Watts, H. L. (ed.) *Focus on Cities.* Institute of Social Research, University of Natal.

32. On the cultural and historical relativity of standards see Choldin, H. M. (1976) Housing standards versus ecological forces: regulating population densities in Bombay, in Rapoport, A. (ed.) *The Mutual Interaction of People and Their Built Environment: A Cross-Cultural Perspective.* The Hague: Mouton (World Anthropology Series), pp. 287-332; Rapoport, A. (1977) *Human Aspects of Urban Form.* London: Pergamon.

33. As an instructive comparison in the evaluation of environments, compare the accounts in Oliver, P. (ed.) (1971) *Shelter in Africa.* London: Barrie and Jenkins, or Denyer, S. (1978) *African Traditional Architecture.* London: Heinemann, with the following extract from the *Annual Report on Medical Services,* 1953-4, Federation of Nigeria, 1955 '. . . the time-honoured, mud-walled compound with its intricate rabbit warren of ill-lit, ill-ventilated and undersized rooms. The more wealthy spend much on beautifying the front of their houses . . . though housing is bad enough in the large towns it becomes more and more primitive

until one reaches the encampments of the nomadic cattle Fulani where large families exist in small wigwam shelters made of grass matting ... During the year a housing survey was made in Argunga town ... to assess what degree of overcrowding existed. The standards of calculation used were those of the England and Wales Housing Act. The results were surprising in that in most of the town there was little or no overcrowding where cubic space per person was concerned'. (*Colonial Building Notes*, No. 41, December, 1956).

34. 'The administrative functions and powers of municipal governments were not conceived as instruments of social service and construction. Instead, municipal laws identified preservation of public health and the exercise of police powers as the prominent functions of the corporation.' Swanson, M. W. (1970) Reflections on the urban history of South Africa, in Watts, H. L. (ed.) *Focus on Cities*. Institute of Social Research, University of Natal.

35. See Atkinson, G. A. (1959) Recent advances in low-cost housing in tropical areas, *Proceedings*, Sixth International Congress of Tropical Medicine and Malaria; Little, A. (1974) *Urbanisation as a Social Process*. London: Routledge and Kegan Paul; King, A. D. (1976) *Colonial Urban Development*. London: Routledge and Kegan Paul, chapter 5.

36. United Nations (1971) *Climate and House Design*. New York: United Nations, p. 12.

37. Blair, T. (1971) Shelter in urbanizing and industrializing Africa, in Oliver, P. (1971) *Shelter in Africa*. London: Barrie and Jenkins, p. 132.

38. White, L. W. T. *et al*. (1948) *Nairobi: Master Plan for a Colonial Capital*. London: HMSO.

39. Davies, D. H. (1969) Lusaka, Zambia: Some town-planning problems in an African capital city at Independence, *Zambian Urban Studies*. Lusaka: Zambian Institute of Social Research; Langlands, B. (1969) Perspectives on urban planning for Uganda, in Safier, M. and Langlands, B. (ed.) (1969) book of same title, Department of Geography, Makerere University College, Uganda; Collins, J. (1980) Lusaka: Urban planning in a British colony, 1931–64, pp. 227–41 in this volume.

40. This is an important distinction. The expatriate elite did not simply 'replicate in the capital the society of their own homeland' (Lloyd, P. (1979) *Slums of Hope. Shanty Towns of the Third World*. Harmondsworth: Pelican, p. 19) as is frequently stated. Had they done this, there would have been little point in them going. The colonial 'third culture' was a subtly modified version of the metropolitan. See King, A. D. (1976) *Colonial Urban Development*. London: Routledge and Kegan Paul, pp. 58–66 and chapter 6.

41. ' "Town and country planning" has been a borrowed phrase which is still much in vogue in India although it appears to be going out of use in the language of its origin in the United Kingdom'. Manzoor Alam, S. (1972) *Metropolitan Hyderabad and Its Region. A Strategy for Development*. London: Asia Publishing House, p.v. See also Parkin, D. (1972) *Town and Country in Central and Eastern Africa*. London: Oxford University Press. On the basic conceptual distinction, its incorporation into linguistic categories and the extension of 'town-country' relations globally, see the seminal works of Williams, R. (1973) *The Country and the City*. London: Oxford University Press, and (1976) *Keywords. A Vocabulary of Culture and Society*. London: Fontana.

42. Meeting of the Third Workshop of the Education for Planning Association, on UK Planning Education for Developing Countries, University College, London, May, 1977.

43. Thus, the Ministry of Overseas Development sponsored Survey and Plan for Kaduna, Northern Nigeria, 1967 (by Max Lock and Partners, published by Faber and Faber, London, 1967) suggests the retention of a small iron bridge erected by Lord Lugard, the previous colonial Governor; the Secretary of the Georgian Group visits the West Indies to advise on the preservation of military officers' quarters from the eighteenth century. In Delhi, various 'sacred' sites, associated with the 'Mutiny' are preserved throughout colonial rule, indirectly affecting the location of the new capital (King, A. D. (1976) *Colonial Urban Development*. London: Routledge and Kegan Paul, p. 234).

44. Dennis, N. (1968) The popularity of the neighbourhood community idea in Pahl, R. E. (ed.) *Readings in Urban Sociology*. London: Longman, pp. 74-94; Bailey, J. (1975) *Social Theory for Planning*. London: Routledge and Kegan Paul.

45. Not everyone links the etymology of Soweto (South West Township) with the black town carefully planned and located away from (but sufficiently close to) the white man's city.

46. McGee, T. G. (1967) *The South East Asian City*. London: Bell.

47. Swanson (1970) Reflections on the urban history of South Africa, in Watts, H. L. (ed.) *Focus on Cities*. Institute of Social Research, University of Natal.

48. Mitchell, J. C. (1966) Theoretical orientations in african urban studies, in Banton, M. (ed.) (1966) *The Social Anthropology of Complex Societies.*London: Tavistock.

49. See Little, A. (1974) *Urbanisation as a Social Process*. London: Routledge and Kegan Paul; King, A. D. (1976) *Colonial Urban Development*. London: Routledge and Kegan Paul; Nilsson, S. (1973) *The New Capitals of India, Pakistan and Bangladesh*. Lund: Scandinavian Institute of South Asian Studies.

50. Oliver, P. (1971) (ed.) *Shelter in Africa*. London: Barrie and Jenkins, *passim*.

51. 'As urbanisation takes effect in Ghana, tribal ties and discipline must be superseded by other loyalites if a coordinated law-abiding society is to emerge. It is therefore important to give the urban Ghanaian a sense of community membership. The policy in Tema has been to discourage racial, tribal, religious or class segregation, in the hope that the citizens' loyalty will be to neighbourhood, community and town. This policy requires non-traditional types of housing accommodation. The tribal compound has no place in Tema and is replaced by the private family dwelling. Differentiation of dwelling standards is purely by income and all income groups are represented in each community', *Tema, 1951-61, A Report on the Development of the Town of Tema,* prepared for the Ghana Government by D. C. Robinson and R. J. Anderson. Russian town planners had also submitted a proposal to the Tema Development Corporation for the development of one community area. This included high flats, communal kitchens, etc. which, at an estimated cost of £8m, was much higher than that of other community developments. However, 'the scheme was not considered at all suitable to the Ghana way of life and it has not been accepted'.

52. Research into pedestrian behaviour and the rules which govern it provides a small but useful demonstration of this. See Goffman, E. (1971) *Behaviour in Public Places*. Harmondsworth: Penguin.

53. King, A. D. (1977) The westernisation of domestic architecture in India. *Art and Archeology Research Papers,* 11 (June), pp. 32–41.

54. In India, the distinction between army cantonments or areas and buildings maintained by the Public Works Department and the 'everyday' Indian environment provides an interesting illustration, even today. See also the discussion of colonial cantonments in King, A. D. (1976) *Colonial Urban Development.* London: Routledge and Kegan Paul, chapter 5.

55. The first paper to be read at the RIBA on 'tropical architecture', for example, was given in 1869 (Smith, T. R. (1869) On buildings for European occupation in tropical climates, especially India, *Proceedings of the RIBA,* 1868–9, 1st series, 18, pp. 197–208. See also King, A. D. (1976) *Colonial Urban Development.* London: Routledge and Kegan Paul, pp. 285–6.

56. Collins, J. (1980) Lusaka: urban planning in a British Colony, pp. 227–41 in this volume.

57. Atkinson, G. A. (1953) British architects in the tropics, *Architectural Association Journal,* 69 (773), pp. 7-21.

58. *Overseas Building Notes,* No. 141, 1971; *Colonial Building Notes,* 1950–7; *Overseas Building Notes,* 1959–present..

59. For example, Housing and Town & Country Planning Section, Department of Social Affairs, UN, ILO, UNESCO, WHO, and various national and regional organizations. See *Colonial Building Notes,* No. 32, 1955.

60. Education for Planning Association, 1977. Government spending cuts from 1979 seem likely to seriously change this situation.

61. *Overseas Building Notes,* No. 141, 1971.

62. The *Third World Planning Review,* edited from the University of Liverpool's Department of Civic Design was begun in Spring 1979. The journal is primarily (though not entirely) directed to 'professionals' and, whilst being 'particularly keen to encourage the submission of papers by authors in less developed countries', it is run by British editors (with an 'international' editorial board).

63. See the comment in *Colonial Building Notes,* No 15, 1953 on Alcock, A. E. S. and Richards, H. (1953) *How to Plan Your Village. A Handbook for Villages in Tropical Countries.* London: Longmans Green. 'They have written this book to help villagers in planning their own villages. The authors explain in simple words which may be understood by men and women who do not know much English and children who will be villagers of the future, the main principles of village planning and improvement. These principles are illustrated by the story of a Gold Coast village and of its village improvement committee led by Kwame who has just returned from studying abroad'.
The role of professional institutes, their examination requirements and syllabus content which is central to these issues is a subject too large to enter into here.

64. They have been discussed at the Overseas Section meeting of the Summer School of the RTPI on a number of occasions since 1957 and, in recent years, in the Education for Planning Association.

65. See also Harvey's comments on 'global metropolitanism' and how this is 'embedded in a global form of economic imperialism' (Harvey, D. (1973) *Social Justice and the City.* London: Edward Arnold, p. 228).

66. See Hebbert, M. (1978) Report of a Survey on the Teaching of Town Planning History. Oxford Polytechnic (unpublished).

67. See Cockcroft, J. D., Frank, A. G. and Johnson, D. J. (1972) *Dependence and Underdevelopment.* New York: Anchor Doubleday; Jenkins, R. (1971) *Exploitation. The World Power Structure and the Inequality of Nations.* London: Paladin; Chilcote, R. H. (1977) Dependency. A critical synthesis of the literature, and Amin, S. (1977) Underdevelopment and dependence in Black Africa – origins and contemporary forms, both in Abu-Lughod, J. and Hay, R. (eds.) (1977) *Third World Urbanization.* Chicago: Maroufa Press, pp. 128-39, pp. 140-50.

68. Oliver, P. (ed.) (1969) *Shelter and Society.* London: Barrie and Jenkins; Oliver, P. (ed.) (1971) *Shelter in Africa.* London: Barrie and Jenkins; Rapoport, A. (1969) *House Form and Culture.* Englewood Cliffs, N.J.: Prentice Hall; Rapoport, A. (ed.) (1976). *The Mutual Interaction of People and Their Built Environment: A Cross-Cultural Perspective.* The Hague: Mouton (World Anthropology Series); Denyer, S. (1978) *African Traditional Architecture.* London: Heinemann.

69. Atkinson, G. A. (1960) Mass housing in rapidly-developing tropical areas. *Town Planning Review,* 31 (2), pp. 62-71; Rapoport, A. (1969) *House Form and Culture.* Englewood Cliffs, N.J.: Prentice Hall; Rapoport, A. (ed.) (1976) *The Mutual Interaction of People and their Built Environment. A Cross-Cultural Perspective.* The Hague: Mouton (World Anthropology Series).

70. For example, the attention given to indigenous building and housing as well as village lay-outs in the *Colonial Building Notes,* 1950–60 and early papers by Dr Otto Koenigsberger and others.

71. Papers of Education for Planning Association, 1976, 1977.

72. See for example, various articles in the *Architect's Journal* 'Kuwait. A Salutary Tale', 'The Middle East. What Chance for You', 'Neo-Colonialist Architecture', 'Destruction of the Middle East', 12 December 1973, 13 August 1975, 15 October 1975, 28 July 1976, 4 August 1976.

11

Lusaka: urban planning in a British colony, 1931-64

JOHN COLLINS

In the 1920s Lusaka was a small agricultural service centre on the main north-south railway line which had been built through this part of central Africa in the early 1900s to carry lead, zinc and later copper from the mines of Northern Rhodesia through Southern Rhodesia to the sea. The capital of the British 'protectorate' of Northern Rhodesia at this time was Livingstone, in the extreme south of the country where the railway line crosses the Zambezi on its way to the south, but since 1929 the colonial government had been looking for a more central (and cooler) location than Livingstone, closer to the emergent copperbelt, but not too close to avoid domination by the mining companies.

In July 1931 the government of Northern Rhodesia decided to build its new capital city close to the old township of Lusaka. This paper is about the planning and implementation of this new capital project during the thirty-three years before Northern Rhodesia became the independent Republic of Zambia. It shows how, as at New Delhi[1], the imported values of the colonial power were translated into the physical form of a city. There are however two important differences from New Delhi. First there was no long tradition of permanent *urban* settlement by the *African* population in this part of Africa. Secondly the *Europeans* who went to Northern Rhodesia comprised not only civil servants cast in the New Delhi mould, but also *settlers* who fully intended to live and die in southern Africa.

These two factors are interrelated. The fact that there was no long tradition of precolonial urban settlement on the West African model—no Ibadan or Benin City[2]—means that the only urban development in Northern Rhodesia was that initiated by Europeans for their own purposes. These particular colonists had economic and institutional links with the

227

south—with South Africa and Southern Rhodesia—as well as with the mother country. Their urban planning therefore reflects not only the imported values of the colonial power but also the attitudes towards the indigenous population which prevailed—and still prevail—in white-dominated southern Africa. In particular it reflects the various attempts by the colonial authorities to dictate the terms on which Africans could partici-pate in urban life—as migrant labourers whose period of residence in an urban area was regarded as strictly temporary.

The first part of the paper covers the period up to the end of the Second World War, when the colonial civil servants were the predominant group and Lusaka came closest to a colonial capital of the New Delhi type. The second part covers the postwar period up to Independence in 1964 when the image was to some extent remodelled to that of a settler city of the Salisbury type. That Salisbury should have replaced New Delhi as the model was no accident, because from 1953 to 1963 Northern Rhodesia formed part of the short-lived Central African Federation of Rhodesia and Nyasaland, and Lusaka lost some of its capital city functions to Salisbury, the federal capital. However, the predominant theme of both parts of the paper is the way in which, even *without* a large indigenous urban settlement comparable to the walled city of Old Delhi, the needs of the two communities in Lusaka were inextricably intertwined and the African population made its presence felt in ways which the colonial planners were ultimately powerless to prevent.

A Colonial Capital, 1931–46

The original plan for the new capital was prepared by a British consultant, S. D. Adshead, Professor of Town Planning at London University, a Past President of the Town Planning Institute and an ardent disciple of Ebenezer Howard whose Garden City planning Adshead had described, in a book published in 1923, as 'a form of organised town development which is likely to have a great influence in the development of England in the future, *to say nothing of the Colonies* [3]. Adshead's report on Lusaka lists the following advantages of the recommended site:

> It is on Crown lands, and the development would be greatly assisted by its proximity to the existing township ... It could hardly be described as a dramatic situation, but covered with buildings it could be seen to advantage from a considerable distance, more especially from along the line of the railway ... It would be easy to sewer and well suited to the requirements of a residential area.[4]

The reference to Crown lands is important. Almost all the land within the modern city boundary has at some time or other been in private and almost exclusively European ownership as a so-called 'farm', but the new capital was located on land which had never been alienated to private individuals as a complete farm. The significance of Crown land was that individual plots could be alienated on terms which enabled the government to determine the types of building erected, by imposing conditions in the leases which were in some ways more strict than those imposed under the Town Planning Ordinance.

Adshead's planning brief was very sketchy by modern standards. From the Governor he received 'valuable advice as to the relative position of the Government buildings, Government House, the town buildings, the Native Compound etc.'[5]. From the Acting Governor he received 'further information, such as that referring to the amount of accommodation to be provided for the different departments of government' together with an approximate indication of the total population to be housed—8000 Europeans and 5000 Africans. It was not the sort of brief which sets out the number of jobs to be provided—the sole economic function of the city was to be that of a 'capital city and government centre'.

The most glaring defect of this brief was the government's failure to appreciate the empirical fact that the towns and cities of this European colony at that time appeared to need an African population about five times the size of the European population. Livingstone for example, the town which Lusaka was to replace as capital, had 7930 Africans to 1596 Europeans in 1931—a ratio of 5.0 : 1; in Lusaka itself there were already 1961 Africans to 470 Europeans—a ratio of 4.2 : 1[6]. A brief for a new city of 8000 Europeans would therefore have been more realistic if it had allowed for say 40,000 Africans rather than the 5000 actually in Adshead's brief.

As a disciple of the Garden City movement, Adshead was anxious to avoid the 'chessboard' plans of Salisbury and Bulawayo[7]. His approach was to provide what he called 'natural growth under the guidance of a plan'; the different functional areas were to develop 'naturally', each in its 'proper' relationship to the other:

Without question the finest position as regards outlook, approaches and conveniences, must be selected for the group of official buildings (the Secretariat). Somewhere between this position, the railway station and the present town of Lusaka, it is natural that there should be a shopping and a business area. Immediately surrounding the government buildings would come the semi-official buildings, clubs, hotels, etc. Perhaps the next most important building for which a site must be found is Government House, which it is assumed will be conveniently situated at a distance of about 2.4 to 3.2 km from the Government Centre. Surrounding Government House, it would seem that suitable sites should be found for the heads of the Government Departments, the intervening area being residential. It is anticipated that as the town develops, its interest as a Municipal as well as a Government Centre will increase in importance. At the same time the town will naturally develop in the direction of the railway line and station. The area bordering the railway will prove to be the natural area for sites for factories and stores, and therefore it would seem that a Municipal Centre would find a natural position somewhere between the seat of government and the railway station.[8]

These functional areas were to be linked together by a 'principal street' 37 m wide, connecting the new and old towns, and by a 'main residential avenue' 122 m wide along the ridge which was to form 'the backbone of the new city'. The main surviving elements of Adshead's plan are in fact this general route of Independence Avenue together with the location of the main government buildings.

It was four years before the Governor and the main government departments were finally able to move to Lusaka, during which time there were many teething problems and modifications to Adshead's plan. Not least of these problems was an underlying shortage of funds because of the world-wide economic depression which hit this part of Africa hardest during the period 1931 to 1933. The new capital project was scaled down in various ways by P. J. Bowling, the government's town planning engineer, in a report and plan which was presented to the Governor in June 1933[9]. It is this plan rather than Adshead's which constitutes the working document from which the colonial capital was actually built. It was designed to accommodate an ultimate European population of 20,000, but gave no corresponding figure for Africans beyond stating that Adshead's provision was inadequate for an expanding town. In one optimistic passage Bowling suggested that the government would be able to recoup its own costs by selling leasehold plots to private purchasers so that the eventual cost to the taxpayer would be nil.

In addition to the government areas, Bowling's plan had seven main zones, in most of which at least one building was underway or completed at the time of the official opening of the new capital in 1935. These zones were:

1. *Special business zone* (i.e. offices, but not shops). The office building erected by the British South Africa Company (now the Ministry of Foreign Affairs) was the first example.
2. *Special shopping zone* (i.e. mainly shops, some offices). This part of the scheme was postponed because of lack of funds to compensate shop-owners moving from the old town.
3. *General business zone* (i.e. shops, offices, etc.) Two areas were given this designation, including the whole of the old town, which suggests that there was never any firm intention to label the existing shops as 'non-conforming uses'.
4. *Light industries zone.* A flour mill was already there; the Government Printer and the Government Mechanical Services Workshops soon followed.
5. *Heavy industries zone.* The abattoir was the first such building.
6. *European residential zone.* This was divided into the 'first class' and 'second class' subzones where most of the early civil service housing was built. A 'third class' subzone with smaller plots was never implemented.
7. *African zone.* A market, and some of the shops in the 'second class trading area' surrounding the market, were among the first buildings to be erected in this zone.

Other significant proposals which were implemented at this time in accordance with the Bowling plan include the old airport and its terminal buildings, the Lusaka Club and the golf club, all of which required the first of many re-acquisitions of land from private persons to whom it had previously been alienated as a farm. The Crown land which had attracted Adshead to the new capital site in the first place was already proving insufficient.

Although in 1935 the layout of roads and location of buildings conformed very closely to the Bowling plan, the plan had no statutory force. This was originally an oversight. A town planning ordinance[10] existed under which the plan could have been made statutory, but it was decided in 1938 to adopt a 'non-statutory development plan'. For enforcement the government was relying on the fact that the majority of land was owned by the government, and therefore suitable clauses could be included in the leases, and on the powers contained in the townships and public health ordinances to make 'by-laws and regulations to control the zoning, siting and conformity and construction of buildings'[11].

Such enforcement methods imply however that control over private development on Bowling's leasehold plots was expected to be the major problem. In practice such controls were hardly needed at this time because there was relatively little private development by Europeans until after 1945. The main result of the adoption of a non-statutory plan was that it was very easy—some said too easy—for the government to amend the plan, usually by displacing residential-type uses whenever a more urgent need arose. Consequently the overall density of development tended to become lower than anyone had ever envisaged.

The new capital also began to have an impact on its immediate hinterland within the modern city boundary. By 1935, certain farms nearest to the new capital had been subdivided into smaller semi-rural homestead plots (freehold) of around 4 hectares. Subdivisions of this type were now controlled by the town planning ordinance, but they were significant because of a tendency, discussed later, for those Europeans who might have been expected to buy plots in the new capital to prefer this semi-rural existence.

Some of the strongest factors which shaped the development of the new capital in the 1930s and 1940s did not however stem from the work of either Adshead or Bowling, or from the formal machinery of town planning. They are the consequences of that complex mixture of legal requirements and accepted practice which applied to the employment and housing of Africans by Europeans—a semi-institutionalized system of *circulatory labour migration* with an extensive academic literature of its own[12].

The underlying assumption of this approach was that the towns (and the Crown land farming areas) were for Europeans and that the rural areas were for Africans. It followed that no African should be in town except to provide labour as and when required by a European employer. Only men were required—wives and children were expected to remain in the rural areas and permanent urban settlement was deliberately discouraged. Urban housing was therefore rudimentary. Employers became accustomed to providing either land on which their employees could build temporary huts (because, they argued, that is what they did in the villages), or to providing rent-free one-room 'native huts' which were specifically exempt from the normal standards of building construction required under the public health regulations. Either way, housing was tied to employment and the employers took the view that they could pay low wages because nothing need be included for housing.

One consequence of these low wages was that African employees could not accumulate the resources with which to provide their own permanent housing in the towns. Even where self-built housing was encouraged, the land was rented with little security of tenure. Elsewhere in the city, the purchase price of a leasehold plot, the costs of surveying and registration, and the stipulation of the minimum value of building to be built on each plot, all combined to put home ownership way beyond the means of Africans, so providing the main method of enforcing an implicit system of racial segregation. There does not appear to have been any legislation explicitly preventing Africans from living in European areas of the towns.

This link between the demand for labour generated by European employers and the housing of African employees was therefore a major determinant of the physical form of the city, but, apart from the obvious defect of not catering for families, it left unanswered the housing needs of three main groups: those seeking work, the self-employed and the retired. Those seeking work had to carry a pass authorizing them to remain in town for this purpose for a specific period of time, but no specific housing provision was made for them, or for the self-employed who simply did not fit into a system based on the Europeans as employers.

By 1944, those who did not fit neatly into the system of circulatory labour migration—the self-employed and the unemployed—comprised 23 per cent of the workforce. Several types of housing area had emerged which were not anticipated at all by the Bowling plan—private locations (defined as 'settlements established on private lands in which plots are rented to Africans to build their own housing'[13]) and unauthorized settlements—which together housed 40 per cent of adult males. Furthermore, in spite of much official discouragement there were already substantial numbers of African women and children in Lusaka. The supposition that Lusaka would develop solely on terms dictated by European requirements was no longer tenable.

Meanwhile, how much progress had the government made in meeting its own requirements for the development of Lusaka? Apart from changes directly attributable to the transfer of the capital from Livingstone, the Second World War of 1939–45 was a period of marking time.

The non-African population of Lusaka and the suburb of Emmasdale in 1946 was 1640, of whom 1254 were Europeans living within the Township

Boundary (i.e. excluding Emmasdale)[14]. There are two important characteristics of this European population which had hardly changed since 1931 or even 1921. First it was still a male-dominated group—the number of males to every 100 females was 138 in 1921, 132 in 1931 and 137 in 1946—suggesting a society which was still in its 'pioneer' rather than 'settler' stage. Secondly, a large proportion of this European population was still living in institutional accommodation—72 per cent in 1921, 31 per cent in 1931 and still 31 per cent in 1946. Hostels were consequently an integral part of the process by which Lusaka was developed.

A detailed analysis of the tenure of European households living in private houses in 1946 reveals two significant points. First it appears that Lusaka had changed from being a town where owner-occupation, at 42 per cent in 1931, was almost as important as renting, to a town where two-thirds of the European houses were occupied by households living rent-free or paying only nominal rents (presumably civil servants). In this respect Lusaka almost exactly mirrors the situation which prevailed in Livingstone in 1931. Secondly, the absolute number of owner-occupiers had hardly increased at all—from 31 to 34—in fifteen years. Both these points are of particular relevance in assessing the success or failure of the Bowling plan. Bowling had talked about the government recouping its costs by the sale of land so that the cost to the taxpayer would be nil. It is clear that by 1946 few sales had been made. The government was virtually the only residential developer, with perhaps a few private companies also renting to their own employees, because housing tied to employment was the norm for the Europeans as well, again confirming that the era of the settler had not yet begun.

A SETTLER CITY, 1946-63

It soon became clear that a new plan was required for the postwar period. Once the war was over, there was an influx of European settlers requiring plots for owner occupation, and there was a growing recognition of the need for more industrial sites. It was also true, but not always fully understood, that any new plan would have to cater for Africans to a far greater extent than ever envisaged in the 1930s. Above all the new plan would this time have to be given statutory force. Non-statutory development plans had proved to have one great disadvantage in that they were too easily amended. It had become increasingly obvious that 'loose development of Lusaka was being permitted to the detriment of the town generally'.

Outside consultants were again appointed. The first, brought in by the government, was Bowling, by then in private practice in Johannesburg, who reported in 1947[15]. The second was G. A. Jellicoe from London, appointed by the Lusaka Management Board, who reported in 1950[16]. Neither of these plans was given statutory force, but each contributed in its own way to the location decisions being taken at the time. The Jellicoe plan was the first to make explicit the approach to transport planning which had been implicit since Adshead's time. One of the plan's basic premises was:

> The maintenance of a standard of living whereby the transport of Europeans is primarily by private cars, with short distances not exceeding half-a-mile by foot; that of natives primarily by foot, but an increasing number by cycle.[17]

It was stated that as African living standards rose, a bus service might be economic but it was to be many years before the inherent link between overall density and the feasibility of the public transport was fully recognized.

It was not until 1952 that the government's own planners produced the first statutory development plan, more than twenty years after the original decision to move the capital to Lusaka. The objectives of the 1952 scheme were clearly stated:

(i) The welding together of the present scattered development into a town with an urban character

(ii) The physical linking of the old commercial centre and the Government Centre with a new Town Centre of a calibre fitting with Lusaka's status as the capital of the territory

(iii) The clear delineation of the extent of urban development necessary to provide a reasonable choice of living accommodation for the estimated future population with all the necessary community facilities

(iv) The provision of industrial areas to the north-west of the town and downwind from the residental areas. By the provision of industrial sites it is hoped to provide the opportunity for Lusaka to become a more balanced community.[18]

The first objective, welding the town together, relied heavily on the new town centre proposal (objective 2). This was yet another abortive attempt to encourage major office and shop development outside the old town. In practice the development of offices and shops on the previously undeveloped east side of the old main street proved to be the only viable expansion of the commercial centre. The fourth objective makes explicit the reason for the emphasis on industrial sites—the new capital of Adshead's day was too imbalanced in the direction of purely governmental activities.

It is however the third objective which led to the most remarkable divergence between stated and actual intentions at the start of the federal era. The residential zones specifically allowed for 22,000 Europeans on 2800 ha but, although the 'optimum' African population was estimated to be 132,000, the plan provided for only 52,000 and even this figure is misleading because it includes 11,000 Africans who were to be 'housed on European stands'—domestic servants and their dependents. It is clear from these figures that no provision was made at all for the remaining 80,000 Africans and the 1500 ha which it was estimated that they would need. In short the Europeans were to have their garden suburbs by ignoring 60 per cent of the estimated future African population.

It is this 1952 plan above all others which determined the location of the main areas required for European expansion during the settler period and, as the number of European settlers increased, there was a gradual shift of control away from central government which had built the new capital, towards the European electorate which eventually ran local government. Even though it was not until 1962 that full *planning* powers under the town planning ordinance were handed over to the council, there were other powers by which a settler council was able to exert its influence, from deciding which roads should be properly made up and tarred to naming the streets. This last example illustrates the shift in influence—central government had tended to name the streets after former governors and civil servants, but now local government favoured English and Welsh counties, cathedral towns, sporting venues and, in the industrial areas, names like Manchester Road and Bradford Street.

However, in spite of all the planning and local government administration of a settler society, the evidence from the census of non-African population for the fifteen-year period from 1946 to 1961 is that Lusaka never really became a European settler city on the Southern Rhodesia model. Indeed the federation with Southern Rhodesia (1953-63) was a major factor in ensuring that Lusaka could never really 'take off' in the way that Salisbury did. Not only was Lusaka deprived of many 'capital city' functions and their related investment which automatically went to Salisbury as the Federal capital, but, later on, political uncertainty over the break-up of the Federation was to slow down for a time even this reduced rate of economic expansion.

The non-African population grew very rapidly at first, reaching 10,758 in 1956 and then much more slowly during the final years of the Federation, to reach 13,300 in 1961. It soon moved out of the male-dominated 'pioneer' stage, the number of males to every 100 females dropping from 137 in 1946 to 112 in 1951, and 109 in 1956. There was a corresponding decline in the proportion of the non-African population living in non-private (usually institutional) accommodation, from 31 per cent of Europeans in 1946 to 13 per cent of all non-Africans in 1961[19].

It is however in the statistics for housing tenure that the main difference between Lusaka and a truly settler society emerges. The thirty-four European households in owner-occupied houses in 1946 had increased to 475 to 1956. At last Bowling's concept of the government recouping some of its investment in the new capital by the sale of leasehold plots to private individuals was being realized and by 1963 there was even a scheme whereby leasehold plots could be converted to freehold on payment of a further fee once building work was complete. Nevertheless, these 475 European owner occupiers should be compared with 1437 European *renters* at the same date. The fact is that, even in 1956, the heyday of the Federation, owner-occupation of private houses still applied to only 25 per cent of European households living in private houses, compared with 63 per cent in Salisbury.

Turning to the geographical location of this non-African residential development, we must first make the important distinction between inner city development (within the old city boundary which was in force, with minor additions, from 1951 to 1970) and peri-urban development within the belt surrounding the inner city up to the modern (post-1970) boundary. The inner city still had relatively little owner-occupation even as late as 1956 (15 per cent if we assume that all flats were rented). The peri-urban belt however had 56 per cent owner-occupation—a level comparable with Salisbury—and virtually no flats. This difference is attributable partly to the different development processes in the two types of area and partly to the preferences of many of the true settlers for a semi-rural life. Anyone with the money to provide not only his own house but usually his own borehole and generator as well could purchase a 'small-holding' of around 4 ha to 8 ha which Kay describes as permitting 'the pursuit of a variety of quasi-rural activities according to the individual's fancy. They offer sufficient space to grow things and to keep livestock (domestic or tamed) and they offer an out-of-doors life'[20].

With the increasing political uncertainty towards the end of the federal era, particularly from 1959 onwards, the pace of non-African residential development slowed considerably. If we compare the distribution of population proposed in the 1952 plan with that for the same areas as recorded in the 1961 census, we find that 60 per cent of the non-African population proposed had been achieved in those nine years, although the continued reliance on institutional accommodation had been under-estimated. It is also significant that only 27 per cent of the intended population in flats had been achieved—again illustrating the recurring tendency in Lusaka for proposals which would increase densities to be quietly forgotten.

Attempts to diversify the economy were fairly successful up to 1956. For example, employment of Africans in manufacturing increased both in absolute numbers (fivefold) and as a percentage of total African employment (from 7 per cent in 1946 to 13 per cent in 1956), while European employment in commerce and finance reflected the growth of such institutions as insurance companies and building societies. Employment in construction, which is heavily dependent on the rest of the urban economy, was particularly high in 1956 when it accounted for 25 per cent of all Africans in employment. After 1956, political uncertainty halted the previous growth in the urban economy. Employment in manufacturing was virtually the same in 1961 as it had been five years earlier, while employment in construction fell by 2000 in five years and accounted for only 15 per cent of Africans in employment in 1961. Public sector employment, although not separately enumerated in the census after 1946, was still the major activity in the capital city and the main component of the 'services' category for Africans and Europeans alike. The links between this growth of employment and the growth of African population and housing can now be examined.

For the first few years after the war it was still assumed that circulatory labour migration was the norm, with the consequent provision of accommodation for single men tied to their employment. It was the Urban African Housing Ordinance of 1948 which finally introduced statutory requirements relating to the obligations of an employer, the provision of married accommodation and the role of the local authorities. In so doing the new ordinance inaugurated a second phase in colonial thinking about the employment and housing of Africans in urban areas; circulatory labour migration was now replaced by *stabilization*, again with an extensive academic literature of its own[21]. It was now recognized that Africans might live in towns for the duration of their working lives, and be accompanied by their wives and children, but it was still assumed that on retirement they would normally return to the rural areas.

The key provision of the Ordinance was that:

Every person who employs an African under a contract of service to perform work within any urban area shall at his own expense provide accommodation for such African and, on such African's request, for one wife.[22]

An employer now had the choice of building houses for his employees on his own land ('licensed private premises'), or of paying the full unsubsidized rent direct to the local authority for accommodating his employees in local authority housing, but large employers (more than twenty-five employees) could be made to build. In either case the housing was rent free to the employee.

Local authorities for their part were required to establish African housing areas where they were to:

provide or cause to be provided suitable accommodation for the housing of every African employed within the boundaries of the area under its control for whom accommodation is not provided in licensed private premises . . .[23]

An African housing area was defined as 'an area set aside within a municipality or township exclusively for the housing of Africans residing in such municipality or township and includes housing areas commonly known as locations and African suburbs'. This definition, together with the requirement in the Ordinance that each local authority must keep a separate African housing area account for African housing and all its associated services (i.e. separate from the usual municipal rate fund services), tended to reinforce the geographical separation of these areas.

It was recognized in the Ordinance that if all housing was tied to employment, something would have to be done for those who were still looking for a job. Local authorities were therefore required to provide married and single hostel accommodation for those seeking work, erected, equipped and maintained by each local authority at its own expense. It was also stated that if an employee was dismissed he could retain his house for up to a month, when he would then have to move into one of the hostels provided by the local authority. The logic of the system was therefore simple: the employer was financially responsible for housing his employees and the local authority for housing the unemployed—but the eventual outcome in Lusaka was more complex.

Work was soon underway on some 4400 local authority houses, and by 1957 there were around 2300 units of employer-owner housing. Nevertheless unauthorized housing continued to flourish. The earlier distinction between 'private locations' and 'unauthorized settlements' had by 1957 disappeared. 'Unauthorized compounds' was the only term used, although in practice most of these were on private land and rent was usually paid to the land owner. Unauthorized compounds accounted for 19 per cent of the inner city population in a 1957 survey. This was the main physical manifestation of the fact that the demand for housing was outstripping that provided under the Ordinance – in other words, in a diversifying urban economy, employment was expanding faster than 'proper' houses could be provided. Other factors were, as in 1944, the continued failure of the system to take account of the retired (1 per cent of the African population was aged over sixty in 1957) and the self-employed (8 per cent of occupied males in 1957), and the inadequacy of the system for housing those seeking work (1500 persons or $7\frac{1}{2}$ per cent of all adult males in 1957). The hostel idea was not entirely forgotten, but by 1962 only 208 single rooms had been provided.

During the period 1957-63 there were two significant departures from the original thinking behind the Urban African Housing Ordinance. When the expansion of employment slowed down, construction and quarry workers were among the first to be affected. Consequently their type of employer's compound began to change in a way which was not foreseen in the Ordinance. There was an increasing tendency for such compounds to be occupied by persons no longer employed by the nominal owner of the compound, and for other persons to build their houses there. This type of housing area was eventually to become virtually indistinguishable from the unauthorized settlements elsewhere in the city. Another significant, and in this case deliberate, departure from the original intentions of the Ordinance was the introduction in 1957 of the 'housing allowance'. This enabled an employer to opt out of his obligation to provide his employees with rent-free housing or pay their council house rents for them. Instead, he was now allowed to pay a cash allowance in addition to the nominal wage and leave to his employee the responsibility for housing himself. In the long-run this tended to increase the number of people looking for a type of housing which only the unauthorized compounds were able to supply.

The 1963 Census of Africans gave the first opportunity to confirm the general picture which had previously been observable only from various sample surveys. Within the modern (1970) city boundary there were 107,000 Africans in 1963, distributed as follows:

Municipal housing areas	51,820	48%
Employers housing (including domestic servants and their dependents)	40,850	38%
Unauthorized housing	14,560	14%
	107,230	100%

The first two categories reflect the general intentions of the Urban African Housing Ordinance—that an African in town should live either in a municipal housing area or in housing provided in one way or another by his employer. The third category, unauthorized housing, is a measure of the imperfections in the system. The 1963 census also revealed that the male : female ratio, which had been 1994 : 1000 in 1931 was now 1272 : 1000; that children aged twenty-one and under were now 52 per cent of the population; and that 6.8 per cent of occupied males were self-employed—each in their different ways indicators of the shift from circulatory labour migration to stabilization[24].

On the eve of Independence, Lusaka was therefore a city of some 121,000 inhabitants, with Africans outnumbering others in a ratio of about 8 : 1. Physically the main built-up area sprawled for 14 km along an axis from north-west to south-east, albeit at a very low density. In both population and employment, Lusaka was now comparable with the largest towns on the Northern Rhodesia copperbelt—equal in size to Kitwe and significantly larger than Ndola. In a country in which 21 per cent of the total population now lived in an urban area, Lusaka had 17 per cent of that urban population.

For the historian of urban planning[25], the big question for the post-Independence period would be the extent to which the majority population would move on from circulatory labour migration and stabilization to a third stage—'urbanization' or permanent urban settlement—and in so doing bring about a change not only in the physical form of the city but also in the very process of urban planning itself. The conventional master plans of an earlier age—of an Adshead or a Jellicoe—were likely to prove increasingly irrelevant to the more demanding processes of urban management which would be required in the future.

NOTES

1. King, A. D. (1976) *Colonial Urban Development*. London: Routledge and Kegan Paul.
2. Mabogunje, A. L. (1968) *Urbanization in Nigeria*. London: University of London Press.
3. Adshead, S.D. (1923) *Town Planning and Town Development*. London: Methuen, p. 118 (emphasis added).

4. Adshead, S. D. (1931) Report on the selection of a site and the preparation of a plan for the new Capital City and Government Centre in Northern Rhodesia. Typescript, National Archives, Lusaka, p. 7.
5. *Ibid.*, p. 1.
6. Northern Rhodesia Census, 1931.
7. Collins, J. (1969) Lusaka: The Myth of the Garden City. *Zambian Urban Studies,* No. 2, University of Zambia, Institute for African Studies, has a more extended discussion of garden city thinking as an influence on Adshead and others responsible for the planning of Lusaka in the colonial period.
8. Adshead, S. D. (1931) Report on the selection of a site and the preparation of a plan for the new Capital City and Government Centre in Northern Rhodesia. Typescript, National Archives, Lusaka, pp. 9-10.
9. Northern Rhodesia Government, SEC/LG/47, Lusaka New Capital: Town Planning: General. File in National Archives, Lusaka, containing report by P. J. Bowling, June 1933.
10. Northern Rhodesia Government (1929) *Town Planning Ordinance,* Cap. 27.
11. Northern Rhodesia Government (1929) *Townships Ordinance,* Cap. 26; and Northern Rhodesia Government (1930) *Public Health Ordinance,* Cap. 96.
12. See for example the publications of the former Rhodes-Livingstone Institute, Lusaka, subsequently the Institute for African Studies of the University of Zambia. See also the extensive bibliography in Boswell, D. M. (1973) Labour migration and commitment to urban residence, in *The Process of Urbanization* (Units 1–5), Urban Development Course DT 201. Milton Keynes: Open University Press.
13. Northern Rhodesia Government (1944) *Report of the Commission appointed to enquire into the Administration and Finances of Locations in Urban Areas* (Eccles Report). Lusaka: Government Printer.
14. Northern Rhodesia Census, 1946 (excluding Polish refugees temporarily encamped in Lusaka).
15. Northern Rhodesia Government, SEC/TP/1, Town planning Board. File in National Archives, Lusaka, containing report by Bowling and Floyd, July 1947.
16. Jellicoe, G. A. (1950) *A Plan for Lusaka.* Lusaka: Lusaka Management Board.
17. *Ibid.*, p. 8.
18. Northern Rhodesia Government (1952) *Town Planning Scheme for Lusaka.* Government Notice 300/1952, p. 3.
19. Northern Rhodesia Census, 1946, 1951. Federation of Rhodesia and Nyasaland Census, 1956, 1961. The 1961 census contains less detail, which is why some time series data cannot be completed beyond 1956. Not all census tables distinguish between Europeans and other non-Africans.
20. Kay, George (1967). *A Social Geography of Zambia.* London: University of London Press, p. 122.
21. Boswell, D. M. (1973) Labour migration and commitment to urban residence, in *The Process of Urbanization* (Units 1–5), Urban Development Course DT 201. Milton Keynes: Open University Press, also covers stabilization, especially the articles by J. C. Mitchell.
22. Northern Rhodesia Government (1948) *Urban African Housing Ordinance,* Cap. 234.
23. *Ibid.*

24. Northern Rhodesia Census of Africans, 1963.
25. Davies, D. H. (1969) Lusaka, Zambia: Some Town Planning Problems in an African Capital City at Independence. *Zambian Urban Studies,* No. 1, University of Zambia, Institute for Social Research, and Sampson, R. (1971) *So this was Lusaakas* (2nd edition). Lusaka: Multimedia Publications, are two other valuable sources for the historian of urban planning in Zambia.

12

The anti-planners: the contemporary revolt against planning and its significance for planning history

ROBERT FISHMAN

Diverse in its goals, experimental in its methods, infinitely variable in its specific applications, city planning has resisted all attempts to impose a single definitive historical interpretation. Yet there exists a set of widely-shared assumptions—all the more pervasive for being rarely articulated—that constitute an unspoken orthodoxy for the field. Historians of city planning tend to assume that planning is one of the progressive forces in modern society. The development of planning theory is presented as one aspect of the rise of modern science and technology: the extension of human rationality to the control of the environment.

And planning is also put forward as an integral part of the rise in social welfare since the Industrial Revolution. The increasing power of the planner means that society is overcoming the blind, cruel and wasteful operation of economic forces. In a planned world, profitability no longer determines and distorts urban structure; the community asserts its mastery over self-seeking individuals. The historian might doubt the wisdom or impugn the motives of specific planners, but the growth of city planning as a whole is assumed to be as beneficial as the growth of public health.

The history of modern city planning, therefore, finds its characteristic focus in the 'rise of the planner'. It starts with the 'humble beginnings' in the slums and sewers of the industrial city; shows the first halting efforts of planners to create more efficient urban forms and more humane urban housing; and traces the successive enlargements of the planners' powers and responsibilities. As one approaches the present, data accumulate to show that control over the environment is moving inexorably away from private individuals toward government agencies; away from profit as the dominant goal toward a bureaucratically-defined 'common good', away from small-scale, uncoordinated, haphazard plans toward increasingly complex and comprehensive programmes. The rise of the planner is as ubiquitous and as comforting a theme in planning histories as the 'rise of the middle class' used to be in traditional economic histories.

This perspective leaves little room for the critics who have challenged the theories and prevented the practice of city planning. These opponents are usually treated in much the same way that histories of medicine describe those who opposed smallpox vaccinations. Their motives are usually reduced to ignorance, a blind attachment to the past, an unwillingness to adapt to inevitable changes, a corrupt self-interest, or an indifference to the plight of the disadvantaged. They provide the unthinking resistance against which successive waves of planners can demonstrate their heroic resolve and—in the end—prove the validity of their innovations. The rise of city planning might require vigorous debate and even a 'loyal opposition', but the more intransigent opponents have been relegated to what Leon Trotsky once called 'the garbage pail of history'.

But is the history of city planning in fact a history of progress? Recently, it has become harder to assert this optimistic conclusion with any confidence. The number and power of planners has indeed increased, but without the benefits that increased planning once seemed to promise. At the same time, a widespread opposition to planning has arisen, better organized and more persuasive than the older opponents. These 'anti-planners' boldly assert that the urban environment needs less planning, not more. Implicitly (and often explicitly) they challenge the optimistic assumptions which have guided planning history. Contemporary planners have already modified their methods in the face of the theories—and sometimes the picket lines—of their opponents. Perhaps the historians of city planning can learn from them as well.

The force of the anti-planners' arguments derives from two fundamental sources. The first is the failure of modern architecture in general and postwar planning in particular to fulfil the great expectations of their creators. The second is the new concern of the 1960s for community and direct democracy, and the corresponding mistrust of outside experts and impersonal bureaucracies. It is, of course, absurd to condemn the whole of planning since 1945; it is too early even to evaluate it. Nevertheless, it is impossible to deny the widespread disillusionment which has caused a crisis of confidence within the planning profession and a cutback in funds from the public. In part this was the inevitable consequence of unrealistic expectations. Those visions of a smooth, shining Machine Age civilization which planners had absorbed from Le Corbusier's *La ville radieuse* (1935) or José Luis Sert's *Can Our Cities Survive?* (1942) or even Lewis Mumford's *The Culture of Cities* (1938) proved disappointing when set down in the middle of an urban slum or a rural pasture[1]. People preferred suburban tract houses constructed by the 'outmoded' speculative builder.

The failure of the planning movement to achieve its most ambitious aims was less damaging, however, than its failure to achieve minimal standards of improvement. The difficulties in slum-clearance programmes were deeply disturbing because such programmes should have provided the most striking evidence of the value of planning. The slum is the embodiment of bad design, poor construction, and a concern for profit over human values. Here, if anywhere, the planner can show that he indeed represents progress. When many projects proved to be worse than the slums they had replaced, confidence in planning was seriously diminished.

Among slum-clearance projects, the American 'urban renewal' programme proved to be the most notable fiasco. One project, the Pruitt-Igoe Towers in St. Louis, can serve as an apt symbol for dozens of others. In 1954 the city administration resolved to spend over 30 million dollars to level a notorious slum and replace it with a modern housing project. Resolved to serve the public good and to show the virtue of public enterprise, planners created a comprehensive design organized around high-rise apartment towers set in parks. Clean, functional, based on the most advanced techniques in construction, the towers were reminiscent of Le Corbusier's designs for Antwerp in 1933[2]. Instead of the inefficient, inhumane, haphazard crowding of the old slums, the towers would guarantee for each resident a civilized standard of light, air and room.

The errors in high-rise housing projects are now all too well understood, and Pruitt-Igoe suffered from all of them. Soon after the towers were constructed, elevators broke down, the plumbing failed, vandalism increased in unwatched public areas while maintenance costs soared. Children urinated in the long, dark corridors and the parks between towers became barren no-man's lands where gangs of youths terrorized the residents. Even the sense of community that had characterized the crowded slum disappeared in the high-rise towers.

Perhaps no design could have overcome the deeper problems of poverty and racism that plagued Pruitt-Igoe and the rest of the urban renewal programme, but the plan of the towers seemed almost perversely chosen to intensify these social problems. The difficulty was not so much a lack of planning expertise but too much of the wrong kind. The men who created Pruitt-Igoe were highly skilled at designing the standardized, large-scale projects that big organizations favour. They produced a plan that satisfied all the bureaucratic criteria for good housing—height of ceilings, number of windows, etc.—and one that presented to the observer an impressive image of order. This was very much planning 'from above' and 'from the outside'.

To the residents however, who saw Pruitt-Igoe from the inside, the towers presented a dispiriting vista of inhuman scale, alienating monotony and anonymity, and a plan that ignored their most pressing needs for sociability and safety. After conditions in the Towers had deteriorated drastically, the city administration first abandoned and then in 1972 decided to destroy most of the project. The towers met their ultimate critic—the wrecker —and in minutes there was nothing left but rubble[3].

Televised 'live' on the network news, the dynamite blasts that levelled Pruitt-Igoe seemed to sum up the bankruptcy of planning from above. The debacle of urban renewal, moreover, came at a time when 'expertise' in all fields was subjected to hostile scrutiny. The loss of faith in political leaders which struck all the Western democracies also undermined confidence in the managerial elite and in the professions. And, if the men at the top were suspect, the bureaucracies that served them were even more disliked and distrusted. Yet planners continued to call for more comprehensive programmes and larger bureaucracies to carry them out. Inevitably, there was a reaction.

If the anti-planners first formulated their ideas in response to the failure of urban renewal, they soon broadened their ideas into a full-scale critique of planning theory and practice. They argued that the ideal of the planner as the scientific manager of the environment, grandly bestowing urban form and social welfare from above, is a false and dangerous delusion. The more comprehensive the plan, the more likely it is to fail. Planning must be reduced to a minimum, and that minimum must be decentralized. The bureaucracies ought to be broken up and their powers returned to neighbourhood communities or to private individuals. This means disorder, but disorder is to be preferred to any planner's hypocritical attempt to impose his own values on everyone else and thus clamp down a sterile uniformity over the diversity of modern life. The anti-planners have no desire to conform to a grand design that leaves people unable to plan for themselves. They put their trust in pluralism and see in urban disorder the last, best hope for individual freedom and self-realization.

The best way to define these attitudes more clearly is to consider the arguments in what is surely the classic of anti-planning literature and perhaps the most influential of all books on planning in recent years, *The Death and Life of Great American Cities* (1961) by Jane Jacobs. The book is remarkable first for its refreshing freedom from pseudo-scientific jargon and for its beautifully rendered observations of the mundane but all-important details of urban life. She sees with a novelist's eye the complex web of behaviour that makes one street lively and prosperous and another a frightening desert; one park a cherished resource of the people who live around it and another a wasteland to be shunned; one neighbourhood a community spontaneously regenerating itself and so many others dismal, decaying slums. She taught a whole generation how to look at the city.

Her individual observations, moreover, lead directly to a tightly-reasoned argument about the limitations of planning itself. She begins from the conviction that the characteristic values of cities—and the qualities that keep them prosperous and healthy—are intensity and diversity. What cities need most, she writes, is a 'most intricate and close-grained diversity of uses that give each other constant mutual support'[4]. Their 'uses', i.e. the thousands of services, skills, and entertainments that a great city offers, form a pattern that is far too complicated to be anticipated or created by even the most powerful planner working from the outside. Big cities, observes Jacobs, are 'just too big and too complex to be comprehended in detail from any vantage point—even if this vantage point is at the top—or to be comprehended by any human; yet detail is of the essence'[5].

What the most powerful planner cannot accomplish, however, thousands of individuals and small groups can. Their independent, unpredictable choices create precisely the vitality the city needs most. Operating without guidance or approval from above, individuals decide to open a restaurant in an abandoned storefront; to convert a loft into a ballet school or a judo academy; to offer a service or product never needed before. Jacobs cites the example of an old building in Louisville which had housed, among other things, an athletic club, a riding academy, an artist's studio, a blacksmith's forge, a warehouse, and was currently a flourishing centre for the arts. 'Who could anticipate or provide for such a succession of hopes and schemes?' she asks. 'Only an unimaginative man would think he could; only an arrogant man would want to'[6]. She concludes that 'most city diversity is the creation of an incredible number of different people and different private organizations, with vastly differing ideas and purposes, planning and contriving outside the formal framework of public action'[7].

The implications for the planner are clear. He must work as modestly and unobtrusively as possible to develop 'cities that are congenial places for this vast range of unofficial plans, ideas and opportunities to flourish'[8]. Jacobs angrily rejects Le Corbusier's concept of urban surgery, the idea that planners must begin by levelling large tracts in the centre of old cities in order to have the space for 'urban symphonies' of skyscrapers set in parks. For Jacobs, this means imposing Le Corbusier's Plan over everyone else's plans. His neatly arranged towers, she argues, are a terrible over-simplification of urban order. Their rigid separation of functions make a true diversity impossible; their inhuman scale and vast empty spaces kill off the close-knit vitality of an attractive city. The high-rise housing projects and business districts are the dying 'unsanitary islands' of the modern city and the dense, complex districts that Le Corbusier wanted to level are the true sources of urban health.

Above all, Jacobs believes that the planner must not try to define the central goals of his society and to offer a comprehensive plan for attaining them. One sees this most clearly in the polemic against Ebenezer Howard that runs through her book. She chose Howard, the founder of the Garden City movement, as her target because he seemed to her to be the source of so many of the anti-urban and paternalistic attitudes toward planning she opposes. Howard, Jacobs claims, 'conceived of good planning as a series of static acts; in each case the plan must anticipate all that is needed and be protected, after it is built, against any but the most minor subsequent changes'[9]. Howard in fact was a flexible and modest man who was very much concerned with allowing the residents of the Garden City to shape their own future. Nevertheless, it is true that he did not conceive his new towns as neutral environments. Howard designed the Garden City to promote the values he believed in—small-scale cooperation, family life, contact with nature—and to discourage those practices he abhorred: large-scale industry, land speculation, accumulations of power[10].

Jacobs regards this attitude as paternalistic or worse. She disagrees not so much with his particular choice of values as with his right to make a choice; for he was necessarily restricting the options of others. The Garden City, she comments pointedly, was very nice 'if you were docile and had no plans of your own and did not mind spending your life among others with no plans of their own. As in all Utopias, the right to have any plans of significance belonged only to the planners in charge'[11]. In Jacobs' ideal city it is the planners who have no significant plans of their own. The common good is served through maximizing the individual's opportunity to pursue his own ends.

Yet, for all her enthusiasm for cities, Jacobs' message is essentially a negative one. Her faith in individual action is more than counterbalanced by an overwhelming scepticism about what people can accomplish together. To go from Howard to Jacobs is to go from a world that can still be radically reformed to one whose physical and social foundations cannot be moved. For Jacobs, the cities are already built. They can be renovated but never transformed. To expect citizens to agree on a better kind of city and unite together for its construction is either a delusion or the self-serving illusion of the 'new aristocracy of altruistic planning experts'. Nor does her very real concern for the urban poor imply a commitment to any economic or social reform. Indeed, the logic of her argument calls for even greater freedom for the capitalist entrepreneur.

Jacobs is especially sceptical about government. We see in her work nothing of Le Corbusier's hopes for a corps of expert administrators who bring order and beauty to the urban environment. Government for her creates more problems than it solves. She depicts a bureaucracy composed of mazes

too labyrinthine even to be kept mapped and open let alone to serve as reliable and sensitive channels . . . of action for getting things done. Citizens and officials can both wander indefinitely in these labyrinths, passing here and there the bones of many an old hope, dead of exhaustion[12].

She recommends that planners be confined to local administrative units where, if the mazes are no less labyrinthine, they are necessarily smaller. At the local level, moreover, planners can be carefully watched by the citizens. Jacobs' most enthusiastic renderings of civic action are always reserved for those occasions when people join together to resist a highway or some other project being forced on them by their own officials.

Even while glorifying the 'intricate and close-knit' city, Jacobs communicates a disquieting sense of an environment out of control, of complexities beyond human capacity to deal with, of systems so huge and unwieldy as to defy any radical attempt at change. In such a world the individual might succeed at creating for himself a comfortable niche, but the planner with great expectations must fail out of ignorance or over-simplification. Her critique of large-scale planning is reminiscent of the work of Joseph de Maistre and other conservatives of the early nineteenth century who damned the insolence of the American and French revolutionaries for presuming to write their own constitutions. Such works, they claimed, are too complex for the human mind. It is no doubt significant that our twentieth-century de Maistre, William F. Buckley, Jr., has included a long section from *The Death and Life of Great American Cities* in his anthology of conservative thought[13].

We must not suppose, however, that Jacobs' conclusions are held exclusively, or even predominantly, on the Right. Her work has had a significant impact on the Left, most notably in a book by the sociologist and urban historian Richard Sennett, *The Uses of Disorder* (1970). Sennett, who identifies himself with the anarchist tradition, accepts almost all of Jacobs' premises and carries them even further. He believes that the planners' search for urban order and harmony is not only bad policy but worse psychology. For him, this goal stems not from altruism but from a 'fear of the sources of human diversity'—it is a refusal to accept the unpleasant truth that conflict and disorder are inevitable in any society. To evade this truth planners unconsciously try to simplify the world and to mould it in their own image. Sennett compares the planner to an adolescent who avoids the pain of growing up by rigidly confining himself within a safe and familiar world.

To the extent that planners actually succeed in homogenizing the environment, they keep not only themselves but the rest of society in a state of prolonged adolescence. Sennett holds that the only path to adulthood lies 'in the acceptance of disorder and painful dislocation'. And this can best be achieved in what he calls a 'dense, uncontrollable human settlement', his phrase for Jacobs' 'intricate and close-knit' city. In such an area there are too many different groups in too small a space for any one group to enforce its values. No one can isolate himself from conflict. Everyone, therefore, is forced to become an adult.

Sennett is concerned, nevertheless, that the municipal authorities in this dense, uncontrollable human settlement might try to impose their own version of order. To counter this he recommends that not only planning but virtually all city services be either eliminated or controlled locally. His aim is to promote what he calls 'a disordered, unstable, direct social life'[14]. Land-use laws would be repealed and 'if a bar down the street were too noisy for the children of the neighbourhood to sleep, the parents would have to squeeze the bar owner themselves, by picketing or informal pressure, for no zoning laws would apply throughout the city'[15]. Police control of civil disorder would be sharply reduced so that the neighbourhoods would be responsible for keeping the peace themselves. Schools would be under direct local control.

Sennett admits that the citizens in such neighbourhoods would experience a 'high level of tension and unease' but he adds that 'it would be better in the end if they did feel uncomfortable, and began to experience a sense of dislocation in their lives'[16]. For their discontents would lead them to confront their problems directly. Without a professional bureaucracy to mediate for them, they would be forced to deal with people different from themselves and to experience in their own lives the movement from conflict to agreement. A disorder that brings freedom, diversity, and maturity is thus preferable to the bland, deceptive pleasures of planning. With Sennett the history of planning seems to come full circle. The early-nineteenth-century planners looked at the 'dense, uncontrollable human settlements' which were the cities of that time and resolved that mankind must be taken away from such environments. Sennett wants to put us back.

Sennett and Jacobs are sometimes extravagant in their arguments, often angry, frequently eloquent. They wanted to shake up a planning profession which was too complacent in its conviction that more slum-clearance projects, more high-rise housing, more highways held the answer to all urban problems. They wrote at a time, moreover, when it was too easy for politicians and planners to override citizens' objections and to impose their own values on people who had neither the opportunity nor the desire to practice them.

To a remarkable extent, the ideas of Sennett and especially Jacobs are now having a significant impact on public opinion and planning practice. Indeed, at the United Nations Conference on Human Settlements (Habitat) held in Vancouver, in June 1976, Jacobs' theories were treated with a respect previously accorded only to those of her *bête noir,* Le Corbusier. The latter's concepts of urban surgery and comprehensive projects were explicitly condemned by planners at the conference. At the same time, Jacobs' call for the renewal of decaying urban neighbourhoods, undertaken without massive new construction and with the participation of the community, was strongly endorsed. From an angry outsider, she has become an honoured authority[17].

Can historians of city planning also learn from the anti-planners? I believe we can. If, as I asserted at the beginning of this paper, historians have tended to view city planning through the perspective of the planners themselves, then the anti-planners can provide an important corrective. For, seen from the planners' point of view, planning history almost necessarily takes its theme from the growth of the profession and the extension of its responsibilities. It focuses on these extensions and takes for granted the corresponding reduction in the initiatives permitted to individuals and community groups. It thus systematically underrates the contributions that non-professionals have made to urban form and vitality; and, consciously or unconsciously, planning history supports the elitist notion that city planning is for experts, not citizens.

With their emphasis on ordinary people working on a small scale, the anti-planners point to a much richer and complex understanding of the evolution of urban form, and one that connects closely with the best research on urban economic and social history as seen 'from the bottom up'. The anti-planners also provide a useful counterpoint to the persistent fascination in planning history with 'the grand design'. (As one who recently completed a study of Howard's Garden City, Frank Lloyd Wright's Broadacre City, and Le Corbusier's *La ville radieuse,* I speak as one who has yielded to that fascination.) Daniel Burnham exhorted planners to 'make no little plans; they have no magic to stir men's blood ...'; and 'little plans' have certainly not stirred planning historians' blood. Planning histories are strewn with impressive monuments which often hide from view the more lasting small-scale activities going on around them.

Le Corbusier relates that in 1922 he was asked to prepare an exhibition on urbanism. 'What do you mean by urbanism?' he asked the director. 'Well, it's sort of street art', the man replied, 'for stores, signs, and the like; it includes such things as the ornamental glass knobs on railings'. 'Fine', Le Corbusier claims to have replied, 'I shall design a great fountain and behind it place a city for three million people'[18]. The anti-planners remind us that planning history has too often dwelt on the fountain and the ideal city to the exclusion of the more mundane world of sidewalk and the storefront which Le Corbusier so grandly spurned. Yet, as Jacobs especially points out, it is precisely the crowded, diverse, intense urban street scene which forms the primary 'image of the city' and offers the best measure of a city's economic prosperity and cultural vitality. The monumental fountains and even the ideal cities succeed or fail in the context of stores, signs and the ornamental glass knobs on railings.

The anti-planners, finally, confront us with a conflict that is inherent in the modern city (and in modern society): the conflict between collective action and individual initiative. The city, in Claude Lévi-Strauss's phrase, is a 'social work of art'[19]. It must have order, but that order must be truly social, built up out of the plans of thousands of individuals. If the anti-planners have underestimated the need for collective action and comprehensive planning, it was because they were reacting against theories that drastically overstated the benefits of professional expertise and control from above. To strike the proper balance between the contributions of governmental planning and individual freedom, between centralized order and community autonomy—that remains the primary task of both the practitioners of city planning and of its historians.

NOTES

1. Le Corbusier (1935) *La ville radieuse.* Paris, translated as *The Radiant City.* London: Faber, 1967; Sert, José Luis (1942) *Can Our Cities Survive?* Cambridge, Mass.; Mumford, Lewis (1938) *The Culture of Cities.* London: Secker and Warburg. Mumford, as an advocate of new towns, disagreed sharply with Sert and Le Corbusier. Nevertheless, all three shared a common faith in the Machine Age.
2. Le Corbusier (1935) *La ville radieuse.* Paris, p. 81.
3. *New York Times,* 19 March, 1972, p. 32; for a comprehensive evaluation of the urban renewal programme see Wilson, James, Q. (ed.) (1966) *Urban Renewal: The Record and the Controversy.* Cambridge, Mass: M.I.T. Press.
4. Jacobs, Jane (1961) *The Death and Life of Great American Cities.* New York: Random House.
5. *Ibid.,* pp. 121–2.
6. *Ibid.,* p. 195.
7. *Ibid.,* p. 241.
8. *Ibid.,* p. 241.
9. *Ibid.,* p. 19.
10. See Howard, Ebenezer (1901) *Garden Cities of Tomorrow.* London: Swan Sonnenschein; reissued in an edition edited by F. J. Osborn (1945) London: Faber and Faber; also Fishman, Robert (1977) *Utopias in the Twentieth Century: Ebenezer Howard, Frank Lloyd Wright, Le Corbusier.* New York: Basic Books.
11. Jacobs, Jane (1961) *The Death and Life of Great American Cities.* New York: Random House, p. 17.
12. *Ibid.,* p. 413.
13. Buckley, William, F., Jr. (1970) *Did You Ever See a Dream Walking?* Indianapolis: Bobbs-Merrill.
14. Sennett, Richard (1970) *The Uses of Disorder.* New York: Alfred A. Knopf, p. xvii.
15. *Ibid.,* p. 144.
16. *Ibid.,* p. 160.
17. Goldberger, Paul, Radical planners now mainstream. *New York Times,* 13 June, (1976) p. 21.
18. Le Corbusier (1960) *Creation is a Patient Search.* New York: Praeger, p. 63; I have slightly modified the translations.
19. Levi-Strauss, Claude (1967) *Tristes Tropiques.* New York: Atheneum, p. 127. Levi-Strauss' reflections on the city strike me as profound and valuable. See especially pp. 125–8.

Index